Leadership, Goals, and Power in Higher Education

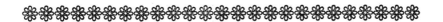

*A Contingency and
Open-Systems Approach
to Effective Management*

✽✽✽

Barry M. Richman

Richard N. Farmer

✽✽✽

LEADERSHIP,
GOALS,
AND POWER
IN
HIGHER
EDUCATION

Jossey-Bass Publishers
San Francisco · Washington · London · 1974

LEADERSHIP, GOALS, AND POWER IN HIGHER EDUCATION
A Contingency and Open-Systems Approach to Effective Management
by Barry M. Richman and Richard N. Farmer

Copyright © 1974 by: Jossey-Bass, Inc., Publishers
615 Montgomery Street
San Francisco, California 94111
&
Jossey-Bass Limited
3 Henrietta Street
London WC2E 8LU

Library of Congress Catalogue Card Number LC 74-9112

International Standard Book Number ISBN 0-87589-235-3

Manufactured in the United States of America

JACKET DESIGN BY WILLI BAUM

FIRST EDITION

Code 7432

The
Jossey-Bass Series
in Higher Education

Preface

Few people would disagree that most universities and colleges are seriously mismanaged. And most people closely associated with academic institutions would probably agree that such organizations are difficult to manage or govern effectively or efficiently these days. The nature of their goals, ambiguities relating to power and authority, financial constraints, and the kinds of professionals that work for academic institutions all contribute to the complexity of managing them.

Few books or studies deal in a systematic, practical, or comprehensive way with the complexities and realities involved in the managerial task. We have developed and utilize here a comprehensive and operational conceptual framework—along with related analytical approaches and methodologies—that can be useful in dealing with an endless and changing variety of managerial problems and situations. In essence, *Leadership, Goals, and Power*

ix

in Higher Education offers a do-it-yourself kit for sound management. The major components of our framework include the goals or outputs of the academic institution as a system, the inputs into this system, the internal subsystems of the organization, and the external environmental constraints and forces surrounding it. Both internal and external relationships are described and analyzed, including the impact of political, economic, and social forces on the institution. Ours is a genuinely open-systems approach to the study of management and organizational behavior.

It is also a contingency approach. There is a middle ground between the view that some theories and principles of management are universally applicable and the view that each organization is unique and each managerial problem is different. The contingency approach takes into account the complex nature of organizations and their managements and attempts to describe how they operate under varying conditions and in different situations. Such an approach can also be directed, as it is in this book, toward suggesting the managerial decisions and practices most appropriate for different sets of conditions or situations. The nature of the people involved, the nature of the task or work, the goals, the resources, and the external environmental factors often determine the managerial approach, plan, or decision most likely to be effective in resolving such basic problems as form of governance, leadership style, organizational design, centralization versus decentralization of authority, human motivation, goals, and choice of technology.

Leadership, Goals, and Power in Higher Education therefore contains many examples, cases, and concrete applications of the conceptual framework, related analytical approaches, and methodologies. In fact, Chapter Two presents a comprehensive case history of a university in crisis. This chapter also illustrates how the conceptual framework can be applied operationally and analytically. Other chapters deal with each of the basic components of the overall framework and focus on the major constituencies of academic institutions.

Because *Leadership, Goals, and Power in Higher Education* is concerned with institutional goal systems, strategy, major policy issues, and power relationships, it is aimed primarily at chief executives and other managers and administrators in positions of major responsibility. It is also aimed at those aspiring to such positions and to the members of governing boards of academic institutions. The book should also be of interest to professors, students, nonacademic employees, and alumni concerned with how universities and colleges are managed, especially their own. Politicians, legislators, private donors, parents, and other members of society who care about higher educational institutions and the quality of their management should gain new insights from the book. Finally, the book is of value to scholars interested in management and higher educational problems, especially from a teaching or research standpoint.

This may be the only book on university and college management to date by two business or management school professors. For this reason alone it provides some new, fresh, and useful viewpoints. We got into the academic management game about fifteen years ago, when we sat through our first dull committee meetings. Like most young faculty members, we were appalled at the trivia under consideration. It seemed incredible that learned and intelligent men and women could waste so much time on so little. Unlike most others, we continued to find university management problems fascinating. Instead of rejecting the whole scheme as a total waste of time, we decided it was well worth analyzing and explaining.

Ever since, we have done research on and observed university management as professors and as department and divisional chairmen at ten different higher educational institutions. One of us (Richman) also served as a faculty dean for a rather brief but quite dramatic period. We have also served on many committees—including search committees for top-level managers. We have sat through interminable meetings, wrestled with budgets, fought for resources, and even made a few major managerial decisions along the way.

We have also held managerial positions in business and have served as consultants to industry, government agencies, educational institutions, foundations, and research organizations in the United States and abroad. And we have been heavily involved in the study of comparative and international management problems in different sectors, fields, and countries. The conceptual and analytical frameworks and methodologies that we have developed and utilized in our comparative management studies, as well as many of our research findings, have had a major influence in the preparation of *Leadership, Goals, and Power in Higher Education.*

In a research project that has gone on in some fashion for fifteen years, more thanks and acknowledgments are required than could possibly be listed. Numerous administrators, staff personnel, professors, and students in academic institutions with which we have been connected deserve mention. However, specific mention is due to the following individuals: Philip Appleman, who got us systematically started on this work; Ragu Nath, whose work we have extensively borrowed in developing some of the basic methodology for this book; and Henry Remak, one of the gifted amateurs in university management, who took time to read some of the chapters and give valuable comments. Particular thanks are due to Bernard Estafen and W. D. Hogue, who argued all the points of this manuscript daily for over a year with us. Warren Bennis deserves special mention for his review of an earlier draft of the book. We also want to thank John Schuster and Donald Williams for their most valuable reviews and suggestions on an earlier draft. James March deserves credit for sending us a copy of the manuscript of his valuable new book on university presidents before it was published, so that we could criticize it here! Finally, we want to express our gratitude to Helen Schwartz and Dawn Amar for the excellent job they have done typing and helping put together various drafts of the book.

Because we are stubborn authors and have often failed to follow the advice of all of this extraordinary talent, the errors, omissions, and defects in the work are our responsibility entirely.

Malibu, California
Bloomington, Indiana
September 1974

BARRY M. RICHMAN
RICHARD N. FARMER

Contents

Leadership, Goals, and Power in Higher Education

*A Contingency and
Open-Systems Approach
to Effective Management*

Chapter I

Management and Mismanagement

This is a book about how to manage universities and colleges successfully. Many would argue that there is no such thing as academic management and that the subtitle is an impossibility. Mismanagement is the only possible outcome. Most American academic institutions now are mismanaged, but this does not mean that their management cannot be improved. It must be, or more and more of them are heading for great crises and problems that will force many to close. The symptoms of gross mismanagement are more obvious than the many subtleties and relative intangibles of truly sound and effective management. We are interested in both in this book.

Our primary purpose is to help university and college managers and administrators do their jobs better. Our presentation goes well beyond the how's, why's, and what's of academic mismanagement. We also consider what to do about it—that is, how to manage effectively and efficiently. In many discussions of higher education, the term *mismanagement* refers to financial misappropriation, embezzlement, payoffs, inadequately determined financial commitments, and the like. Our conception of mismanagement—and hence of management as well—goes far beyond this limited financial dimension. We are interested in such critical things as: articulating goals and priorities and making them operational and effective; effective and wise use of power; conflict avoidance and conflict resolution; improved long-term and strategic planning, as well as improved shorter-term planning and budgeting; improved information and control systems; effective staffing and organizational design; effective leadership, direction, communication and human motivation; and bringing about constructive change and innovation.

We present a comprehensive open systems approach to academic management. We also develop operational taxonomies (classification schemes of important variables) in a systematized manner. More will be said about this later in this chapter.

Our major focus is on strategy, not tactics. Many volumes cover the nuts and bolts of academic administration, but few deal with strategy in a truly comprehensive or open systems manner. Strategy involves primarily the higher levels of an institution—usually the presidential and vice-presidential levels, and quite often deans as well. It also involves the trustees, although we are more interested in the president or chief executive. The key administrators or managers get hanged in effigy and perhaps threatened personally; they have to face irate legislators, rabid editors, and baffled parents. They have to make decisions about cutting back faculty or department X, expanding interdisciplinary program Y, or firing that obnoxious Professor Z. They decide to build buildings and they find the funds to finance them.

With major university budgets ranging from $25 to $500 million per year, and with faculties of one to three thousand, plus as many or more other employees, along with tens of thousands of students, these administrators manage extremely complex organizations. Even most of the smaller universities and colleges have multimillion dollar budgets, several hundred faculty members and other employees, and over a thousand students. They have problems as complicated as those faced by managers of major private firms or bureaucrats administering major government departments. Yet not that much has been said about how they actually do or should do their jobs, and very little truly systematic analysis of university management, or of universities, has been done. We consider middle management—deans, individual schools and faculties, department chairmen, and support services. The men and women in middle-management positions must carry out decisions made by others or finalized higher up, but they also must show considerable management creativity, especially with regard to academic programs. Without reasonably able middle management, top-level administrators cannot get much done. Our middle-management analysis also focuses on key strategic issues. Finally, we look at trustees, professors, students, and various external groups since they all represent basic constituencies in the academic world.

This study is directed primarily at administrators, so it looks at the academic world largely from their point of view. At times this may make our comments seem Machiavellian to some—administrators want to survive too, and compromises may be necessary. But we are trying to look at the real world of complex decision-making, not the theoretical one of perfect justice, truth, and brotherhood.

Because we are writing for administrators, we need to take a look at what they want out of the system. Being a university or college administrator these days is tough, and the reward system is frequently obscure. But they basically want to survive, to achieve personal success and institutional success, and to attain personal satisfaction.

Few persons are suicidal, university administrators, like everyone else, want to hold on to their jobs. Given present pressures on academic administrators, often the problem comes right down to this fundamental issue. Personal success includes gaining some reputation and prestige personally for being a capable person; some money income gains; and the development of optional employability. If one gets fired or is forced to resign, it is nice to know that some other job is available.

Most administrators are proud of their institutions and would like to make them better. We still have to define *better,* but if others agree that the institution has been made better, personal success will be assured. Many persons need what a good university has to offer. The administrator who can improve a good institution will have a sense of personal satisfaction. This is what motivates a gifted man, with lots of alternatives, to take on the difficult and often painful tasks of university or college management. Something can be done—I can do it.

Although this book focuses on academic administrators— especially the president—it is also directed at professors, students, trustees, and alumni who have much interest in how universities and colleges are managed, particularly their own. It is also directed at scholars who are interested in educational and comparative management problems, as well as government officials and intelligent laymen concerned about academic institutions.

Key Terms and Concepts

A comment on our use of some terms and concepts is in order. Unless otherwise noted, we use the terms university, college, and academic institution synonomously. The same is true for administration and management and their derivatives. Many readers probably use these terms synonomously, and some functions are performed by both administrators and managers. However, later in this chapter we discuss some significanct differences in our conception of these terms in reality. The terms trustee, regent, and governor as applied to the governing boards of academic institutions are also used synonomously, unless otherwise stated. The same is true for president, chancellor, or chief executive.

A word of explanation is also in order here with regard to our use of the terms *open system* and *contingency approach.* A system is an arrangement of things or people related to form a whole. Closed system perspectives stem primarily from the physical sciences and are applicable to mechanistic systems. A closed system is self-contained and deterministic. Traditional or classical management and organization theories—including those dealing with bureaucracy—have been based essentially on a closed system approach. This approach can be useful under some conditions even in the study and practice of management. For example, it can be useful at the technical core of an organization to reduce uncertainty and create more efficient subsystem performance. It takes as fixed or assumes away many external factors.

With an *open system approach,* the organization and its management is conceptualized as a continuously importing-transforming-exporting system (Mauer, 1971). The system remains in dynamic, not static, equilibrium—if it survives—and continuous feedback can lead to changes in inputs, transformation processes, and future outputs. The organization is viewed as transacting with external environmental elements with respect to the importing and exporting of money, people, energy, material, goods and services, information, and so on. An open system does not simply engage in interchanges with its environment. The exchange is an essential factor underlying the system's viability, its reproductive ability or continuity, and its ability to change. An open system seeks multiple goals, and the individuals, constituencies, subunits, and subsystems involved often have different values and objectives.

There is always an expectation of uncertainty in open systems. They typically contain more variables than we can comprehend at one time, or some variables subject to influences we cannot control or accurately predict, or both. A university is a set of interdependent parts that together make up a whole because each contributes something and receives something from the whole which, in turn, is interdependent with some larger environment. The whole is not just the sum of the parts—there is synergy—but the system itself can be explained as a totality. Changes in one subsystem, or in the broader environment, frequently infringe on other subsystems.

Most analyses of university and college administration have a predominantly closed system orientation. Many writers on academic life study merely the internal operations, problems, and relationships, those within academic institutions—for example, the power relationships among faculty members, administrators, and students. Similarly, external factors bearing on the institution's goal system and priorities are treated peripherally, if at all. Such an approach considers the institution as much more of a closed system than it is in reality. In contrast, an open system approach examines both internal and external relationships, including the impact of political, social, and economic forces on the institution and its management.

All organizations are comprised of various subsystems—for example, functional or structural, informational, social, political— that are coordinated by a managerial subsystem designed to give direction to the overall endeavor. The managerial subsystem is superimposed on the other subsystems and is supposed to exert conscious and active influence and control over them. The *contingency approach* seeks to understand the interrelationships within and among the subsystems, as well as between the organization and its external environment, and to define the patterns of relationships or configurations of variables (Kast and Rosenzweig, 1973). It emphasizes the multivariate nature of organizations and attempts to understand how they operate under varying conditions and in specific circumstances. Contingency views are ultimately directed toward suggesting managerial practices and organizational designs most appropriate for specific situations.

Urgency for Better Management

The financial crisis and serious budget squeeze confronting an increasing number of universities and colleges is a main factor in the need for much more effective management and leadership (*Governance of Higher Education*, 1973; Committee for Economic Development, 1973; Lee and Bowen, 1971; *Statistical Abstract;* Cheit, 1971). Both private and public institutions have been hit hard by inflation, costly expansion programs, and the recent leveling off of enrollments. When resources are abundant, an institution can survive and even flourish without very effective management. However, when the financial crunch comes, inadequate management and ineffective leadership can perpetuate crises and lead to very severe problems. Management and leadership become more critical with scarce resources, which lead to conflicts. Moreover, effective and creative management can often prevent or head off serious crisis, or at least keep it to a minimum.

Total expenditures for higher education in the United States have skyrocketed from about $7 billion in 1959–1960 to $30 billion in 1971–1972. (Public expenditures alone now account for over $15 billion.) They have risen from 1.3 percent to 2.7 percent of the gross national product during this period. Although the budgets of many universities and colleges—especially public ones—have continued to increase in recent years, if price inflation is taken into account they have probably gone down in real terms or stagnated in most cases. In any event, the rate of growth in both budgets and enrollments generally has slowed down, often dramatically. Since 1970 the enrollment of students in the traditional college age group has declined as a percentage of the total population in that age bracket. The rate of cost increase per undergraduate student (in constant 1969–1970 dollars) has risen from $1523 in 1960 to about $2152 in 1972, significantly exceeding the rate of inflation.

With the tremendous increase in capacity in American higher education since World War II, in conjunction with a shift from eltite to mass and now toward universal higher education—which means financial aid for more and more students—students are becoming more selective about where they go to college than they were in the past. They are also expressing increasing dissatisfaction with traditional and irrelevant (at least in their view) academic programs, policies, approaches, and goals. Getting into college has become a buyer's rather than a seller's market. The dropout rate among students of traditional college age has increased sharply at many schools. With significantly greater choice, many students are becoming the employers at institutions that depend on enrollments for most of their funds.

More interest groups are now vying for power and influence in higher education. Sharply rising cost is a major reason for this, especially with regard to state supported institutions. This means a bigger stake for all, including external parties such as politicians, legislators, government administrators, parents, and taxpayers. Much of the power has been shifting outside of such institutions. At the same time, numerous private schools find that they can no longer compete with public universities and colleges that have much lower tuition. Many private benefactors have become much less generous for various reasons, including dissatisfaction with what some institutions seem to be doing and how they use their resources.

In the 1972–1973 academic year alone, more than forty-five independent private schools shut down. They went bankrupt, merged with other institutions, or were taken over by the government. This represented more than 3 percent of all private colleges and universities. There are nearly 2600 higher educational institutions of all types in the United States; of these, about 1475 have been private. Private schools account for only about 25 percent of the student population, and some projections by experts indicate that by 1980 that figure may go down to 15 percent or less.

Effective marketing and salesmanship by academic institutions can help matters somewhat, but not nearly enough. At the heart of the problem, and even deeper than the general financial situation, are the goal systems and priorities of such institutions, in conjunction with pervasive mismanagement. Different constituencies —both internal and external—frequently have quite different views about what the goals and priorities of colleges and universities really are and should be. This often leads to conflict and misunderstanding. Outsiders are often unclear or unhappy about what universities seem to be doing or should be doing, and how they do it. The whole area of goals and priorities in higher education—what they really are and should be at most academic institutions—has been obscure, inoperative, and unverified. Now more written sources are gradually coming to recognize this as a problem of utmost importance, but there have been very few studies that have focused on this problem in a systematic or comprehensive way (Petersen, 1973; Gross and Grambsch, 1968, and 1974; Gross, 1971). This is one of the major concerns of this book.

A key task of management—especially of the president— and perhaps the most importane one, is to define, articulate, operationalize, and insure the effective implementation of goals and priorities that are relevant, realistic and attainable. Of course, this should involve adequate participation of all the major constituencies, and it is the job of management and effective leadership to achieve a workable consensus. It involves a careful analysis of the strengths, weaknesses, and limitations of the institution, and selection of a suitable niche in higher education that leads to institutional viability and success.

Relatively few academic institutions can or will be able to effectively pursue a very wide range of goals and priorities simultaneously. There are very few Harvards or multicampus universities like the University of California. Many institutions try to emulate them, without success. Many schools could vigorously pursue various potentially lucrative, relevant, and important goals, priorities and programs related to significant educational needs in society, but to date they have not. If they did they could gain a reputation for excellence and relevancy in a limited but still important part of American higher education. We are thinking of such things as part-time and work-study programs, various types of adult education, special kinds of vocational or career training and retraining, open university approaches, taking the classroom off campus, and other programs discussed later in this book.

Top management, in the final analysis, is responsible for getting an adequate mesh between what the outside world wants, needs, and expects from a given institution in terms of its goals, priorities and related programs, what the internal constituencies want, need, and expect, and what the faculty is capable of delivering. If the institution is wholly alien to its external environment it cannot function or survive. But if it yields completely, it fails in its ultimate educational purpose or task. This delicate balancing requires effective and creative management and leadership.

Scarce resources in conjunction with the goals problem is at the heart of serious power problems and conflicts at numerous colleges and universities, both internally and with regard to external interest groups. Only recently has a growing number of published works paid any significant attention to power and conflict as a critical issue in the real academic world. And only a few authors have done so in a systematic or comprehensive manner (Baldridge, 1971a; Hodgkinson and Meeth, 1971; Baldridge, 1971b; Gross and Grambsch, 1968 and 1974; Demerath, Stephens, and Taylor, 1967). This, too, is of central concern in this book. A primary task of management and, again of the president in particular, is to understand the nature and sources of power, to use power wisely, and to minimize conflicts and resolve them effectively.

A third critical task of management is to increase the institution's productivity and operating efficiency, without seriously hindering academic quality. This is often expressed quantitatively in such measures as teaching loads, student credit and contact hours, class sizes, student-faculty ratios, cost per student, cost per professor, use of space and facilities, and cost of support services. Public concern about the inadequate productivity of universities and colleges has increased sharply, and is also at the heart of many conflicts. The adequacy of financing in the future will depend in large part on how efficiently resources are managed and used.

Much more has been written about the internal management and operations of academic institutions than about goals and priorities or power and conflict. More universities, especially large ones, have been implementing such things as management information systems and computers, planning-programming-budgeting systems (PPBS), full-time offices for institutional research, operations research and various kinds of mathematical models, and other modern managerial methods and contemporary innovations that are still much more widespread in business and even in government than in universities. However, a current Carnegie Commission study concludes that institutions of higher education in general have not yet put very substantial effort into such modern management techniques, in spite of mounting social and economic pressures for accountability and efficiency. A survey (Bogard, 1972) of 1873 universities and colleges in the United States revealed that only 13 percent had established a management information system, 31 percent were using PPBS in some form, 24 percent reported a full-time office for institutional research, and only 2.8 percent (or 1.5 for private schools) had all three. Private schools seem to have the same posture as public institutions regarding innovative and modern management, and are no more efficient (McCloskey, 1972). This is rather foreboding since most of them do not have very significant endowments and they are supported mainly by tuition—which is typically considerably higher than at state institutions.

Although we consider the productivity and internal efficiency of academic institutions, these are not treated as centrally as goal systems and priorities or power and conflict. Improving internal operating efficiency is, of course, now extremely important to universities, but not quite as important, we feel, as the problems of goals, priorities, power and conflict. The allocation and use of the institution's resources should be directly related to its goals and priorities. If the goals and priorities are obscure, the allocation and utilization of resources are not likely to be very effective or efficient.

We are much more interested in the relationships between external environmental factors and their impact on internal management and operations than in treating internal factors in a closed-system manner divorced from the larger environment. Very few of the mathematical models being experimented with and used by academic institutions are capable of predicting and accounting for critical, external environmental effects (Bell, 1972b).

The writing is clearly on the wall for all to see if they would just look. Something must be done now, or the administrators and faculties of numerous academic institutions will lose much more of their independence, autonomy, and initiative to outsiders, especially to the government, taxpayers, voters, and other financial benefactors. Many will close their doors for good or be taken over. Top management must take the lead in doing those things necessary to insure institutional viability and success. No amount of wish fulfillment will make the problems disappear. There are certainly various critical environmental constraints, such as the financial problem. However, all of them are at least partially controllable through effective management and creative leadership, and management can adapt to them with varying degrees of effectiveness.

Reasons for Cautious Optimism

There clearly seems to be a need for immensely more educational diversity and innovation in our society, rather than for more homogeneity. Those institutions that can articulate, operationalize, and in many cases reformulate their goals and priorities in ways that enable them to build a viable niche and a distinctive campus will prosper. There are many opportunities that have not yet been adequately capitalized on.

A recent survey involving university and college goals (probably the most comprehensive such study ever undertaken in the United States) has found that there is quite a bit of agreement among the different constituencies on what the goals—both internal and external—of various types of higher educational institutions should be (Peterson, 1973). There is much less agreement about what the goals and priorities really are, thus clearly indicating the seriousness and pervasiveness of the problems of obscurity, ambiguity, and lack of verification and accountability regarding the actual goal systems of academic institutions. On the other hand, this same study suggests that in many cases top management could get a workable consensus on the articulation, restructuring, operationalization, and pursuit of institutional goals and priorities. This would require creative and courageous management and effective leadership. In this way the president could build confidence in and support for his institution. Although the above survey dealt with 116 college and university communities only in California—including public and private schools, junior colleges, state colleges, and the multicampus university—many of the findings and conclusions have national implications.

Public confidence in higher education is apparently again on the rise, at least for now. A recent Louis Harris Poll for the Senate Subcommittee on Intergovernmental Relations—involving a survey of a representative cross-section of 1596 Americans—indicates that 43 percent expressed confidence in higher education as an institution in 1973. This compares with only 32 percent in 1972; but this is still far less than the 61 percent in 1966 (*Time*, 1973; *Newsweek*, 1973). Higher education rated higher than almost all of the other major American institutions. However, in 1973 there was general disillusionment and dissatisfaction with almost all institutions, most notably the nation's presidency and federal government. The main implication here is that the public currently views higher education as better than most other basic institutions. This means there still may be time for many schools to restructure, reformulate, and operationalize goals and improve their management sufficiently, before the severity of the financial crunch increases and they lose much more of their autonomy and initiative.

With the campus turmoil of the late sixties and early seventies now pretty much played out, there seems to be an increased willingness among students, faculty, trustees, and even many government officials to grant more decision-making powers to an effective university or college president (*Governance of Higher Education*, 1973; Gross and Grambsch, 1974). The key word here is effective, and this implies effective in terms of goals or ends as well as means. The president will also have to earn this power in order to keep it. If the actual and potential providers of funds have confidence in the management of a given academic institution, they are willing to allow for more discretionary funds and qualitative factors in its budgets than if they do not.

Finally, there seems to be growing recognition, even within academic institutions, not only that they are seriously mismanaged but also that something should and must be done about it. Most people still do not seem to know what to do, however. One thing that needs to be done is to articulate, at least partially redefine, and take a different view than the common traditional views of what management should be in a university or college, including the president's job. In order to do this, one must also give consideration to what administration or management in academic institutions really is at present, and how the institution really functions.

Management versus Administration

The terms *administration* and *administrator* are still much more commonly used with regard to academic institutions than *management* or *manager*. Most academic executives and officials probably consider themselves to be, and behave much more like, administrators than professional, modern managers. This suggests much about why so many universities and colleges are in so much trouble. The term *management* is universally used in business organizations in the United States, and this may be a chief reason for the distasteful and negative connotations it arouses among academics.

The term management has become widely used and accepted in business organizations throughout the world, including public sector firms in developing countries and state enterprises in the Communist countries (China and the Soviet Union included). It is also widely used and favorably viewed by government agencies in the United States and abroad. Moreover, it is becoming common in social service organizations, the human service professions, religious institutions, artistic organizations, and even hospitals. Quite a few schools of business administration have become schools of management dedicated to training managers for all major sectors of society, not just business. As a result, many public administration programs have been hard hit or phased out, because they have clung to the traditional administrative and institutional approaches in their curricula. A growing number of management schools—including some that still are called business schools—are adding new programs in educational, arts, public health, government, and urban management.

The words *management, managerial,* or *manager* appear in the titles of far more books today than do *administration, administrative,* or *administrator.* The reverse was true only fifteen or twenty years ago. And this is true not only of books that focus on business and industry but also, increasingly, of books on higher education. There are also far more books about mismanagement than misadministration—in fact, we have never seen one with misadministration in the title (Weissman, 1973). This implies that mismanagement is a more serious problem than misadministration. Many more words with positive or favorable connotations are more commonly associated with management or its derivative than with administration. These include participative, democratic, creative, innovative, change, revolution, strategy, science, theory, information systems, planning, goals, professional, and management by objectives or results. Such terms and their connotations are often reflected in the career behavior and performance of those who see themselves as managers rather than as administrators.

Some functions are performed by both managers and administrators, in different ways. Management involves strategy, innovation, initiating and bringing about change, creative problem-solving and decision-making, actively seeking out alternatives and opportunities, reformulating goals and priorities, redeploying resources, negotiating, resolving conflicts, dynamic or active leadership, diplomacy, statesmanship, and a high degree of risk-taking and entrepreneurship. Administration implies more routine decision-making and operations, and the implementation of goals, priorities, and strategies, usually determined by others. It is more concerned with following predetermined policies, procedures, and regulations. It tends to be much more adaptive, passive, and reactive than management, and it is much more of a closed system concept primarily concerned with internal efficiency and operations. It is also more concerned with internal monitoring and control than with external environmental change and strategic planning. To us, at least, administration implies bureaucracy. That is not to say that it is not important. It is, and effective management needs the support of competent administration and administrators. However, in the turbulent environment in which most academic institutions now find themselves, effective and professional management is more critical than competent administration.

Andrew Sloan Draper's quote of several generations ago—"Groups legislate; individuals execute"—is still widely accepted in the academic world. This implies that those who are responsible for running or governing a university are administrators, not managers. It also has much support among those who favor the collegial model of academic governance, to be discussed later. Philosophically, and in terms of idealism, this is a nice democratic concept with which we partially agree. However, in the real academic world, where conflicts are not mere aberrations but tend to be quite normal, it is often not possible to wait for groups to legislate—and legislate wisely—if an institution is to be kept functioning properly. Management, formal authority, and effective leadership must step in eventually to resolve conflicts, which increase in frequency when resources decrease. There are various kinds of decisions and some situations where group decision-making can work, and work well. What is required is a contingency approach, which we stress in this book.

The government can typically afford to wait for legislators to legislate. Often a university cannot afford to wait for widespread group decisions, especially decisions about financial matters. The government has vast resources and power, as well as many options at its disposal, and it is able to incur large deficits that can be perpetuated if need be. In an academic institution, even where groups should and do legislate—for example, on academic matters—top management can have the final say on major institutional decisions, as long as it maintains budgetary control.

Another more recent statement which also still has much acceptance in the academic world also represents an administrative rather than a managerial mentality. Daniel Griffiths (1959, p. 89) wrote, "It is not the function of the chief executive to make decisions; it is his function to monitor the decision-making process to make certain that it performs at the optimum level." This philosophy may be workable when there is a high level of organizational harmony and resources are abundant. Then active leadership and effective management is not nearly as crucial as they are in a situation of significant conflict and scarce resources.

How Universal Is Management?

Back in the 1950s, then Chancellor Edward Litchfield of the University of Pittsburgh was one of the first prominent educators to espouse the universality of the managerial or administrative process or functions, regardless of the type of organization involved. He wrote, "Administration and the administrative process occur in substantially the same generalized form in industrial, commercial, civil, educational, military, and hospital organization" (1956, p. 28).

The aim of Robert Lahti's *Innovative College Management* (1973) is to bring professional managerial knowledge to educational institutions from business and industry. His major emphasis is on management by objectives. Although he focuses primarily on the two-year or junior college, his book has broad implications and is a very worthwhile work. It is quite different from our comprehensive open systems approach, however.

Although the universality of management and the applicability of many managerial concepts from business to academic institutions have gained acceptance in academic circles, there are still a great many who support the position of John Millett, former president of Miami University. He has written, "Ideas drawn from business and public administration have only a very limited applicability to colleges and universities" (Millett, 1962). John Corson in his important book, *The Governance of Colleges and Universities* (1960), also has taken the position that management processes and the president's role are basically different in academic institutions and business. However, he may modify this position in the forthcoming revised edition of his book, particularly in view of his more recent experience as president of Fry Consultants.

Corson and other writers have done a thorough job of presenting and analyzing various factors that account for differences in the management and functioning of academic institutions as compared to business and even governmental and other types of organizations (Perkins, 1973). There certainly are a number of significant differences, as well as some valid reasons for them. However, in the normative or prescriptive sense—rather than in terms of description or even explanation—the necessity for such differences tends to be grossly exaggerated. In fact, they often seem to be used as an excuse for mismanagement and inaction—in other words, a cop-out.

Increasingly, business corporations are facing many of the problems that make effective academic management so difficult, albeit often not to quite the same degree. For example, goal systems and priorities in business are becoming much more difficult to define clearly, operationalize effectively, or verify, because of growing concern in society about corporate social responsibility and the quality of life (Richman, 1973). Major firms in particular are under pressure to pursue social goals, in addition to such traditional economic goals as profitability, much more vigorously and seriously. These goals relate to such things as pollution abatement, employment and advancement of minorities and the underprivileged, consumerism, urban renewal, the quality of working life, and philanthropic activities. In response to this, a growing number of progressive companies—as well as various government agencies—are trying to develop meaningful social audits and social indicators to be used for decision-making purposes along with the more traditional economic criteria. John Corson has recently been heavily involved in this.

Participative or democratic management and group decision-making have also become much more widespread in business. Many companies have experts, highly specialized in diverse fields, who are often more committed to their profession or discipline than to the organization. Many business and other organizations also produce fairly intangible services where cost-benefit analysis, goal verification, and accountability are rather messy and difficult to apply very effectively—but they make a serious attempt.

Furthermore, numerous corporations now find themselves confronted with active, vocal, and independent interest groups who can exert power and influence. These include conservationists, consumer advocates, minority and community groups, and community based legal groups. Corporations find that effective management and leadership is needed if they are to achieve consensus and workable compromises—both externally and internally—instead of relying on an authoritarian or formal power approach.

Not all business firms are dealing with such problems and changes very effectively. However, a growing number seem to be trying to make significant changes and innovations in their management processes in order to deal with problems that are more complex and difficult than those ordinarily faced by academic institutions.

We agree with Clark Kerr, who has stated, "There is no reliable model for university organization that surpasses the model set by the best universities themselves. Universities are clearly a genus apart" (Kerr, 1973). Both managerial and institutional success are indeed relative rather than optimum concepts, and there are vast differences among institutions. However, this does not mean that many managerial, organizational, and system concepts, approaches, methods, practices, and techniques cannot be effectively applied—albeit often in modified form—from business or government to universities and colleges. On the other hand, not everything can be applied. What is needed is a contingency approach that depends on the actual situation, circumstances, conditions, and problems. It is clearly not a totally yes or no or black or white issue—it is a gray one that can be best determined empirically, by trying, by experimenting, and often by trial and error.

Business organizations and academic institutions can learn much from each other; we are not talking about a one-way street. There is likely to be an increasing convergence of the managerial concepts and practices applied by the successful and progressive organizations in both sectors. Academic institutions are becoming much more concerned about improving their productivity and efficiency, while business corporations are becoming much more concerned with and involved in social problems and improving the quality of life in society.

Basic Functions

The management process is comprised of basic interrelated managerial functions. *Managerial functions* are the activities managers (or administrators) perform as managers, regardless of what they manage. The relative importance of each function, and precisely how and how well these functions are performed, may differ dramatically among organizations and among managers. However, these functions can be viewed as universal, and they provide a useful classification scheme for studying management. We base our claim about the universality of some managerial functions not only on what we have read and our own practical experience but also on the empirical research we have undertaken in many countries.

A useful division of managerial functions is: planning and innovation; controlling; organizing; staffing; and direction, communication, leadership, and motivation. If an organization is to continue functioning, regardless of its nature, these functions must usually be performed in one fashion or another, be it consciously or unconsciously. Some goals and plans must be formulated; operations must be controlled to at least some extent; organizational structures of some kind must be designed; at least some authority must be delegated in multilevel organizations; personnel must be recruited, selected, trained, appraised in some way, communicated with, and motivated and led at least to some extent. Management is also often expected to take the initiative in improving operations and results through innovation and change. All of these functions can be carried out in either a relatively democratic (participative) or an authoritarian manner. Let us examine each of these interrelated functions in more detail.

The planning function involves the determination of goals and the plans, and of the strategies, policies, programs, schedules, procedures, tools, techniques, and methods for achieving them. Planning is decision-making for the future, although decision-making is also part of the other managerial functions. Planning involves choosing among alternatives, and it encompasses innovation—one must do some planning in order to innovate effectively. Planning tends to be the most crucial function with regard to the organization's external environment. The control function includes those activities designed to compel events to conform to plans or to recognize deviations therefrom. This involves measurement, feedback, monitoring, and, if necessary, corrective action. It also entails the gathering of information required for evaluating performance and provides critical inputs for subsequent planning. Often the best control is futurity or forward oriented, rather than after the fact. A close and continuous link between planning and control should exist in all parts of the organization and in all major functions. Information systems and budgeting arc at the heart of this process, and they deal with the external environment as well as with the internal organization.

The organizing function involves the determination and enumeration of activities necessary to carry out plans; the grouping of these activities; the assignment of groups of activities to units headed by managers or administrators; and the delegation of authority to carry out the activities. Sometimes all of these are included in the term *organizational structure* or *design;* sometimes they are referred to as *authority relationships.* In any case, it is the totality of such activities and relationships that make up this function. The question of centralization versus decentralization is a major organizational design problem. So are the nature and degree of work specialization; spans of management; number of organizational levels; basic departmentalization; program organization; the use of staff specialists and service units; and group decision-making and the use of committees.

The staffing function includes those activities essential to manning, and keeping manned, the positions in the organization structure required to achieve the organization's goals and plans. Thus, it involves defining the human requirements for the jobs to be done and the inventorying, recruiting, appraisal, and selection of candidates for positions, as well as training candidates and incumbents and helping them to develop and perform well. It also includes the provision of adequate compensation to attract and maintain the needed personnel; the definition of the jobs to be done; and dismissing or laying off of personnel for various reasons.

Some management writers lump directing, leading, motivating, and communicating activities under the single concept of directing, leading, or supervising. They can also be viewed as separate functions or subfunctions. They are so intimately connected in reality that we prefer to put them in the same overall category, although we do make distinctions among them. We also prefer not to place them under a single category like direction, because we feel that this has too much of a hierarchical, inorganic, or mechanistic connotation. Much of the important communication that actually takes place in an organization is not from the top down, or along formal vertical or hierarchical lines, whether it be up or down. Communication need not follow only hierarchical lines and, in fact, when this happens it can be detrimental to organizational effectiveness and efficiency. Similarity, there is often much motivation, including self-motivation, that has little or nothing to do with formal direction, hierarchical leadership, or supervision. Motivation involves the use of hierarchically determined incentives of penalties, or both, to get people to perform in desired ways. But it also involves much more, as will be discussed later in the book, especially when we consider the social and political subsystems of academic institutions.

Direction and leadership can take different forms and it is a basic task of sound management to employ those styles, approaches, and techniques that obtain the best results in specific situations. Effective leadership, especially in relatively democratic organizations, often depends on much more than formal authority and official power, although these, too, are very important. It also depends on providing an environment and structure that adequately satisfy important human needs, on various personality factors, on mutual respect, trust, and confidence, on knowledge, information, and wisdom, and more.

Leadership and communication are critical with regard to external relationships. A major task of management—especially of top management—is to ensure that adequate contributions—goods, services, funds—are obtained from the various external participants or interest groups in return for inducements at the disposal of the organization. Such inducements include money and concrete goods and services, and also much less tangible things like social and psychic satisfaction. A primary responsibility of management is to balance inducements and contributions to provide for the viability and success of the organzation, and also to maintain effective communication and alliances with external participants. This is frequently a complex and difficult task, especially in an environment of scarce resources.

Direction, leadership, communication, and motivation are essential to getting things done through and with people and interpersonal relations. It is the job of effective management to maintain a suitable balance between individual motivation and adequate cooperation and support, both internally and externally. Clear and sound goals and plans, efficient and effective controls and information systems, sound organizational design, and proper staffing set the stage for coordinated and efficient efforts. But management must also provide effective leadership, direction, communication, and motivation, if people both inside and outside of the organization are to work together in ways that achieve the organization's goals efficiently.

Top Management and the Presidency

The university or college president cannot rely on any one model of governance or management if he is to succeed. Much has been written about the presidency of academic institutions, but relatively few works take a very systematic view of either the president's role or of the organization for which he is responsible. (A current selected bibliography on the college and university presidency is available from American Council on Education, One Dupont Circle, Washington, D.C. 20036. See also Cohen and March, 1974.)

At most schools it seems that more, not less, presidential influence is needed to initiate and guide change. There are more conflicts to be understood and resolved. Fiscal stringency requires more presidential authority, which must be earned through effective leadership and management. Financial stringency almost forces a competent president to play a central and forceful role, as do the clearly perceived conflicts between the insiders whom he represents and the outsiders he must count on for institutional support. Therefore, usually it is wisest to seek and appoint an active rather than a passive president, one who will lead rather than merely try to survive (*Governance of Higher Education*, 1973; Gross and Grambsch, 1974). He should be granted adequate authority in his difficult task of dealing with financial problems, goals and priorities, and encouraging constructive change. At times he will need to act and decide even if a broad consensus cannot be obtained. This takes both wisdom and courage. The president of an academic institution must also have a high tolerance for ambiguity, and he must be able to cope with it without disrupting the institution unduly.

The president must often be a negotiator and a mediator, jockeying among power blocs, trying to carve out viable futures for his institution. He should not be either an autocrat or bureaucrat, or merely an administrator. He should be a professional manager, an active leader, and often an entrepreneur as well. He must understand and effectively use both formal bureaucratic and informal expert and participative structures and processes. He must also maintain channels of communication and influence between the formal and informal structures. The faculty should have a major say regarding academic matters, and the students regarding matters that directly involve them. However, when conflicts cannot be resolved in a reasonably timely fashion, and when there are not enough resources to meet all demands, the president must resolve conflicts either through his overall budgetary powers or some other means.

Many academic institutions have run headfirst into acute problems and crises because of serious deficiencies in the managerial, leadership, or entrepreneurial abilities of their presidents. If the president does not possess all of these basic abilities to a relatively high degree, it is important that he (or she) and his key deputies, working as a team, do. A good balance is needed between overall managerial competence regarding the basic functions of management, relatively active if not highly dynamic leadership, and entrepreneurship. Let us cite some actual examples to illustrate this point more vividly (Riesman and Stadtman, 1973).

The president of Antioch, James Dixon, has been a dynamic entrepreneur and risk-taker, but not apparently a very effective overall manager or leader (Grant, 1973). He has embarked on one of the most lively and stressful experiments in higher education. It involves a network of several campuses, more than twenty field centers, and widespread job and foreign linkages. Dixon has deliberately escalated the level of crisis involving his institution, because he believes change comes through personal confrontation. His encouragement of so much competition among both faculty and students may prove him to be too much of a risk-taker. Dixon has great tolerance for ambiguity, but this has taken a big toll on many others. He realizes that neither his own nor Antioch's survival are assured, and he even stated in 1963 that Antioch "has no obligation to pursue its own survival as an end." Dixon has managed to remain in office even with the loss of faculty support. Most of the faculty (about 75 percent) supported the views of a respected dean—views that were more cautious and conservative than Dixon's regarding the dramatic network expansion. Dixon fired the dean and relied for a time on a coalition of innovative administrators and more or less radical students in opposition to scholarly faculty members. His virtuosity has been enhanced by his position as heir to a tradition of institutional innovation. President Dixon may be the ultimate academic entrepreneur. But he has seriously threatened both his own survival as president and the institution's viability and future success because he apparently has serious limitations as a manager. This includes serious deficiencies in such areas as systematic, strategic, and contingency planning, effective control and information systems, organizational design, staffing, and leadership, motivation, and communication.

In 1966, Chancellor Sam Gould of the State University of New York launched Old Westbury as a new experimental college (Dunn, 1973). Its charter involves admitting students who are not high school graduates, granting degrees without regard to length of study, participation of students as full partners, and much reliance on mechanical teaching aids. Most of the students have been Blacks and Puerto Ricans from low-income families. The main educational purpose was to "pay heed to the individual student and his concern with the modern world." This program failed and Old Westbury I became Old Westbury II within three years. Mismanagement and ineffective leadership were the primary causes of this failure. The president was too permissive and tried to follow a purely collegial style of governance. The faculty and students had no experience in institution-building and very little in management. There was far too much unplanned and poorly thought out improvisation, with everyone wanting "to do their own thing." Consensus became increasingly difficult to achieve without effective leadership, and conflicts became acute. The president became the focus of all conflicts and disagreements but could not handle them.

In May 1970, John Maguire became the new president of Old Westbury II. He continued to work within the basic terms of the original charter. However, he chose as the single guiding theme for organizing the curriculum "the riddle of human justice." He felt this was an adequately operational concept capable of knotting the overall program together, giving it coherence and viable purpose. Maguire has thus far apparently proven himself to be an effective manager and leader. Much effort is being devoted to spelling out and clarifying the powers, authority, and roles of the college council, the president, SUNY officers, and various other constituencies. Maguire has brought in some new, experienced, and evidently competent administrators. He has set up a planning group consisting of administrators, faculty members, and students (including some prospective students) to develop an overall academic program and curriculum. There is now widespread awareness of the need for perceptive evaluation of programs and people (administrators, faculty, and students). The president has felt it necessary to deal with academic details much more than he had expected. However, he has been willing to make decisions where needed.

John Dunn, who has studied the Westbury case firsthand, expresses cautious optimism about the future of this college. A major concern is for the preservation of the human justice theme. But a serious split could emerge between those with intellectual (traditional) academic interests and those who wish to stress professional (applied) skills. The development of the SUNY system has been guided by the need for variety to meet educational needs, but budget pressures and regionalization could homogenize the system.

San Francisco State University has been a classic case of gross mismanagement and ineffective leadership since the early 1960s (Henderson, 1973). A few years ago it emerged from a three-year period of extreme crisis and conflict, which included the longest strike at any American university or college. It is still not out of the woods, however. President S. I. Hayakawa remained in office for a considerable period of time with little faculty support. He was relatively inactive and uninvolved in this job. For most faculty members, his presence was no more than symbolic, and the trustees did not want to fire him because of the symbolic role he played during the crisis.

The University of Wisconsin is another good example of gross mismanagement, ineffective leadership, and inadequate entrepreneurship (Altbach, 1973). Most of the administrators have been Wisconsin faculty members or graduates. This has led to excessive inbreeding and homogeneity in the administration of the university. The institution has gone from crisis to crisis in recent times. Crises have been met by short-term compromises or, more often, by outside action. Rather conservative senior faculty-administrators and the regents have been in charge, with the strong conservative majority of the regents playing an increasingly active role. The internal system of governance, which is both conservative and complicated, has been able to perpetuate itself. Because the university has not had effective top management or leadership, it has not been possible to implement major changes and innovations that are needed in the administrative structures, academic programs, student participation, faculty participation, and creative planning. Evidently the system has really served only the interests of the senior faculty. Without effective management and leadership there is little institutional commitment or conviction, and responses to challenges and problems are inadequate. The will to adapt to new situations and environmental change is lacking, and the administration spends most of its time on budget crises. Neither the financially strapped state government, nor dissatisfied and relatively radical students, nor the younger and more progressive faculty members can be expected to support the traditional academic governance and the orientation of the University of Wisconsin much longer.

Fortunately, there are also examples of relatively well-managed academic institutions. UCLA is one example of a relatively efficient university with a pretty good balance of professional management, effective leadership, and entrepreneurship in its top management (Bell, 1972a). At Princeton, President Goheen presided through recent crisis and change with sense and sensibility (Sigmund, 1973).

The University of Pennsylvania made great strides under the strong leadership, entrepreneurship, and generally effective management of President Gaylord Harnwell, who served in that job from 1953 until September 1971 (Goddard and Koons, 1973). The new president, Martin Meyerson, has already found that he is confronted with significant problems. He came from Buffalo, which underwent great turmoil years ago. Before that he was the chancellor at

Berkeley. It is still too early to tell how he is going to fare in his new chief executive job.

Wesleyan is a model of how to adapt gently to an increasingly turbulent environment. The moral capital and institutional identity of Wesleyan offer reserves that can be spent in a crisis before it gets out of hand. As Clark (1973) states, "A college which strongly believes in itself can withstand stresses, shocks, and even shortages of resources and carry on so effectively that it is widely heralded as a success." But institutional self-belief, character, and commitment do not just happen. One important reason for the existence of these characteristics at Wesleyan—in addition to large endowment—has been effective management and sound leadership over many years. And these seem to be continuing under Colin Campbell, who became president in 1970–1971. Because of the strains at Wesleyan during the 1968–1970 period, Campbell wisely took a hard look at priorities and reexamined purposes and basic goals. This examination led to a reaffirmation of the dedication of Wesleyan to excellence in undergraduate education. Campbell decided that it was essential to align innovations with regard to this goal. He then openly ranked programs according to their importance in the undergraduate curriculum. Top priority was given to the core program and to financial aid to undergraduates—including many minority students. At the same time, the master's program in teaching was phased out, and the Wesleyan Press was put under careful review.

Swarthmore has been one of the least altered colleges in the last decade (Mangelsdorf, 1973). Its Quaker inheritance of co-education as social egalitarianism is suddenly right in step today. Over its history, Swarthmore has developed a clear sense of mission and character in conjunction with the pursuit of effective goals and priorities. By concentrating on a restricted clientele of bright students for whom the academic orientation has proven highly suitable for over fifty years, it has developed a solid place in higher education. There is relatively little emphasis on expensive graduate programs or research. There have been problems, but not very serious ones compared to other institutions. Top management and the presidency seem to be relatively easy and nice jobs at Swarthmore. There appears to be a good fit between the key administrators' personal values, goals, and styles and the institution's goals, capa-

bilities, and needs. However, these jobs are easy today—as compared
management positions at most other colleges and universities—only
because of effective management, leadership, and institution-building
over a long period of time.

Models of Governance

Three basic models of university and college governance are
well known among specialists in higher educational administration.
These are the bureaucratic and collegial models and the more recent
political model developed primarily by J. Victor Balridge (1971a,
1971b). An important fourth model, *organized anarchy*, has been
developed by Michael Cohen and James March (1974) in their
study of university presidents. The bureaucratic model relates to the
traditional and formal organization and management theories of
Max Weber (1947). It focuses on hierarchies, predetermined procedures, rules, and regulations. It is basically a closed system,
mechanistic and relatively authoritarian approach.

The collegial model is based on the notion of a collegium or
community of scholars (Millett, 1962; Demerath, Stephens, and
Taylor, 1967). It is a rather ambiguous concept that favors full
participation in decision-making, especially by the faculty. It is a
utopian prescription of how the educational process should operate,
and it is favored by many—professors in particular—who are discontent with bureaucracy. The community of scholars administers
its own affairs, while bureaucratic officials have little influence. It
is reflected in the statements of Draper and Griffiths quoted earlier.
It is essentially opposed to hierarchy and structure. There are few
actual examples of such a round-table democratic organization in
the real American academic world, although some small liberal arts
colleges not confronted with a scarcity of resources resemble this
model. In the collegial model, the faculty's right to govern stems
from its professional or technical competence, not from any formal
or official authority. Talcott Parsons (1947) was among the first to
focus on the importance of technical competence to attainment of
leadership, power, influence, and decision-making, but he focused
on the physician. John Galbraith, in his *The New Industrial State*
(1967), also considers group decision-making and technical expertise

as important factors in the management and functioning of industrial corporations.

The main flaw in the bureaucratic model is that when applied (and it still is widespread in organizations of all types), it often does not work very well. One main reason for this is that human needs—especially social, psychological and self-actualization needs—are not adequately fulfilled. Another reason is that the bureaucratic model creates serious informational problems. On the other hand, there are still many situations where a relatively bureaucratic or authoritarian approach is called for and does work better than other approaches. These include situations in which human need fulfillment does not suffer very seriously, where routine and preprogammed decisions are involved, where standardization is appropriate, where a quick decision is clearly needed, and particularly where the organization or a given part of it functions in a stable environment and is not confronted with very significant uncertainty. Many people still prefer to work in structured settings and work better in them.

We do not prefer bureaucracy over more democratic forms of organization and management, either philosophically or in practice where we are directly involved. However, we recognize that there is an appropriate place and need for it, at least to some extent, in the governance of universities. In other words, we take a contingency approach regarding different models, and we feel that this is the wisest and most realistic approach. It depends on the situation. Some type of adequately balanced multidimensional model tends to be most effective in the governance or management of academic and other organizations.

The collegial model confuses normative (what ought to be) with descriptive, explanatory, and predictive (what the situation really is or what can be effective) organizational concepts. It has a very strong harmony bias that assumes away the possibility of conflict. It is only likely to work well when the organization has abundant resources, and where virtually all of the participants— especially the more active ones—have a strong spirit of genuine cooperation, similar values and personal goals, and a deep commitment to the institution and its goals and priorities.

This by no means implies that we are against participative

management and democratic organizations. We do favor a high degree of participation where decisions have a significant impact on those directly involved, where the inputs and ideas of the participants can lead to better decisions, and where they genuinely want to participate. We generally favor group decision-making on various purely academic and student matters—involving students as well as faculty in the process where appropriate. However, we do not favor a total abdication of official authority, formal power and structure, or all forms of hierarchical management, leadership, and decision-making. If this were to be done, the institution would function poorly, over time, and would probably not even be able to survive for long.

We feel that Baldridge's political model is an important contribution (Baldridge, 1971a, 1971b). It was first developed during an analysis of decision-making at New York University in the late sixties. Since then it has been applied to the conversion of Portland State College to university status and to a study of the growth of a radical student movement at Stanford. The Stanford Center for Research and Development in Teaching has been supporting further work on the application of this model since 1971. The political model takes conflict as a natural phenomenon and focuses on problems involving goal-setting and values, rather than on problems of maximizing efficiency in carrying out goals. It takes into account the role of interest groups and power blocs, and has thus far found that small groups of political elites tend to dominate major decisions but that different elite groups dominate different decisions. There is, however, a democratic tendency in universities toward more participation. Baldridge's studies have also revealed that formal authority is often severely limited by the political pressure and bargaining that groups can engage in. Decisions are often negotiated compromises among competing groups. External interest groups can have great influence, and internal groups do not have the power to make policies in a vacuum. The model also gives much attention to legal and decision-making phases that translate pressures into policy. And it can provide for an analysis of change processes and the adaptation of an institution to its changing internal and external environment. In essence, it is a relatively open systems model, unlike the other two, and we see this as its major strength.

The political model has contributed significantly to our thinking and to some of our work in this book. However, development and application of the model thus far have focused on organizations and situations where there has been a great deal of conflict and turmoil, as well as unique circumstances. One can by no means make sweeping generalizations from these applications. Also, this model cannot be applied to all aspects of university governance or administration. It is a good model for understanding, explaining, and even dealing with conflict, power, and important aspects of decision-making. But it is not useful in all situations and under all conditions. The political model does not attempt to deal with the management process, especially the functions of management, in a comprehensive way; nor does it focus on what the president should and should not do. It is not intended to be a normative or prescriptive model and, thus far, has been essentially descriptive and explanatory.

The latest model is that of "organized anarchy," developed by Cohen and March (1974). They studied the presidency of forty-two universities and colleges of different types. They interviewed forty-one presidents, thirty-nine chief academic officers, thirty-six chief financial officers, forty-two presidents' secretaries, twenty-eight other officials close to the presidents, and student leaders or editors on thirty-one campuses. In their book they briefly examine eight metaphors of academic governance and conclude that academic institutions can best be described as organized anarchies that only vaguely resemble conventional notions of what universities and colleges are.

The basic properties of organized anarchies include ambiguity of purpose and problematic goals; unclear technology; fluid participation; ambiguity of power; ambiguity of inability to learn from experience; and ambiguity of success, in particular presidential success. Cohen and March believe that organized anarchies should not be viewed as vehicles for solving well defined problems, but more as a collection of choices looking for problems, issues and feelings looking for decision situations in which they might be aired, solutions looking for issues to which they might be the answers, and decision makers looking for work. Hence, the choice of a new football coach becomes a debate over liberal education, and a committee on curriculum revision becomes a forum on the values of experiential education.

Cohen and March's decision-making model is based on a "garbage-can" theory, according to which participants throw their solutions into the can whenever the need to make a decision arises. When the garbage-can model is measured against a conventional normative model it does seem pathological, but Cohen and March point out that the great advantage of trying to see gargage-can phenomena together as a process is the possibility that this process can be understood and, to some extent, managed.

Given this model, they are skeptical about how much meaningful and effective institutional planning for the future can be done. They also feel that for sound evaluation of performance, criteria need not be specified in advance, and that evaluation in terms of what is presently felt to be important may be best. They advocate the need for "sensible foolishness" and organizational "playfulness" in academic institutions. Their book is policy oriented only to a limited extent. The most prescriptive parts deal with leadership responses to anarchy, elementary tactics of administrative action, and eight tactical rules for those who seek to influence decisions (pp. 203–219).

Cohen and March seem to feel that the basic ambiguities which make academic institutions function like organized anarchies are an inherent, inevitable part of them. Although it does not seem to be a major purpose of their book, their study does provide many vivid insights about why so many universities and colleges are in trouble today. But the book is, in our view, of only limited help to those institutions and their managements which are or will be in deep trouble since it does not provide many guidelines or prescriptions about what they might or could do to alleviate their serious problems. The garbage-can model, although relevant and realistic for many organizations, invites a "garbage-dump" approach to the allocation and utilization of scarce resources. As descriptive organization theorists, Cohen and March do not seem to be interested in or concerned about economic problems. Their book has little to say about genuine conflicts that arise over scarce resources or about the serious financial and economic problems confronting academic institutions. Despite these drawbacks, however, Cohen and March's descriptive-explanatory study can be a valuable point of departure for developing predictive, prescriptive, and operational theories, guidelines, and approaches.

Our own position, which is demonstrated in this book, is that it is possible to operationalize goal systems and related priorities, to verify goal performance, and to make viable and effective goal and priority choices at academic institutions generally. We also feel that power and participation need not be ambiguous and that authority, power, and participatory roles and relationships can be clarified considerably more than they typically are. Technology and experience also need not be ambiguous, and neither must presidential, managerial, or institutional success.

Although much needs to be done with regard to the development of management and organizational theories—especially predictive and prescriptive theories—for universities and colleges, various contingency theories and approaches can be effective and useful; there will never be one universally applicable theory of management.

Need for a Comprehensive Open Systems Approach

The administration of an individual college or university has been the subject of many investigations since James Perkins pointed out, in 1960, that administrative theorists were interested in all kinds of organizations except the academic organizations that house them (Perkins, 1960). Most administrative theorists have focused on institutional functions such as academic and student affairs, public and governmental relations, business affairs, budgets, finance, and fund-raising (Barzun, 1968; Brown, 1969; American Council on Education, 1968). A limited but growing number of them have focused on general administration, including some of the basic functions of management discussed in this book (Lahti, 1973; Lumsford, 1963; Olive, 1967). However, most of these have taken an administrative rather than a managerial point of view.

Few studies have utilized a comprehensive systems approach, especially an operational open systems approach (Millett, 1968). And few studies utilize a contingency approach to any significant extent. Moreover, we have not personally come across any book on higher education that has developed comprehensive taxonomies of the various systems, subsystems, interrelationships, and environmental constraints that bear significantly on the functioning and management of universities and colleges. We have found one significant study which focuses on the development of taxonomies of organizational behavior in the administration of primary and secondary schools (Griffiths, 1969). This study draws on general systems theory, nonmathematical decision theory, compliance theory, and Weber's theory of bureaucratic behavior. However, it is basically quite different from our approach, which focuses on the management of higher educational institutions.

In this book we take a comprehensive open systems approach to the study of universities and colleges and their management. This is coupled with a contingency approach. We are interested in the predictive and prescriptive dimensions of management and organizational behavior, as well as the descriptive and explanatory aspects. We consider the outputs or goals of the system, the inputs into the organization, the internal subsystems and relationships involved in the transformation process, and the external environmental constraints that surround the organization. We classify the critical elements or components of each of the above, and also deal with the interrelationships within each category or set of elements, as well as the relationships and interfaces (or interactions) among them. This will hopefully provide an overall framework for more effective management and better decisions.

Of primary importance is the vexing problem of institutional goal systems and priorities. Conflict situations frequently result from goal divergence among different groups or constituencies—both internal and external to the organization. If goals and priorities are obscure or are not adequately operational, it is not possible to get the most suitable inputs or to use them very efficiently and effectively to achieve the goals. Much of the environmental constraint action confronting academic institutions stems from attempts by interested outsiders to establish and change the institution's goal system and priorities. A paramount task of management is to structure goal systems and priorities in ways that minimize disadvantages and maximize advantages to the institution. This requires systematic consideration of the goals problem.

Because our approach attempts to be both realistic and dynamic, it also pays much attention to the concept of power, as well as to conflict among the various individuals, constituencies, and units that have major interests in the institution and its management. We classify and analyze power in managerial and political terms, not merely in a legalistic or formalistic manner.

In sum, we attempt to: (1) build a useful taxonomy of the overall system and its major parts; (2) raise important questions about what goals and results the system is supposed to achieve; (3) analyze interrelationships within the system, as well as external environmental constraints; (4) determine what the system is actually doing and whether it is doing what it should be doing; (5) show what could be changed to correct significant deviations if the system is not doing what it should or is supposed to be doing; and (6) show management how to get better results.

In the next chapter we present an actual case of a university in crisis, before proceeding with the above overall approach. We consider the origins of the crisis, the kinds of serious mismanagement problems involved, and what effective management might have done to minimize the crisis. At the end of the case we apply some important aspects of our approach and related taxonomies in an illustrative and operational manner. The following chapters will describe in more depth the comprehensive open systems approach.

Chapter II

Mismanagement and Crisis

This chapter presents a case study of a university in crisis—a government-supported public university with an annual budget of about forty million dollars, fifteen thousand students, and more than one thousand faculty members.* This case contains significant implications for universities and colleges in general and also provides a backdrop for the concepts, problems, and guidelines discussed in the rest of the book.

* Student and faculty figures are approximate full-time equivalents. This university has many part-time students and quite a few part-time faculty members.

We feel that it is fruitful and interesting to highlight what not to do in preventing and dealing with crisis, rather than focusing only on what to do—although we also do give consideration to what might have been done. There are many different ways to head off and handle crises effectively and to achieve desired results, depending on the specific circumstances. And there are some things that, if done, entail a high probability of contributing to and perpetuating crisis. This is the art of true mismanagement! The university in this particular case failed to avoid several basic pitfalls common in academic mismanagement. It also acted contrary to many of the positive guidelines and approaches discussed at various points throughout this book.

Table 1 presents in summary form the highlights of this crisis and related management problems. The first column lists the critical events in chronological order. The second column outlines the basic managerial problems relating to each time period. The final column indicates those chapters in the book which deal with or relate to each of the managerial problems. The chapters indicated present further discussion and analysis of these problems, as well as techniques for avoiding or, at least, minimizing them.

Origins of Crisis

We focus on the 1972–1973 academic year, when the crisis reached its peak. However, some discussion about the origins of the crisis is in order. There seem to have been at least ten critical factors. They were (in no particular order of importance): (1) the government's funding formula, which has been tied directly to the number of students of different types enrolled; (2) the selection of a compromise candidate for president and also several years before a compromise chairman of the board of governors; (3) poor management and ineffective leadership, particularly by the president, which increased the overall crisis; (4) serious deficiencies in the abilities, training, and skills of several of the president's key deputies and personal staff; (5) unclear goal systems and the lack of operational priorities; (6) poor planning and forecasting, especially of enrollment projections, and the absence of contingency plans; (7) grossly deficient information systems; (8) ineffective control and

Table 1.

CHRONOLOGY OF CRITICAL EVENTS AND
MAJOR MANAGERIAL PROBLEMS

Chronology of Critical Events	Major Managerial Problems	Key Chapters Relating to Managerial Problems
1960s: First President		
Dynamic entrepreneurship Enrollment growth Abundant resources	Inadequate attention to articulation and operationalization of institutional goal system and priorities	3, 13
	Inadequate **long-range** planning	8, 13
	Failure to develop and apply adequate efficiency criteria and cost-benefit analysis for resource allocation and performance evaluation	5, 13
	Inadequate development of information, control, and other management systems	6, 7
	Ineffective managerial staffing and organizational design (especially in the central administration and with regard to staff support and service functions)	9, 10
1970: Selecting New President		
Power struggle among deans vying for presidency Board selects a compromise candidate for president in haste	Failure to clearly define and communicate suitable criteria and procedures for selecting new president	9
Apparently board also settles on compromise candidate for its new chairman	Miscalculation of faculty reaction and motivation in conjunction with inadequate provisions for faculty consultation	11

Table 1. ,(Cont.)

CHRONOLOGY OF CRITICAL EVENTS AND
MAJOR MANAGERIAL PROBLEMS

Chronology of Critical Events	Major Managerial Problems	Key Chapters Relating to Managerial Problems
	Ineffective presidential and board leadership and direction	9
	Ineffective use of power and failure to understand critical subsystem relationships and interfaces	3, 6, 7
1972–1973: Acute Crises		
Financial (budgetary) crisis leads to disastrous managerial and leadership crisis that compounds financial crisis	Deficient overall functioning by president and central administration; also major problems involving goal system and priorities, as well as power and authority	All chapters
Summer 1972		
Emerging awareness of a likely significant enrollment shortfall	Deficient forecasting and , projections as well as unclear goals and priorities; inadequate analysis of external environment and potential student interests and desires	4, 8, 12, 13
	Inadequate contingency planning and lack of comprehensive systems approach in management	3, 4, 5, 13
	Deficient information and control systems and budgeting criteria and methods	5, 7
October 1972: Regular Classes Resume		
Enrollment shortfall significantly greater than anticipated	Deficient planning, lack of contingency planning	4, 9, 13

Table 1. (Cont.)

CHRONOLOGY OF CRITICAL EVENTS AND
MAJOR MANAGERIAL PROBLEMS

Chronology of Critical Events	Major Managerial Problems	Key Chapters Relating to Managerial Problems
Confusion mounts as to true magnitude of budget deficit and crisis	Ineffective leadership and use of power and authority	6
Critical data of central administration revealed to be in error by part-time college dean	Staffing, organizational, and authority-delegation deficiencies, especially in central administration and with regard to staff support and service functions	9, 10
President's statements ambiguous and inconsistent		
Conflict between president and board revealed in senate	Deficient information and control systems	3, 5, 7
Faculty begins to panic about retrenchment and other budgetary consequences	Inadequate understanding of critical interfaces and subsystem interrelationships	3, 5, 7, 8, 11, 12
	Poor communication	9
	Inadequate efficiency criteria and use of cost-benefit analysis for resource allocation and performance evaluation	5, 13
	Inadequate comprehension of faculty motivation and reaction	5, 11
November 1972		
Financial and leadership crises become acute and emotional	Same managerial problems as in October	All of above chapters
Senate creates Joint Committee on Alternatives (JCOA) to deal with crises; president's council to deal with budget formulation suspended; chairman of sen-	Loss of much of president's formal power and authority and those of other key administrators to committee; central decision-making	6, 7, 9, 10, 13

Table 1. (Cont.)

CHRONOLOGY OF CRITICAL EVENTS AND
MAJOR MANAGERIAL PROBLEMS

Chronology of Critical Events	*Major Managerial Problems*	*Key Chapters Relating to Managerial Problems*
ate becomes chairman of JCOA	and especially implementation of decisions at near standstill	
December 1972		
JCOA reports to senate on financial situation	All managerial and leadership problems continue, with president's leadership, authority, and direction becoming even more ineffective	All chapters
Senate votes to extend life of JCOA to prepare a comprehensive final report		
President informs JCOA that he would resign if a significant majority of its members did not support him; also instructs committee to discuss his "essential conditions" for remaining in office	President's ultimatums come from position of increasing weakness; unwise uses of power and failure to comprehend or be informed about critical interfaces and subsystem interrelationships	3, 6, 7, 13
Board chairman tells dean that the board would accept president's resignation if he submits it	Breakdown of communications between board and president	9
Vice-president of finance reveals that deficit for current year is likely to be significantly greater than anticipated	Senate creates new crisis committee without accurate or sufficient information	7, 11
	Faulty and inconsistent information and ineffective public relations; president, board and university in general presented to public in poor light by media	7, 8
	Lack of operational goal system; unclear institutional priorities; inad-	4, 5, 6, 7, 9, 10, 11, 13

Table 1. (Cont.)

CHRONOLOGY OF CRITICAL EVENTS AND
MAJOR MANAGERIAL PROBLEMS

Chronology of Critical Events	*Major Managerial Problems*	*Key Chapters Relating to Managerial Problems*
	equate contingency planning; absence of meaningful criteria, techniques, and data for allocating resources and evaluating performance; poor communication; misuses of power and authority	
JCOA majority votes for president to stay in office, but does not vote on essential conditions		
President, at JCOA meeting, gives dean of the part-time college five-minute ultimatum to promise to cooperate with him in the future or else resign or be fired		
Several board members indicate informally that they would support president if it comes to a showdown between him and the part-time college dean		
President writes the troublesome dean a conciliatory letter and meets with him briefly; dean's faculty is strongly behind him		
President's demand for a "loyalty oath" hits mass media		
JCOA recommends creation of new small task force to follow up work of JCOA		

Table 1. (Cont.)

CHRONOLOGY OF CRITICAL EVENTS AND
MAJOR MANAGERIAL PROBLEMS

Chronology of Critical Events	Major Managerial Problems	Key Chapters Relating to Managerial Problems
when it is dissolved; task force could act only under authority delegated by president		
President tells various JCOA members that he feels proposal regarding task force is vote of no confidence in his presidency		
President presents JCOA with two alternatives for staying in office		
JCOA passes a motion combining elements of both proposals		
President strongly endorses creation of new task force and proposes members		
Coordinating Committee on Alternatives (CCOA) created		
Informal emergency meeting of members of dissolved JCOA and executive committee of board arranged without president's knowledge		
Majority of former JCOA members present express nonconfidence in the president, several board members indicate that matter of the presidency is likely to be appropriately resolved within a month or at most two		

Table 1. (Cont.)

CHRONOLOGY OF CRITICAL EVENTS AND
MAJOR MANAGERIAL PROBLEMS

Chronology of Critical Events	Major Managerial Problems	Key Chapters Relating to Managerial Problems
Chairman and some other board members ask president for his resignation; he strongly refuses		
Articles begin appearing regularly in the press about university crisis		
Dean who had earlier been a strong supporter of the president submits resignation; vice-president for academic affairs and controller also resign		
January 1973: Mismanagement Resumes		
Board seeks to work out some arrangement by which the president would resign	Power, authority, influence, and leadership effectiveness of president suffer further	3, 6
President has little contact with deans, CCOA takes over major functions of JCOA and president's council	External environmental constraints and pressures and gross internal mismanagement and inaction cause board to take strong stand on budget	5, 6, 8, 9, 10, 13
Board makes it clear to president that budget for next year has to be cut substantially		
	Ineffective handling of student problems by president	12
	Board must resort to ultimate authority and force president to resign; no other staffing or organizational changes initiated or implemented	6, 9, 10, 11

Table 1. (Cont.)

CHRONOLOGY OF CRITICAL EVENTS AND
MAJOR MANAGERIAL PROBLEMS

Chronology of Critical Events	Major Managerial Problems	Key Chapters Relating to Managerial Problems
Student problems related to an increase in tuition; president vacillates in his support of students versus government		
Board finally gives president choice of resigning or being fired; president submits resignation effective immediately		
Acting president takes over, but within less than twenty-four hours submits resignation		
Second acting president appointed		
Remainder of 1972–1973 Academic Year		
CCOA plays major advisory role to acting president and central staff in formulating budget, which still entails large deficits over next several years	Few JCOA recommendations effectively followed-up or implemented; not much done generally to overcome managerial and organizational problems	5, 6, 7, 9, 10, 11, 13
Senate establishes new budget committee which again excludes all deans and most central administrators	Power, authority, and other important role relationships remain highly ambiguous	6, 7, 9, 10, 11
Vice-president of finance fired; some other administrators also leave Search committee and set of procedures are established to select new permanent president	Adequate criteria not defined for getting a good fit between goal system and priorities and the individual to be selected as president; goal system and related	4, 9, 13

Table 1. (Cont.)

CHRONOLOGY OF CRITICAL EVENTS AND
MAJOR MANAGERIAL PROBLEMS

Chronology of Critical Events	Major Managerial Problems	Key Chapters Relating to Managerial Problems
	priorities themselves still not defined or operationalized in any systematic or clear manner	
Fall Term 1973–1974		
Overall university enrollment drops by about 3 percent compared with 1972–1973	Presidential choice questionable	6, 9, 13
New permanent president selected to take over in July 1974	Serious budgeting problems related to goal system, priority, power, and serious internal mismanagement problems, as well as external constraints and not enough students	All chapters

budgeting systems; (9) faulty communications, including a breakdown in effective communication between the president and the chairman of the board of governors; and (10) a dean who wanted but failed to become president—and was out to get the president.

This university was created in the late 1950s. In less than a decade it had gained a warranted reputation as a relatively high caliber, innovative, and creative academic institution. Benefiting from the undercapacity of universities and colleges in this particular region to meet the needs of all those desiring a higher education, abundant financial resources from the state government, substantial research grants, and the academic recession already affecting many other institutions, this university managed to attract many high-quality faculty members. And it did not have significant problems attracting enough qualified students, except in one or two faculties.

Most funds for the university come from the state government, which has been using a rather simple formula that relates funding to student enrollment (body count) on December 1 of each academic year. Each type of student—undergraduate, honors, graduate, PhD, part-time—is worth so many income units. When enrollments are increasing steadily and continuously this is an advantageous formula. However, when enrollments stagnate, and especially when they decline, such a formula causes serious problems. This has in fact occurred only in the past few years at most of the universities and colleges under the jurisdiction of this particular state government. But because funds for a given year are not actually allocated until the academic year is well underway, faulty enrollment forecasts can compound an institution's problems.

Only after the financial crisis at this university—and at some others in the same state—had reached dramatic proportions did the government begin to seriously consider more rational, stable, and effective funding formula alternatives. It also did eventually grant some supplemental funds for an interim period to institutions in serious trouble. In the future, actual enrollments for a given year might become a budget floor for the next year should enrollments drop. This would be an improvement over the existing formula, but a more rational formula should be developed to enable long-range planning and to ensure greater stability.

Until 1972, most of the faculties and schools of this university experienced steady and substantial enrollment growth. For some years total enrollment increased by 15 percent and even 20 percent or more each year. In fact enrollments, and hence resources available, grew so much and so fast that no one really seemed very concerned about university goals and priorities. Resources were usually adequate to do most things that the board, the administration, and the faculties felt should be done and wanted done. No meaningful contingency plan was prepared for a time of scarce resources.

First President

The first president, who held office for about a decade, came from a top university in the same region. There he had been involved in senior-level management. He had a doctorate in economics. He was a very dynamic, entrepreneurial type, and was instrumental in building up a first-rate institution in a remarkably short period of time. He hired first-rate and dynamic deans gave them leeway to build their schools and faculties. After all, money was really not much of a problem. However, this first president never did build a very effective central administration, information systems, support services, effective controls, and the like. As long as there were ample financial resources, these deficiencies did not create very serious problems. Management tends to be relatively easy and need not be that effective when there are abundant resources.

The president got along well with the board and its chairman, who was a respected, effective, and powerful individual. Even though this is a government-supported public university, the board has been self-perpetuating. Both the president and the board chairman were ideally suited to this stage of the university's growth and development. The main weaknesses were probably in not building up more effective central management systems, not defining goals and priorities over time more clearly and operationally, and not developing any real contingency plans.

Selecting a Successor

The first president decided to retire in 1970. Both he and the board wanted the dean of the management school to succeed him as president. However, no clear criteria or procedures were established for selecting a successor, and not much genuine faculty participation in the selection process was provided for by either the board or the first president. Many influential members of the academic senate had been opposed to the appointment of the management dean as president and felt that they were not adequately consulted; they did not want the board to force a new president on them. The academic senate gave their support to the dean of the faculty of arts for president. The dean of the large part-time college of the university, which had a good reputation in the community, also wanted to be president, but he had minimal support and then suffered a heart attack. During the presidential campaign he sent telegrams and other communications reaffirming his candidacy, but to no avail.

The board in the end was divided. Members rather hastily put together a list of possible outside candidates and finally appointed the dean of the graduate faculty at a much smaller university who had expressed a strong interest in the job. This appointment met with adequate, but not particularly enthusiastic, faculty support. Some board members, mostly supporters of the management school dean, resigned, and several others became less actively involved with or concerned about the university. Apparently the new board chairman who took office at about the same time as the new president was also a compromise choice. He had a Ph.D. in economics, was a senior executive with a large bank, and was also a long-time friend of the new president.

The new president had a good reputation as a scholar and economist and was prominent and influential in the banking world. However, he had not been a distinguished manager or leader in his previous administrative job. He soon gained a favorable reputation at the university for his honesty, integrity, open-mindedness, dedication, and hard work. But he tended to get deeply involved in detail and did not delegate authority adequately or effectively. The central administration and the way it functioned left much to be desired when he took over, but he made little headway in improving the quality of personnel or in developing new and more effective information, control, and other systems. These deficiencies did not result in severe problems in his first few years as president because student enrollment was still growing. Continued growth also prevented his problems with deans, faculty members, and the academic senate from reaching crisis proportions.

Acute Crisis and Mismanagement

Then, in 1972–1973, the crunch came. A financial crisis led to a disastrous managerial and leadership crisis that compounded the financial crisis. With more effective management and leadership, including a clean definition of priorities, good information systems, and effective contingency planning, the financial crisis would not have reached the proportions it did. It might have been possible to work out an interim arrangement with the government, to get the board to agree on a sizable deficit without panic, and even to get the board to help in raising other funds to cut the deficit. It would also have been possible, over a period of years, to devise new ways to raise additional revenues and cut costs considerably. If this planning had been done in advance of, and in anticipation of, the crisis, it would have been more effective than the coping that was done in a panic situation.

As late as midsummer of 1972 the president and his central staff expected enrollment to increase from 6 to 9 percent. An even higher increase had been anticipated earlier. Some steps were taken to get the deans to agree to freeze a modest part of their faculty budgets, which had been drawn up and approved on the basis of the higher enrollments expected earlier. This modest reduction was, at the time, viewed as a contingency plan to be used only if the higher figures were not realized. It was the only contingency plan developed (and ultimately used) by the president or others in the central administration throughout the crisis.

By early October, classes had begun and enrollments were clearly short of even the revised targets. There were a number of reasons for this, including much higher drop-out rates than had been anticipated. Better information systems and analyses would have significantly reduced the errors in forecasting and planning.

The president's council, the key budgetary and management committee at that time, was made up of the president as chairman, all of the senior executive officers, and all of the deans. The executive committee of the academic senate and the senate committee on academic planning and policy (APPC) were the two most important senate committees. APPC was the one most directly concerned with budgetary matters and the financial crisis. During October these bodies met often to discuss and try to come to grips with the large deficit and financial crisis that had emerged.

However, there was much confusion about the magnitude of the deficit and the crisis generally, because there were many major deficiencies and inconsistencies in the information available on such things as actual enrollments, costs, and revenues. Moreover, the president and his staff were ineffective in making much headway in establishing operational or meaningful priorities, criteria, guidelines, or contingency plans for what should be cut and by how much, if necessary.

The part-time college dean revealed on a number of occasions that figures and other data provided by the central administration were in error. He was assisted by some of his faculty members, who did a thorough analysis of the accounting data, records, and other information available. For example, they proved at one point that, although all faculties had agreed during the summer to freeze a part of their approved budgets, the actual expenditures to date by the central administration significantly exceeded the figures originally approved in the spring of 1972.

This group was also later to prove that actual enrollments were higher than the central administration's figures revealed—because of a significant error in the computer printout—and that other figures used were also significantly in error. The net result was that the revised projected budget deficit for the year, although still considerable, was significantly less than had been estimated by the central administration. All of this was made public in meetings of the entire senate and even in the press. Although most people at the university sympathized much more with the president than with the part-time college dean, it did become clear that the latter and his group were usually right on their computations and the central administration was wrong. This damaged the president's credibility and undermined his leadership.

Even though the President's leadership left much to be desired during the growing crisis in October, most of the deans agreed to substantial additional cuts in their faculty budgets. Moreover, the central administration was pressured into making substantial cuts in its own budgets. However, a sizable deficit still remained for the current year, and there was much uncertainty about future enrollments. The president and his staff were not very optimistic about the enrollment prospects for the next few years, and there was not much information available to use in making meaningful projections.

At one point the president presented data and projections indicating that the total number of faculty would have to be reduced significantly during the next few years, and that some cuts would be required during the current year. The APPC came to the same conclusion—although the part-time college dean and his group strongly disputed this. In a meeting of the senate-at-large, the data indicating the magnitude of retrenchment were presented and much panic, confusion, and conflict emerged.

At another senate meeting a resolution was received from the Board and distributed publicly. The resolution requested the president to cut faculty budgets by an additional 10 percent, and this clearly implied large cuts in academic personnel. A member of the board of governors who attended this meeting stated that the resolution was based on data provided to the board by the president, who agreed with the resolution. Then the president made some rather ambiguous and unclear statements to the contrary. This open dispute between the board and the president greatly intensified the crisis.

The president began to back off on his statements about the seriousness of the crisis and the need to dismiss a sizable number of faculty members. But he and the new vice-president for academic affairs got their signals crossed, and the vice-president continued publicly to support retrenchment. This greatly undermined his credibility and effectiveness and eventually led to his resignation in December.

Since rules and procedures regarding faculty dismissals were far from complete or clear, various Senate Committees started holding meetings about this and reported to the Senate-at-large. The Senate, as well as faculty union leaders, consistently tried to get a formal statement from the President that there would be no faculty members dismissed on financial grounds, at least during the current year. The President did eventually make an unequivocal statement to this effect in December.

If operational rules and procedures for faculty retrenchment had been determined earlier in a noncrisis environment, and had been ready to be applied if and when needed, the crisis would not have become as emotional or acute as it did. Moreover, sound forecasting and contingency planning could have led to more contractually limited appointments and to more forceful application of academic standards in faculty tenure and promotion decisions. This, in turn, would have led to increased flexibility, more retrenchment on purely academic grounds, and significantly less overstaffing. Because resources had been abundant in the past, many marginal or substandard faculty members had not been required to leave and quite a few had received tenure and promotions. The general atmosphere of live and let live could have been tightened up without fanfare through effective leadership and managerial foresight.

As the fall term progressed, operational priorities, criteria, plans, and procedures for dealing with the crisis were still not established. Some of the deans urged the president—without success—to develop a contingency plan that would indicate budgetary priorities and would spell out which programs and courses should be cut back first. They made recommendations such as these:

1. Much could be done to determine which departments and specific courses consistently have very small or negligible enrollments, teaching and work loads, and so on. If there are no realistic prospects for a significant improvement in the future, it would be wise to make the first budgetary cutback in these areas.

2. It would be possible to consolidate various courses and sections and get rid of duplication.

3. It would be possible to redeploy quite a few faculty members to various courses and new programs for which there clearly is student demand.

4. New initiatives of various kinds can be developed and implemented to improve the financial situation.

5. If dismissals are required, the president, in close consultation with the president's council, should decide on priorities on the basis of financial constraints and other pertinent information. He should then give quotas and deadlines for cutbacks to the appropriate deans, and, in turn, to the appropriate department chairmen and faculty committees. They would be responsible for implemening specific cutbacks.

6. A thorough analysis should be made of the central administration to see what kinds of services and functions were really needed, how effective they are, and how they can be reorganized, economized, and improved.

The president did not take meaningful action on any of these recommendations when they were offered to him. If he had, the crisis may well have not gotten out of hand, and he probably could have saved his job. He continued to make unclear and inconsistent statements. For example, at times he implied that all faculties and schools should share substantially in the cutbacks according to some undefined, uniform formula. At other times he stated that the stronger and growing faculties should not be expected to make substantial cutbacks or unduly subsidize those that were in the most trouble.

Arguments about what criteria to use in making budgetary decisions—for example, student-faculty ratios, cost per student, expenditures in relation to revenues, or student contact hours—typically resolved nothing, largely because adequate information and comparable data were not available. Virtually no attention was given to a determination of the goals and priorities, or the strengths, comparative advantages, and weaknesses of the university or individual faculties, or to an analysis of the feasibility of, and degree to which, these goals and priorities were being and could be realized. This kind of analysis is difficult and involves many qualitative factors; but if done properly it could have led to meaningful decisions.

President's Loss of Power and Influence

By November both the financial and leadership crises had become very emotional. Several deans, with the backing of some key senators and the president, presented a motion to the senate. The motion was designed to create a special committee to help resolve the crisis, to compile accurate data, and to come up with recommendations for action and alternatives. This was to be the joint committee on alternatives (jcoa), and it was created with a virtually unanimous positive vote of the senate. jcoa consisted of all of the members of the president's council (senior administrators, deans, and so forth), representatives from the faculty union and staff association, and a few other administrative officers and senators, including a student senator. However, the president was not to be named chairman of this crisis committee, and its members chose the chairman of the senate as chairman of jcoa. The committee was to report back to senate on its progress within about a month. jcoa eventually took over the functions of both the president's council and appc, and those groups discontinued their regular meetings.

jcoa met frequently and for long hours and made some significant progress—albeit slowly. The president abdicated much of his leadership and authority to the committee, in a sense putting the university in committee trusteeship. The actual financial and enrollment situation of the university was finally agreed upon by the committee. One of the part-time college dean's deputies played the key role in gathering and analyzing the data available.

The members of jcoa decided to set up various subcommittees for such things as getting at the true existing situation, new initiatives, enrollment projections, how to get economies in the central administration, early retirement and voluntary staff opportunities, liaison with the board, and overall budget preparation. Consideration of nonvoluntary academic dismissals was to be postponed until all of the subcommittees had finished their work. However, this issue was never really discussed in an operational sense in JCOA.

When JCOA reported to senate in December, the only concrete information it agreed on unanimously and presented was on the actual financial situation of the university. Some preliminary reports on other matters were also given. The senate voted overwhelmingly to extend the life of the committee for another several weeks, at which time its final report was to be given and it was to be disbanded.

Shortly after JCOA reconvened, the matter of procedures to be followed after the committee's life terminated was brought up and discussed. The various subcommittees continued their intensive studies and investigations and compiled much data. The president prepared a position paper on the procedures to be followed after the committee was disbanded. He urged a return to normalcy and recommended that the president's council should resume its functions. He also suggested that some kind of budget advisory committee might be created. The president asserted that he intended to resume his functions as chief executive. And he listed other conditions and recommendations, some of them rather unclear and confusing. He stated that if he was to remain as president, JCOA would have to agree on the basic points of this memo of essential conditions.

At about this same time the president agreed to implement a proposal made earlier by a few of the deans. This involved setting up a special committee or task force under the chairmanship of dean of the arts faculty, who would report directly to the president. This task force would be responsible for following up and implementing the recommendations adopted by JCOA after it was disbanded. It would also make some additional studies and undertake certain other tasks. However, this proposal was never implemented. The dean of the arts faculty refused to take the chairmanship because the president presented to different people widely divergent

views on what this task force was really going to do and how much
authority its chairman would actually have.

Vote of Confidence

On a Saturday morning in the second week of December,
while JCOA was in session, the president decided to meet privately
with all of the deans and a number of influential senators, several
of whom were not on the committee. His purpose was to see how
much support there was for his presidency. He also informed JCOA
that he would resign if a "significant majority" of its members did
not support him and if he felt that there was not broad support for
him generally. He also instructed the committee to discuss and
hopefully adopt his memo of "essential conditions" he would require if he was to stay on as president.

While that meeting was going on, one of the deans received
a telephone call from the board chairman, who said that the board
would be willing to accept the president's resignation if he submitted it. The caller also said that it was all right for the dean to
use his discretion in informing other members of JCOA, particularly
some of the deans, of the board's willingness to accept a resignation.
The chairman emphasized that the president did not know and
should not learn of the phone call, which was to be treated in strict-
est confidence. The dean then told other deans and a few other
members of JCOA who supported the president of the phone call.

During the JCOA meeting held that day, it was revealed and
acknowledged by the vice-president of finance that, as a result of
various miscalculations and overexpenditures, the deficit for the
current year was likely to be more than $500,000 greater than an-
ticipated. This revelation was made after the committee had agreed
on and reported a significantly lower deficit figure to the senate.

By that evening, the President had finished his private ses-
sions and the Committee turned its attention to his memo on
essential conditions. Many members did not even want to discuss
this memo, and the discussion got nowhere. Finally, one member
suggested that a straw vote be taken to see how much support there
was for the President, and if there was enough, then the memo
would be taken up again. The following motion was voted on after
much discussion and debate: "It is in the best interests of the Uni-

versity for the President to stay on in office." The motion carried
12 to 7, and all but two deans supported it. The opposition included mainly backers of the part-time college Dean who had
formed a kind of coalition.

The outcome was then reported to the President. He said
that he felt there was generally enough support for him, and that the
committee should again take up his memo for the next day.

At the outset of the meeting the following day, the President
read a prepared statement. He asserted that in his view he had
adequate support. He then gave the troublesome Dean a five minute
ultimatum to promise to cooperatet with him in the future or else
resign or be fired. The Dean left the room and a discussion followed in which even several of the President's strongest supporters
pointed out that the straw vote was not really a vote of confidence
for him to serve out his full term—he was appointed for a 5 to 7
year term—and that there were some serious reservations about his
leadership ability and managerial effectiveness. It was really only
a vote to see how much support there was for him to stay on for
the time being.

A number of the Joint Committee members—seven deans
along with the head of the APPC committee—determined that it
would be wise to arrange an emergency meeting with the board
chairman to make an accurate, factual presentation of the events
of the past two days and to prepare the board for any adverse
publicity which might and soon did—arise from these events.
After the meeting broke up, several key board members indicated
informally that they would support the president if it came to a
showdown between him and the part-time college dean.

The following day, the President wrote the troublesome dean
a conciliatory letter and met with him briefly. The dean's faculty
—who were strongly behind him—were in emergency session all
day and later sent a strong statement to the board condemning the
President's behavior. The outcome was that the President did not
force him to resign. Shortly thereafter, the president's demand for
a loyalty oath hit the media and continued to do so for some time.

Reply to "Essential Conditions"

That evening the committee again took up the president's
essential conditions for staying in office. This discussion got nowhere

until a small group of individuals got together during a recess and prepared a proposal and related motion which was to be accepted overwhelmingly and without dissent by the committee. This proposal involved the creation of a new small task force or committee to follow up the work of JCOA once it was disbanded. However, the president was to still have final authority on all important financial and administrative matters and the proposed committee could only act under authority delegated to it by the president. This proposal was very similar to the one the president had agreed on a few weeks earlier, but which was not implemented. It was also agreed almost unanimously by the committee that the arts faculty dean would chair this task force and report directly to the president. The other members included the management school dean, the vice-president of finance, the student member of the JCOA, and one member to be elected by the senate. The members were proposed and approved overwhelmingly because of their expertise and abilities to make this task force work effectively. This approved motion was then communicated to the president.

Early the following day, the president met with some senior senators not on JCOA whom he considered to be "loyal and trustworthy." He then began telephoning people. First on his list were the deans he felt were most responsible for this motion and several of the members named to the proposed new task force. He was very upset and he stated that he interpreted this proposal as one of nonconfidence in his presidency. It was pointed out and explained that this was by no means the intent of the motion, although, as it turned out, some committee members who were not that familiar with managerial terminology and authority concepts did apparently view the motion as essentially one of non-confidence. It was suggested to the president that an emergency JCOA meeting be called that night where he could state his position and clarify the situation, and this meeting did take place.

At the outset, the president stated that he took the proposal and motion dealing with the new task force as one of nonconfidence, as did a number of loyal senators he had met with earlier that day. He then presented two of his own alternatives for staying in office, one of which he called "most preferable," and the other "least preferable." When he finished his presentation, he left the meeting. None of the members even wanted to discuss his "most preferable" proposal which they generally found to be very confusing and far from sound. His "least preferable" proposal was basically similar to the motion adopted the previous day. However, he wanted to delete any reference to specific members named to this task force. He also wanted a number of word changes as well as a preamble which more forcefully asserted his own authority and powers.

It was clear that if anyone had raised a straightforward non-confidence motion then and there against the President it would have passed easily, if not overwhelmingly. But no one did this out of compassion for him. People started getting restless and several indicated that they intended to leave. One eventually did. Then the chairman of APPC began to work on some wording changes desired by the president. He said that the committee must come to the senate meeting the next day with some kind of procedure to follow up on the work of JCOA which was to be dissolved then, and that the senate was expecting this. Finally, his somewhat revised and amended motion passed, but without any reference to the new Committee's membership or selection procedures.

The vote was only five in favor and two against in a committee of twenty-one members, almost all of whom were present. It was clear that most if not all of the abstentions were expressions of non-confidence in the President. Even some of those voting for it did not really want the President to remain in office. A motion to adjourn the meeting passed before the new committee's membership could be considered, and the President was then informed of the outcome of the meeting.

Another Crisis Committee

Near the outset of the senate meeting the next day, the president stated that he strongly endorsed the motion on administrative procedures following the termination of JCOA passed by that committee the previous night. He implied that it had strong JCOA support and made no mention of the five-to-two vote. He then proposed that the members of the new committee be three senators elected by the senate and two people appointed by him. Some of his loyal and trusted senators took the lead in getting these proposals passed. Eventually, the motion on the new committee—called the Coordinating Committee on Alternatives (CCOA)—along with the membership selection procedures proposed by the president passed by a solid majority. However, there were a significant, but uncounted number of abstentions. Not more than a few members of the JCOA voted in favor. The JCOA was then officially dissolved.

The JCOA generally did a dedicated and good job, given time constraints, the magnitude of the problems involved, the dearth of pertinent information at the time of its creation, and the diverse constituencies represented (in fact, all the major constituencies within the university). The various subcommittees came up with potentially fruitful recommendations involving new initiatives; vigorous ways to attract, recruit, and keep students; concern about jobs for graduates; ways to increase enrollments and revenues in the future; and ways to effect economies, cut costs, and improve services. The JCOA generated and compiled much information of potential value. However, apparently only a small number of the recommendations have thus far been followed up effectively or implemented.

The JCOA did come up with a global budget—broken down only in broad categories—for 1973–1974 and some preliminary projections for later years. The global budget was presented to both the board and senate. It contained provisions for both significant faculty additions and across-the-board salary increases. It projected a large deficit for the following academic year and somewhat smaller ones for the two subsequent years.

The JCOA also did finally come up with enrollment projections for the next several years. However, various deans managed to have the projections for their own faculties raised quite significantly with little or no justification. Moreover, some of the impact that new initiatives were likely to have on increasing revenues and enrollments and the impact that various recommendations if implemented, would have on bringing about economies and cost savings were overprojected if not entirely unrealistic.

Emergency Meeting with Key Board Members

During the day of the senate meeting which ended with the termination of the JCOA, the board chairman, who was out of town, was on the phone with various deans and the secretary of the university without the president's knowledge. Some of the other board members also spoke to certain individuals at the university. The board chairman decided to have the secretary set up an informal emergency meeting without the president's knowledge in the late afternoon of the next day. Members of the executive committee of the board and most of the members of the now-dissolved JCOA attended.

The board chairman asked each non-board member present to candidly state his views regarding the presidency. An overwhelming majority expressed nonconfidence. All but a few felt that it would be best for him to resign or be removed from office immediately or as soon as possible. One dean said that he had recently sent a letter to the president in which he in effect resigned from all matters external to his own faculty, including any further dealings with the president. A new dean had already been appointed as of the following July, and he would immediately take over the external functions. Two other deans had just communicated to the president their great disappointment in and dissatisfaction with his recent behavior. Another acting dean asked that his confirmation as permanent dean be postponed until the problem of the presidency was cleared up.

It was also pointed out that most of the senators who voted in favor of the motion involving the creation of the new CCOA did not have adequate information upon which to base their decision. Several people pointed out that the senate was deceived with regard to the amount of JCOA support there was for the CCOA and the membership selection procedures adopted. There was also considerable concern that this new committee was likely to be primarily political in nature and would lack adequate expertise and knowledge to perform effectively.

Several board members indicated that the matter of the presidency was likely to be appropriately resolved within a month or at most two months. In fact, one key member stated that January 15 would be a reasonable target date.

President and Board Clash

The next day, the board chairman consulted with a number of influential senators and faculty members who were not at the informal board meeting and most of whom had not been members of the JCOA. Quite a few informal emergency meetings also took place among small groups of influential people at the university.

On the weekend, some board members, including the chairman, met with the president. They told him about the informal meeting with board members and university representatives and the overwhelming expression of nonconfidence in his presidency. They asked for his resignation, but he strongly refused. He was understandably extremely upset and angry. He was willing to have an open confrontation with the board if necessary. The chairman of the board decided that the president should stay on at least until around the end of the academic year, although all board members did not agree with this decision.

One of the deans who had earlier been a strong supporter of the president then submitted his resignation to the board Chairman. This resignation followed shortly after the vice-president for academic affairs had resigned. The controller had also recently resigned, although it is not known how important the leadership and financial crisis was in his decision.

Articles were by then appearing in the press speculating about whether or not the president would resign. In some cases, conflicting statements were made by the president, various (usually unnamed) board members, and even certain government officials involved with higher education.

The president did not attend the final senate meeting just before Christmas vacation. At that meeting, the resignation of the management school dean was made public, and a mail ballot was announced with regard to the election of members of the CCOA. During the Christmas break, a tremendous amount of coverage—mostly unfavorable—was given to the university and its problems in the media.

Mismanagement Resumes

Shortly after classes resumed in the new year, the membership of the CCOA was determined and announced. It comprised mainly senators whom the president considered to be loyal and trustworthy. Many senators did not vote, and an uncounted number of protest ballots were intentionally filled out improperly. The total number of votes and the breakdown were never made public, although the individuals receiving the most valid votes did go on the CCOA, which included no deans, senior executives, or former members of the JCOA.

In January, various meetings took place between the president, the board chairman, and other board members in an attempt to work out an arrangement by which the president would step down. At times, the president apparently did agree to resign, but heated conflicts arose about the specific timing and terms.

In the meantime, the president had little contact with the deans; CCOA members took over as his key advisors and, in effect, took over the major functions of both the JCOA and the president's council. The board made it clear that the budget for the next year, which had thus far been prepared primarily by the JCOA and presented by the president, would have to be cut substantially. However, in the first several weeks in January, little meaningful progress was made in this regard.

In January, the president was also confronted with student problems related to an increase in tuition. Some student activists and leaders were trying to get all students not to pay their fees or tuition for the term to protest the hike in tuition. There were some disruptions, including a takeover and sit-in at one of the colleges. The president vacillated in his support of the students versus the government, which called for disciplinary action against those withholding their payments, including not giving them course credit. The president made some public statements that conflicted with those made by government officials. In the end he took the government position, and the students gave in. Apparently past events and the strain were taking their toll on his capacity for effective leadership on all fronts by this time.

Around the third week of January, the board demanded the president's resignation and said he would be fired at the next board meeting if he did not comply. (A while later, the press printed stories about the president's being fired rather than voluntarily resigning.) Right after this meeting, the board chairman met with most of the key administrators (including deans), members of the CCOA, and a few other influential academic personnel and informed them of the president's resignation. He also informed them that the board intended to appoint as acting president a history professor who had some undistinguished middle-level administrative experience at the university. He asked for their support and said he wanted to consult with them before making this appointment official. The history professor had already agreed to accept the job. General support was given by this group, although a number of reservations were raised. The secretary of the university was also appointed to a newly created vice-presidency.

The next day, the new acting president took over, but within less than twenty-four hours he submitted his resignaion to the board chairman for health reasons. Apparently, the acting president was advised by his doctor not to take on the onerous job because of his medical history. This may well have been the true chief reason, although there were a lot of surprised people on campus that day.

The new acting president was a philosophy professor who had been chairman of his deparment as well as chairman of the senate. He was currently a senate representative on the board of governors. Before making this announcement, the board chairman sought the support of more or less the same group as in the previous appointments. This group again gave its general support and significantly more enthusiastically than in the case of the previous acting president. The university community at large also seemed to be happier about this appointment.

After the new acting president took office, a general mood of calm and cautious optimism emerged. The worst of the crisis seemed to have passed. The unfavorable media publicity soon disappeared, except for occasional articles. But there was still the urgent matter of the budget for the next year.

During the rest of the year, the deans never regained much of their former authority and also lost much—probably most—of their influence in the higher administrative affairs of the university. The vice-president of finance was fired on short notice, and a few other middle- and lower-level administrators also left their jobs, either under heavy pressure or by choice. However, no first-rate new administrators were brought in.

The ccoa remained in effect and played the major advisory role to the acting president and his central staff in finalizing the budget. On a number of occasions, deans as well as others in the central administration were called in to defend their budget requests to the ccoa. The deans had, in a de facto sense, been purged. Eventually, in the spring, a revised budget entailing some major cutbacks was finalized and approved by the acting president and then by the board. It still entailed a large deficit, and substantial deficits—amounting to several million dollars—were expected for the next several years. The senate established a new budget committee at the end of the 1972–1973 academic year which again excluded all of the deans and most central administrators.

Selection of New President

Near the end of the 1972–1973 academic year, a Search Committee and a set of procedures were established with regard to the selection of a new permanent president. This committee consisted of two Board members, a representative of the non-academic staff association, two students, and three faculty members, the latter five being nominated and elected by the Senate. Its chairman, a professor, was elected by the committee's members.

The Committee came up with a "short" list of candidates which was reported to the Senate as a whole. Eight candidates—including two women—eventually made this list, and meetings and informal interviews with each were open to all interested senate members and others at the university. Two or three of these eight candidates decided to drop out of the presidential race before the senate vote was taken. Through a written senate vote the field was eventually narrowed down to two candidates—the president of a much smaller university in another region, and a senior state government official who was also on the Advisory Council of the Management School, and who does not have a doctorate degree. In November, 1973 the Board selected the government official to take over as the new President as of July 1, 1974.

In theory, the process of choosing this new President at this university was about as democratic, participative and consultative as any we know of. In practice, it also turned out to be relatively democratic. Every effort was made to obtain as many inputs about and contacts with each candidate as possible. However, the percentage of faculty members who availed themselves of this opportunity was quite low. The proportion of senators who cast ballots was somewhat higher—an estimated two-thirds or more voted. One wonders seriously whether many other truly first-rate and potentially better presidential prospects may have been willing to be considered for this job, if they did not have to go through such a public and visible process and vote in open competition with other candidates. There was not a great deal of enthusiasm for any of the candidates who let their names stand on the ballot. This was evident from the results.

Taxonomy of the Crisis

The whole crisis can be sorted out and analyzed by applying the concepts, factors, and methodologies presented in later chapters. What was at stake, in the last analysis, was who had power when the chips were down, and what goals and priorities were really being pursued. Because budgets were to be cut, whoever controlled the cutting would emerge on top when the battle was over. In a purely technical or official sense, the president and board held the trump cards, but as the case suggests, the board and especially the president could not play them effectively when needed.

Table 2 suggests a taxonomy of this crisis highlighting some of the most critical factors. The problem areas are the system taxonomies discussed in Chapter Three (see Figure 1 in that chapter). The role-players are those persons or groups who are part of the university taxonomy in its various subsystems.

The origins of the crisis are to be found in large part in the absence of reliable information and data in conjunction with deficient planning and inadequately defined goals and priorities. No one could really take charge because no one really knew what the relevant facts were. This was a failure of both data-processing and planning. This failure was the responsibility of the central administration. And so the failure to hold power really stems from the inability early in the game to realize that—if the president or the board really knew facts and had some sound contingency plans—

the professors and deans could be outflanked. Note that real data was necessary, because any dismal statistics will be carefully scrutinized by others concerned, especially in times of crisis.

When the data were not available, the deans and the faculty senate set up their own groups—both formal and informal—to find out what the problem really was. If the president had been able at the beginning to present all of the critical facts, along with a sound contingency plan for the future, the crisis may have well been over in a few days. But lacking this information, he surrendered power, in huge chunks. Notable also is the collapse of the social subsystem. When a university is growing and healthy, personal relationships can help get and keep things going well. But when the chips are really down, the buddy system often collapses— too much is at stake.

Because no one in the central administration had really forecast the problem, there was no contingency planning. There could not be, until someone came up with structured data showing what the problem was and what options might realistically be followed. You cannot get there from here, if both here and there are undefined.

None of the participants in this struggle really reckoned with the grapevine. Professors were to be fired, immediately, or so the rumors went. One predictable result was that everything stopped short while many nervous faculty wondered if they would have a job next week. Productivity in the academic sense declined significantly. Interestingly, the whole show ran with negligible student input, the major exceptions being the student representatives on the JCOA and the presidential search committee, even though a shortage of students was the core of the financial shortfall. The students were generally impotent because they did not deal with the one key problem, which was the budget.

Comparison of Table 2 with Table 7 in Chapter Six shows that the only significant participants in this problem were the top half of those power rankings—central administration, the board (trustees), deans, schools (or individual faculties), public relations, social subsystem, the academic senate or faculty council and data-processing in particular. And here the power vacuum was quickly filled by the senate, deans, and schools. Public relations, which was a rather casual activity at this institution, fell apart when the press

Table 2.

THE TAXONOMY OF A CRISIS

Problem Area	Major Roleplayers
1. *Functional Subsystem:*	
Dismissal of personnel: Who does it?	Schools and departments
Planning/control system	Central administration
Lack of contingency planning	Board
Priority goal system lacking	
No plan for cutbacks	
No planned work loads/norms	
Lack of information for planning	
No budget planning flexibility	
Deficient central administrators and staff specialists	
2. *Information Subsystem:*	
Poor forecasting	Data processing unit
Lack of key data	Public relations
Disorganized data	Central administration
Computer errors	Professors
Grapevine problems— dismissal rumors and reactions	Senate
3. *Social Subsystems:*	
Collapse of buddy system when pressure mounted—problem too important to be solved by informal lunches or phone calls	Various deans, central administrators, board members
Communication breakdown between board chairman and president	
4. *Political Subsystem:*	
Last resort moves—for example, get rid of president when all else failed	Deans, senate, faculty committees, informal faculty groups, faculty union, board members
Seizure of power by key faculty and administrative committees when faculty legally did not have such statuatory authority	
Collapse of presidential authority, *de facto*	
Clashes between president and board members	

Table 2. (Cont.)

THE TAXONOMY OF A CRISIS

Problem Area	Major Roleplayers
5. *Inputs:*	
Budget cuts led to crisis	Government (budget),
Professors get very nervous	professors, students
Students upset	
6. *Environmental Constraints:*	
Government refused to provide temporary budget relief; decided to stay with existing rules, thus provoking crisis	Government
7. *Goals or Outputs*	
One critical top priority clearly threatened, namely pay and position of faculty	Professors, administrators, students (re teaching)
Teaching in various programs and probably research suffered to at least some extent	

began to show interest in what was happening. There never was any real effort to coordinate news releases issued by interested parties. One result was that the central administration and the board looked rather bad to outsiders. Throughout the crisis the one operational goal (or output) that was clearly of greatest general concern within the institution was the protection of those within the system, especially the faculty. This involved their jobs, pay, prestige, and other prerequisites.

A Lesson from the Past and the Future

If the president had acted in the following ways, the crisis probably could have been contained and the president would most likely have survived in his job: Through his leadership he could have obtained a workable consensus and taken steps to operationalize the goal system, especially priorities, effectively before the crisis ever emerged. He could have forecast problems from the signs that were present months before the crisis. Then he could have developed contingency plans with adequate consultation and participation. If the financial crunch still came, he would by then have already put together hard data and resource allocation criteria relating to the problem, including such items as faculty work loads, expected norms on work loads, class size trends, and prospects for individual courses and departments, costs per students by schools, support staff and service costs and allocations, optional budgets given expected declines, and similar matters. He could have called meetings of interested parties and presented the above data. Then he could have asked for advice and counsel. The deans, professors, and schools would then have been on the defensive (some of them would look pretty bad by comparison with others). The long series of follow-on meetings would have been devoted to extricating the schools and departments from the problem, questioning data, trying to figure out the best of bad alternatives, and struggling with other schools and deans. The president could have sat quietly above the hassling, ready to accept whatever compromise solutions (within his chosen contraints) he wanted. Faculty, aware that their jobs were in jeopardy, would have frantically done about what the schools and deans were doing. Unless someone could show that the data and projections were seriously in error, faculty would be faced with dismal options that they would have had to resolve.

Instead, we find one failed president, a fired vice-president for finance, several resignations of other key administrators, an embarrassed discredited board, and a lot of very unhappy faculty and deans. Moreover, power drifted to the faculty—but only a very small group of senators—who gained a part of the authority to determine budgets but none of the responsibility to raise the cash. More troubles may well be in the offing for this university.

In this case of crisis and mismanagement, virtually all the critical events in Table 1 guaranteed major problems for top administrators and the board.

The future of this university remains uncertain. It did really seem to have the seeds of greatness before the crises. If it were not for the high quality and relatively visible reputations of a significant number of its faculty members, its strong professional schools, some of its more innovative and truly relevant programs in other schools and faculties, and various other positive aspects of its reputation and performance, the crises would no doubt have resulted in deterioration from which the institution would never have recovered. It would have drifted into mediocrity. Fortunately, there still seems to be a chance for it to become an even greater university than it has been anytime in its relatively short history. However, this will depend in large part on the quality and effectiveness of its management and leadership.

Effective management and leadership can usually overcome —if not prevent—even a serious financial crisis; but poor management and deficient leadership can result in financial and other problems becoming much more damaging than need be.

Chapter III

Components of the
Open System

To get at problems of mismanagement and how to improve management in the academic institution, we utilize some basic open systems concepts. Figure 1 suggests the pattern. The university or college has the following components:

1. Inputs: These include money, students, labor, materials, equipment, land, and so on. Without inputs, nothing happens, so these are one key element in the whole power system. Later we will organize these inputs more systematically for analysis.

2. Internal systems: These are the various processes that go on in the university, including such diverse things as class work,

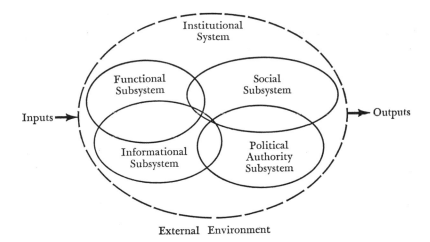

FIGURE 1. An Open System.

research, information processing, purchasing of grass seed, and committee meetings.

3. Outputs: Many things come out of the university, including published papers, graduates, and public services. As with the other elements in our model, we will be taxonomizing these in some detail shortly. (It should be noted that we treat *outputs* and *goals* synonymously.)

4. Environmental constraints: These are the constraints that the environment places on the university or college. Examples are many: athletic rules are in part imposed by the relevant conferences; the state legislature imposes money constraints and legal sanctions; the federal government states in its research grants how the money is to be used; private donors give gifts under various conditions.

5. Subsystem interfaces: These are interactions among the various components of the system. There is a key interface between the faculty and students; between faculty and administrators; between the trustees and administrators; between the legislature and the administrators. Note that critical interfaces can be internal (between two parts of the university); or external (between someone outside and someone inside).

We spell out these system components in an effort to determine who does what and who has the power to do what. Unless we carefully note the various groups, factions, and elements within the university, it is unlikely that we can ever sort out who might be powerful or for what reasons.

Taxonomies for Academic Management

As far as we know, no one has looked closely at the taxonomies used in universities and colleges for any of the categories suggested in Figure 1. We know what many of the categories are—we have for example, schools, departments, professors, and students in the systems taxonomy. We have alumni and various government agencies in the environment. We have inputs of capital, labor, and land, and our outputs (among others) are research and (hopefully) better trained minds. But it is not immediately clear that these are the best taxonomies available for analysis. Indeed, it is possible that we miss many significant things by not considering our taxonomic problem systematically.

Moreover, we rarely consider interface or interaction problems systematically. When a president goes to the legislature to ask for funds, or when a professor handles an irate parent, we are working at critical interfaces, but rarely are all significant interfaces considered. Another problem here is that of disaggregating variables or deciding in what detail they should be spelled out. We can talk about schools generally, break them down into departments, into smaller groupings, on down to the individual. For some kinds of problems (for example, pay of individuals), this is necessary, but for others, such fine divisions may confuse more than help. Good operational theory should attempt to unpack the variables to the proper level for the problem at hand.

The four classifications—System Taxonomy, Input Taxonomy, Environmental Constraints, and Output Taxonomy—below present one possible taxonomic division of a university. This taxonomy is an intuitive one that has been developed with much help from the real world and the literature. After all discussion and consideration of how to build a good university taxonomy that properly covers all relevant categories and variables, we are forced back to considering what has already been done, plus what already exists. Thus, most of the systems noted in our system taxonomy are no more than a list of what already exists. The input set is largely derived from economic considerations, while the environmental constraints are nothing more than a list of typical real world organizations and constituencies that seem to affect universities. One major reason for developing the sets in this way is that they seem to be relevant. That is, these divisions do appear to affect the ways universities and colleges operate, and the various blockings are found (sometimes slightly modified) in numerous academic institutions in many situations.

The system is broken into four parts, only two of which are usually considered separately—the functional subsystem, and to a lesser extent the political subsystem, which includes formal authority relationships. We all know that social interaction occurs constantly and rather messily through a large organization, but rarely is this sort of interaction, along with its implications, considered as a factor in what goes on. The informational system is also known and talked about, but rarely in any systematic fashion. These variables could be abstracted or broken down as much as desired. The system taxonomy suggests one possible degree of detail. Thus schools (S1.1) could be divided down as far as necessary, and so on. These four basic subsystems overlap each other to some extent. Each one has separate components, but all have parts in common. Thus, the functional subsystem performs many informational subsystem operations, and indeed is a critical part of the information system. But this subsystem also is in part a social subsystem and a political subsystem.

The numbers or weights assigned to each item in the four parts indicate the relative importance of each during two time periods. (For more details, see Chapter Six). The weights are based on what seems to have been happening at one multicampus state university within the last several years. A great deal of intuition is involved, of course, but because of Farmer's extensive and quite intimate knowledge of this particular university, the weights are probably a pretty meaningful reflection of reality. And even where there might be some significant margins of error in some of the assigned weights, this is not likely to be crucial to the policy implications or the power and interface ranking orderings to be presented later.

Moreover, our chief purpose here is not to present precise numbers, but rather to provide a useful framework and methodology for understanding and dealing with power. We have already found this technique to be quite useful in analyzing our own and other organizations. The weights would no doubt be different at other colleges and universities, and they are likely to shift over time at a given institution. In fact, some of the weights have shifted in significant ways at this particular university, as is discussed in Chapter Thirteen. The assigned weights range from 1 to 15 except for budget, which has been given a value of 20 because it clearly was the most important item with regard to power at this university.

The exercise presented here has the following major purposes: (1) to provide a framework and methodology for locating and analyzing power; (2) to provide useful insights about how an individual might gain power; (3) to provide insights about how, when, where, and why to form coalitions to accomplish something desired; and (4) to enable a better understanding of critical relationships involving shifts in power and institutional change—what kind of power shifts are likely to bring about specific changes, and what impacts various kinds of changes are likely to have on the power structure.

All of these purposes have descriptive and explanatory dimensions, and the last three also have predictive and prescriptive aspects. However, it is not our primary intention to state what should be done in given situations. The reader must decide this for himself. But he hopefully will find our analytical framework, taxonomies, and methodologies useful and relevant in this regard. Our primary aim is to provide a widely applicable do-it-yourself power kit that can be useful in an endless variety of situations and changing conditions. With this in mind, let us proceed with the taxonomies.

SYSTEM TAXONOMY

S-1: Functional Subsystem. The functional subsystems include the activities involved in each and their relative importance to the institution as a whole. They do not include the formal authority or formal power elements. However, the relative importance of a given functional subsystem item tends to be one important indication of how much power or influence it may exert, because its importance to the overall system, or the institution's dependency on it, is a source of power. The number or weight after each item is an indicator of its relative importance.

S-1.1: Schools or faculties: This category includes all graduate and undergraduate schools or faculties within the university. It could be subdivided down into departments, areas, and so on, down to individuals (15, 14).

S-1.2: Interdisciplinary groupings: Such areas as cross typical disciplinary lines. Examples would be environmental studies, Latin American affairs, or West European studies (9, 10).

S-1.3: Central administration: Centralized activities dealing with the operation of the university, including such functions as fundraising, central purchasing, accounting, auditing, and the housing office (12, 13).

S-1.4: Placement (5, 8).

S-2: Social Subsystem (4, 2). This general category includes the relevant social relationships that occur within and outside the university. Who knows whom, who drinks or talks or plays tennis with whom, and similar relationships are included. The weight suggests the relative amount of inherent power and influence exerted by social subsystems at one university.

S-3: Political and Authority Subsystem. The scores here reflect the formal authority or official power of each subsystem, as well as the inherent power and influence each has because of leadership and personal qualities and political effectiveness.

S-3.1: Student government: The formal government set up by the university and run by students (4, 5).

S-3.2: The AAUP: The American Association of University Professors, which normally represents the professional interests of the faculty. In some cases, the relevant group would be the American Federation of Teachers (AFT), and in a few cases, both of these groups could be considered (7, 6).

S-3.3: Unions: The trade unions representing nonacademic employees on the campus (4, 4).

S-3.4: Central administrative groupings: The president, vice-presidents, chancellors, vice-chancellors, and so forth. This category represents the power structure of the central administration (rather than its activities, which are considered in the functional subsystem category) (15, 14).

S-3.5: Deans (12, 9).

S-3.6: Department chairmen (7, 5).

S-3.7: Faculty council (university senate, or similar title): The formal organization of the faculty to act, consult, and advise the administration on various affairs relevant to faculty interests (7, 6).

S-3.8: Other student groups: Organizations of students, both formal and informal, that push for various interests and ideas. Examples range from special professional interest groups (such as Spanish clubs and marketing clubs) and student publications through social movements (free love societies) to politically oriented bodies (such as SID, Young Republicans) (5, 5).

S-3.9: Trustees, regents, or similar governing boards (15, 18).

S-4: Information Subsystem. Information is frequently a major source of power itself, and the weights reflect the amount of inherent or independent power and influence each element seems to have.

S-4.1: Data-processing: The various organizations that formally process data for use by other groups (11, 13).

S-4.2: Public relations and information: Groups charged with informing insiders and outsiders about activities within the system (9, 10).

S-4.3: University press: The formal publisher of books and paper items under the university imprint (4, 2).

S-4.4: Other publications: Books, pamphlets, journals, newspapers, newsletters, and other items printed by various organizations within the university (8, 7).

S-4.5: Television and radio communications (to outsiders): The university organizations that form and broadcast items to the outside (7, 7).

S-4.6: Library system: All formal libraries within the university (11, 11).

S-4.7: Registrar: The group responsible for maintaining records on students, processing information about new students, and similar matters (5, 6).

INPUT TAXONOMY

The weights reflect the relative importance of each input, both in terms of how critical each is regarding institutional decision-making and as a source of power.

I-1: Budgets—cash: The flow of money into the system in terms of amounts and sources. Both capital and operating funds of all sorts are included (20, 40).

I-2: Professional manpower: Professors and other professional level manpower, such as accountants, auditors, medical doctors, planners, and public relations specialists (15, 15).

I-3: Other manpower: Skilled, semiskilled, and unskilled manpower, such as machinists, electricians, plumbers, junior technicians, tractor operators, guards, police, and clerks (5, 5).

I-4: Fixed plant: Capital plant required for the university, including buildings, roads, and power plants (5, 3).

I-5: Equipment and supplies: Equipment needed, such as laboratory instruments, autos, tractors, and light bulbs (3, 2).

I-6: Land: Real estate needed for operations, including both developed and undeveloped land (3, 2).

I-7: Students: All types, including graduate and undergraduate, special, adult, and postdoctoral (6, 15).

ENVIRONMENTAL CONSTRAINTS

The weights reflect the relative importance of each environmental set with regard to the functioning of the university, especially in terms of organizational decision-making.

C-1: Alumni: All persons who have attended the university (6, 5).

C-2: Body politic: All voters within the jurisdiction within which the university operates (3, 6). For private schools the relevant constituency (for example, the relevant religious group). Major private donors could be placed here, in C-3 below, or in a separate category, and in many cases the weight would be quite different.

C-3: State government and legislatures (8, 11).

C-4: Federal government (5, 5).

C-5: Local government units around or close to the actual physical location of the university (2, 1).

C-6: Other pressure groups: Any groups, political or otherwise, that interest themselves in university activities or performance (3, 4).

C-7: Users of university trained manpower: Any group or organization that hires persons educated in the university (6, 12).

C-8: Other colleges and universities (6, 8).

C-9: Secondary schools (3, 7).

C-10: Professions and professional groups: All such groups that have direct relationships with the university (for example, in training of future professionals of the group) (4, 7).

C-11: Parents of students (3, 4).

OUTPUT TAXONOMY

In Chapter Four we deal with thirty-one institutional goals. To deal with such a large number in our analysis here would be far to cumbersome and complex. Therefore, we have chosen to deal with a limited number of important representative goals, and to combine some of them for illustrative purposes, in connection with the application of our comprehensive framework and methodology. The weights assigned to each output (or goal) is a reflection of its relative importance to the pursued and actual goals of this university.

O-1: Truth: A shorthand term for all types of searches for learning, including scholarly and faculty and student activities toward this end (3, 2).

O-2: Graduate students: The production of graduate degree holders in all relevant fields (8, 6).

O-3: Undergraduates: The production of undergraduate degree holders in all fields (5, 8).

O-4: Athletes: The production of intercollegiate teams in competition with other schools (3, 3).

O-5: Protection, income, prestige, perquisites, and freedom, of professionals (faculty, major administrators, some high-talent staff specialists) in the system: This involves the goal of maintaining and providing such things for professionals (9, 5).

O-6: Protection, income, perquisite and prestige of other employees in the system: Similar to O-5 (3, 2).

O-7: Public and community service activities: Includes such items as faculty service, professional training programs, adult and extension education, summer programs, and cultural events and facilities open to the public (5, 8).

O-8: Research activities and output: Both practical and theoretical (6, 5).

O-9: Cultural assimilation (3, 2).

O-10: Jobs for students (2, 8).

The system taxonomy relates to what goes on in the university in transforming inputs into outputs—the functional subsystems deal with the formal kinds of activities involved. The social subsystems deal with informal behavior. The political subsystems involve authority, power, and influence directly. The informational subsystems deal with getting, processing, and disseminating information both internally and externally.

The input taxonomy follows conventional economic analysis. To accomplish the job, the system needs money, capital, manpower, and so on. As with the system taxonomy, this one can be subdivided as far as necessary to get the detail necessary to attack the problem.

The environmental taxonomy follows what appears to be a useful pattern for universities and colleges. That is, these appear to be the relevant constraints with which a university must deal. These external constraints are the facts of life with which an administrator must deal. The word *constraint* may be misleading, because it implies some sort of restriction on action. In most cases this is correct, in the ultimate sense. One ultimately is constrained by his environment. But if the legislature gives more money, or alumni become more avid boosters of the university, the constraints become less negative.

And finally, the output (or goal) taxonomy is based on a limited number of important representative goals from Chapter Four. This division reflects what an academic institution tries to achieve. As we will see later, this is a very critical set, because one has to have some idea of where he is going before he can organize anything or use power to get there.

Now, why bother with all of this? Consider the achievement of one accepted goal, that of educating an undergraduate. Presumably we would like to perform this task as efficiently and well as possible. Putting aside for the moment the tricky semantics of *efficiently* and *well,* it is clear that most of this taxonomy would be relevant for analysis of how well we do this particular task. The student, in his untrained state, is an input. In his trip through the system, he will be exposed to various functional subsystems (schools, departments, and courses). Other inputs (professors and teaching assistants) will work on him in this subsystem. The information subsystem will keep track of him, and he will be involved in innumerable social subsystems of varying importance. He will be affected by, or become a part of, various political subsystems, for better or worse. Various environmental factors (legislative rules, alumni, and parents) will influence both him and the subsystems in which he operates. What kind of input he is (in terms of intelligence, and motivation) will in part determine what he becomes as an output. We cannot say very much about how well or efficiently we do the job of education until we thoroughly consider all critical things that may affect the student, which is why it is necessary to put together this taxonomy and system.

Assigned Weights

In the four classifications, weights or number values are assigned to each item suggesting the relative importance of each at one university. These earlier weights are the first in parentheses after each item. Schools or faculties as a group received the highest weight of any functional subsystem because their overall activities are the most important in connection with the goals and functioning of the institution. The activities of the central administration are next in importance, followed by interdisciplinary studies. Student placement activities have not been very important at this university because career preparation and jobs for students has been a relatively low priority goal. These weights have been changing in the past few years, however, and the new weights are the second numbers in parentheses after each item. The new weights are discussed in detail in Chapter Thirteen.

The social subsystem at this university is not very important in terms of power or goals. It is, however, a source of referent power and information, and it does contain informal leaders of various kinds. But when the chips are down and self-interest is involved, the social subsystem is not likely to be critical to major decisions—as was illustrated in the case in Chapter Two.

The political and authority subsystems involve legitimate power centers and special interest groups that exert varying degrees of power and influence. While formal authority, official power, and rights are important, so are leadership (both formal and informal), power, and influence derived from personal qualities, manipulative ability, political effectiveness, and situational factors. The central administration at this university has considerable formal authority, but its overall power and influence exceeds its formal authority considerably because of these other factors. The trustees have had more formal authority than the central administration, but the overall power and influence they have been exerting appears to have been about the same. However, this seems to be changing as the trustees exert even greater power.

The deans have had quite a bit of formal authority, although professional school deans have typically been more powerful compared to the other deans. The deans as a group now seem to be losing some of their power. The other parts of the political subsystem have some official rights and formal authority, but the power and influence each exerts also depends on quite a few other sources of power discussed earlier. The department chairmen as a group seem to have about the same amount or degree of power as the faculty council and the AAUP, although some chairmen exert significantly more power than others. Student organizations in total seem to have somewhat more inherent power and influence stemming from their activities than does the student government.

At the time the weightings were assigned, the power and importance of the nonacademic union was quite low. If the union were to successfully organize a strike it could exert considerable power, although only in a limited area relating to its members' economic and working conditions. Nevertheless, this would mean greater institutional dependency on the union, and the weight for this item would increase somewhat. The same might be true if a student group took some kind of forceful action.

Some of the informational subsystem items were assigned fairly high weights. Information can often be a significant source of power and influence. Moreover, information is very important internally for decision-making, management, teaching, research, and many other activities. It is important externally in connection with the acquisition of inputs, institutional image-building, disseminating relevant and interesting information and knowledge, public relations, and building institutional support generally. Information is also critical to the institution's goal system.

At this particular university, data-processing and the library system seem to be the most important and powerful information subsystems, followed by public relations and public information, other university publications, university TV and radio, and the registrar. The university press appears to be the least important item.

As for inputs, budgets are the most important at this particular university, and the same is probably true at most other academic institutions. The budget is highly critical to this university's goal system and resource allocation. Budgetary control is a very important source of power. Professional manpower is also given a high weight, because many sources of power, as well as their influences on the goal system, are involved here. If enough departments and schools have great difficulty over time in attracting enough students, the weight given to students would, or at least certainly should, increase significantly.

Nonhuman resources have not been presenting very critical problems at the university, because they have been adequate. However, these items—as well as nonprofessional manpower—could present more serious problems in the future, if the institution cannot get enough resources for badly needed replacements and additions. Then control and influence over these items will become a more important source of power, even apart from direct budgetary control.

None of the environmental constraints are really very important in an overall sense. Their formal authority over the university is limited. However, some of them do exert considerable power and influence in critical areas, such as the budget. The state government and legislature are examples of this. The body politic can also exert much power, although this may be indirect power as voters and through their elected representatives. In private institutions, major private donors often exert considerable power, especially with regard to the budget. Employers of graduates have not been exerting very much influence over this university. This is not surprising because jobs for students as an institutional goal, and student placement as an activity, have not been considered very important. However, this may change in the future, especially if the university is faced with a persistent acute shortfall of students. And the weight assigned to parents could well go up.

As noted earlier, the weights assigned to the goals or outputs of this university reflect their relative importance in terms of pursued and actual goals. The goal rank ordering here is quite similar to that for state multiversities, presented in Chapter Four, although many more goals are considered there. Shifts in the university's goal systems and priorities will inevitably lead to shifts in power, and shifts in power will be required in order to change the goal system.

We have assigned weights to the various parts of the university system without focusing on or really considering critical interfaces involving the total system (both internal and external). To get a more meaningful and total power score for each of the internal subsystem items, it is necessary to consider critical interfaces, because they can provide many sources of power.

Interface Problems

If we tried to follow even one student, faculty member, or administrator through his entire university or college career, dealing with all possible items that affect him, we would quickly bog down in the total complexity of the problem. We are interested in relevant and significant interrelationships, not all of them. Such interrelationships usually occur at the interfaces of the model, between different subsystems, between the environment and one internal factor, or between the input and a subsystem. One way of visualizing this problem is to reflect on university problems generally. Normally, they occur where one item intersects with another. This would be a critical interface.

No interface taxonomies were given earlier, because these would be defined by the set of relationships among the various other taxonomies. They can best be indicated as shown in Tables 3 and 4. In Table 3, the various subsystems of the institution are listed vertically. The environmental constraints, outputs, and inputs into the system are listed horizontally. Within this matrix, the places where the subsystems and the other items tend to be closely related and in continual ways are indicated by Xs. These are the critical interfaces that require administrative and managerial attention. The weights and scores contained in each table are discussed in Chapter Six.

Thus, to take one obvious relationship, schools (S-1.1) are directly concerned with producing undergraduates with proper qualifications (O-3). They are also directly concerned with and

Table 3.

External Interface Relationships

SUBSYSTEMS	_INPUTS_ Budgets (20)	Professional Manpower (15)	Other Manpower (5)	Fixed Plant (5)	Equipment and Supplies (3)	Land (3)	Students (6)	_ENVIRONMENTAL CONSTRAINTS_ Alumni (6)	Body Politic (Private Donors) (3)	State Government (8)	Federal Government (5)	Local Government (2)	Other Pressure Groups (3)	Manpower Users (6)	Other Colleges and Universities (6)	Secondary Schools (3)	Profession Groups (4)	Parents (3)	_OUTPUTS OR GOALS_ Truth (3)	Graduate Students (8)	Undergraduates (5)	Athletics (3)	Benefits and Protection of the Professional (9)	Benefits and Protection of other Employees (3)	Public and Community Service (5)	Research (6)	Cultural Assimilation (3)	Jobs for Students (2)	TOTAL EXTERNAL INTERFACE SCORE
Functional S-1																													
1.1 Schools	X	X	X	X			X		X	X	X	X	X	X	X	X	X	X	X	X	X		X	X		X	X	X	139
1.2 Interdisciplinary Studies	X	X	X				X		X	X	X	X	X	X	X	X	X		X	X	X		X			X	X		78
1.3 Central Administration	X	X	X	X	X	X	X	X	X	X	X	X	X	X	X	X	X	X		X	X	X	X	X	X	X	X	X	147
1.4 Placement								X						X	X	X	X	X		X	X	X	X	X	X		X	X	75
Social S-2	X	X	X				X	X					X					X	X	X	X		X	X			X	X	65
Political-Authority S-3																													
3.1 Student Government	X	X	X				X						X							X	X	X					X		28
3.2 AAUP	X	X	X				X						X		X		X	X	X	X	X	X	X	X		X	X		84
3.3 Unions		X	X	X													X				X		X	X					32
3.4 Central Administrative Group	X	X	X	X	X	X	X	X	X	X	X	X	X	X	X	X	X	X	X	X	X	X	X		X	X	X	X	145
3.5 Deans	X	X	X	X	X	X	X	X	X	X	X		X	X	X	X	X	X	X	X	X	X	X		X	X	X	X	120
3.6 Department Chairmen				X			X													X	X	X				X	X		65
3.7 Other Student Organizations							X													X	X	X					X		28
3.8 Faculty Council	X	X	X	X			X			X	X				X		X	X	X	X	X	X	X	X		X	X		66
3.9 Trustees	X	X	X	X	X	X	X	X	X	X	X	X	X	X	X	X	X	X	X	X	X	X	X	X	X	X	X	X	154
Informational S-4																													
4.1 Data Processing	X	X	X	X	X		X	X	X	X	X	X	X	X	X	X	X	X		X	X	X	X	X	X	X		X	104
4.2 Public Relations and Information								X	X	X		X	X	X	X	X	X	X		X	X		X	X	X	X	X		99
4.3 University Press		X		X	X		X	X							X		X		X	X	X		X	X	X	X			61
4.4 Other University Publications		X		X	X		X	X							X		X		X	X	X		X		X	X	X		97
4.5 University TV and Radio											X				X					X	X	X			X	X	X		55
4.6 Library System	X	X	X	X	X	X	X							X	X		X	X	X	X	X	X	X		X	X	X		78
4.7 Registrar	X	X	X	X	X	X	X	X											X	X	X						X		45

Table 4.

SUBSYSTEM INTERFACE RELATIONSHIPS

SUBSYSTEMS	S.1.1	S.1.2	S.1.3	S.1.4	S.2	S.3.1	S.3.2	S.3.3	S.3.4	S.3.5	S.3.6	S.3.7	S.3.8	S.3.9	S.4.1	S.4.2	S.4.3	S.4.4	S.4.5	S.4.6	S.4.7	A Total Subsystem Interface Score	B Subsystem Weight (From Figure 2A)	C Total Power Score (AxB)
EXTERNAL INTERFACE SCORE	14	8	15	8	7	3	8	3	15	12	7	3	7	15	10	6	10	6	8	8	5			
Functional S-1																								
1.1 Schools		X	X	X	X		X		X	X	X	X	X	X	X					X	X	151	15	2265
1.2 Interdisciplinary Studies		X	X	X	X		X		X	X	X	X	X	X	X	X				X	X	116	9	1044
1.3 Central Administration	X	X	X					X	X	X	X	X	X	X			X					165	12	1980
1.4 Placement	X	X	X	X		X	X	X	X	X	X	X	X	X	X	X	X	X			X	102	5	510
Social S-2																								
2 Social	X	X	X	X					X	X	X	X	X	X								140	4	560
Political-Authority S-3																								
3.1 Student Government	X		X	X	X				X	X	X	X		X							X	119	4	576
3.2 AAUP	X	X	X	X	X				X		X	X	X	X								110	7	770
3.3 Unions					X																	57	4	228
3.4 Central Administrative Group	X	X	X	X	X	X	X	X	X	X	X		X	X	X	X	X			X	X	162	15	2430
3.5 Deans	X	X	X	X	X	X	X	X	X	X	X		X	X	X	X	X			X	X	131	12	1572
3.6 Department Chairmen	X	X	X	X	X	X	X	X	X	X			X							X	X	122	7	854
3.7 Other Student Organizations	X	X	X	X	X	X	X	X	X	X										X		108	5	540
3.8 Faculty Council	X	X	X	X	X	X	X	X	X	X	X	X	X	X	X	X	X	X	X	X	X	125	7	875
3.9 Trustees	X	X	X	X	X	X		X	X	X												158	15	2370
Informational S-4																								
4.1 Data Processing	X	X	X	X		X	X	X	X	X		X		X				X		X	X	112	11	1232
4.2 Public Relations and Information	X	X	X	X		X	X	X	X	X				X		X	X	X		X		142	9	1278
4.3 University Press	X	X	X		X				X			X					X				X	55	4	220
4.4 Other University Publications	X	X	X		X	X								X			X			X	X	101	8	808
4.5 University TV and Radio	X	X	X						X	X				X			X					65	7	485
4.6 Library System	X	X	X	X	X	X		X	X	X	X		X	X	X		X	X		X		105	11	1155
4.7 Registrar	X	X	X	X					X	X	X				X		X		X	X	X	73	5	365

must administer relations between the professions and new students
(C-6). In both these boxes, an X indicates a critical interface for
schools within the university, as do all other Xs in that row.

Where there tends to be no relationship or a tenuous one
between a subsystem and various inputs, outputs, and constraints,
the square is left blank. This particular subsystem does not deal with
the item in question. Hence one political subsystem—the AAUP
(S-3.2)—does not deal with budgets (I-1), so this square is left
blank. Note that in this case some potential or actual policies and
behavior of the AAUP may eventually have some effect on budgets,
so there may be some relationship, but it is much more tenuous and
indirect than the budget relationship to the deans (S-3.4), where an
X is placed.

Table 4 shows the interface relationships within the system,
between the various spbsystems. Deans relate critically to professors,
while student government relates to the central administration. But
not every possible internal subsystem relates significantly to every
other subsystem, so many squares are again not marked.

These tables suggest that critical interfaces exist, but they do
not show how important any given interface may be. Moreover,
what is critical may change through time—through natural evolution of the system, changes in various elements of the system, or
perhaps because of changes in the personalities of the persons holding key roles within the various subsystems. And even a relatively
unimportant relationship can temporarily become very important if
role-players within such systems become aggressive. It is typically
true that various student organizations, for example, are not too
significant to the total system—but if one group takes over the
administration building, it is temporarily extremely important. Or,
trade unions of nonprofessional employees do not influence the
system very much—until the food processors go on strike. Indeed,
one sure sign of a viable, active university is the universal trend
toward empire building, which in this context could be interpreted
as an effort of some leaders in a given subsystem to develop more
critical interfaces with other elements, or to make those now critical
still more critical.

The numerous critical interfaces within Tables 3 and 4 also
suggest another problem. Technically, the trustees (or similar

group) and the university president are responsible for all of the interfaces. Practically, no small group or individual can ever handle more than a few critical problems at one time. Moreover, at any given moment, only a few of the interfaces are highly significant or have reached the crisis stage. Thus, top officials necessarily delegate the responsibility for dealing with interface problems to subordinates. Rarely do more than a few in the university worry about who buys the meat for the dining hall, although this type of problem is significant to a number of people (for example, budget makers, student diners, and actual and potential vendors). Someone in the central administration handles this detail—which may, in a big residential university, amount to spending a million dollars or more a year. Or the function may be further delegated to individual dining units or dormitories. It somehow gets done, and rarely do many people care.

However, if there is a student riot protesting poor food, or if an official is embezzling the meat money, the problem may assume considerable short-term significance. The administrator in effect has the problem of deciding, out of all the possible things he should be looking at, which are important enough to merit his attention. He also has to know how to audit less critical ones so that they will not become critical. Given the propensity of many subordinates and opposing power groups to try to expand their power (often by fair means or foul), such critical interfaces shift through time.

Here is where the genius of the manager or administrator comes into full flower. A good one knows not only what is important today but what is likely to become important tomorrow. He monitors carefully the results at these key interfaces, so that he at least has some tentative plans of action to correct significant deviations from norms.

Now that we have outlined the key elements of our overall conceptual framework, let us focus in depth on each set of variables. We first consider output, or goal, systems since they are—or should be—basic to academic institutions and their management.

Chapter IV

Goal Systems

The first question to ask when beginning an analysis of any complex organization and its management is: What is the organization trying to achieve? That is, what outputs, outcomes, or results are sought and expected? Further, how can it be determined if these outcomes are actually obtained? These questions lead to considerations of goals systems and the evaluation and measurement of results.

Any complex organization has multiple goals, and universities and colleges are no exception. Some goals are quite precise and easy to measure. Others are complicated and difficult to evaluate. But evaluation must be done. If no one knows whether goals have been achieved, the organization is likely to function inefficiently and ineffectively. Management and leadership must be goal-directed in order to answer the basic question: "Management for what purpose?"

Moreover, if goals are open-ended and impossible to evaluate, the outputs are undefined and the system seems to require infinite inputs. We could spend the national income on trying to get better poetry, for example, without any assurance that the goal would ever be achieved—unless *better* is defined. We might get more poets, but not necessarily better ones. And *better* can be remarkably hard to define.

The need for clearly defined goals and for evaluation of outputs has been widely discussed in the business management literature, but rarely has it been considered for university management. The reason is simple: It did not matter too much what universities did, because they were minor activities in the total social setting and used relatively few resources. If they occasionally put too many resources into poetry, and not enough into medical or business schools, the error was not seen as important to society.

But the years since 1945 have brought changes. Universities were minor operations of interest only to a small elite. During the past thirty years they have grown, their budgets have grown, and interest in them has grown. In many states, the costs of higher education now are the single largest budget item. But now competing pressures for both state and private funds are stimulating serious questions about educational costs. Sizable cutbacks are being discussed—and are being made with increasing frequency. Financial supporters are wondering what they are getting for their money, and university administrations have to respond.

The inability of nonbusiness and not-for-profit organizations to fix money-oriented goals and decide whether or not they have been reached creates two very fundamental problems. These are the *infinite resource problem* and the *achieving problem,* and in both cases the only common denominator is money. These problems pertain not only to academic institutions, but also to various kinds of governmental organizations, social welfare agencies, churches, hospitals, and so on. However, a growing number of nonbusiness organizations are probably doing a better job in operationalizing, evaluating, measuring, and verifying their goal systems and priorities than are most universities and colleges.

If goals are infinitely desirable (ethically), then it follows that infinite resources should be put into them. If it is agreed that education, learning, truth, knowledge, and research are infinitely good, then these activities warrant infinite resources. So far nothing unusual—until the bill has to be paid. We may find that millions of dollars were spent last year on medieval history. Are the results worth the cost?

Similarly, we may agree that human life is infinitely precious and that we should do all we can to protect and preserve it. Thus, if at great cost for expensive emergency equipment, hospitals and medical personnel can save a few more lives, the equipment should be purchased. However, we may find that tens of millions of dollars have been spent on complex, expensive equipment that is used to save four lives a year. Do the results justify the cost? If education and medical care have infinite value, then our medical and educational systems deserve infinite resources.

Questions of this sort typically annoy people, because such questions fly in the face of deeply held ethical beliefs. We should do these things—until costs are counted. Actually, much of hospital and academic administration is like the management of a business firm— limited resources have to be allocated among competing goals. A school or hospital with a large—but finite—budget must decide whether to hire a few first-rate doctors or research scientists and add equipment for them, start a new prenatal clinic, build a new hospital wing to handle more bedridden, dying patients, or build a new lab for the physics department. These are very hard choices, yet they must be made. Far too often, because objective criteria have not been determined, these major decisions are made without adequate analysis.

Often budget requests—for education, health, welfare, or national defense—run two to ten times any reasonable or available amount of money. So, cuts are made, and the losers emit loud cries of doom or gloom. All is lost, because society is unwilling to put up enough cash to reach our most cherished goals. Then, next year, we discover that our academic institutions, hospitals, and armies are still operating, and many of them reasonably well. Their chief executives will shrug their shoulders, state that they are doing the best they can, and point out what they could do if they had more funds.

The second fundamental problem is the achieving problem. How do we evaluate how far an academic or other social institution has come toward achieving its goals? If output is not quantified, how do we really know if we are doing anything useful, or how much we are doing? Universities and colleges have this problem. Students are educated; research is performed; and professors may do some university or public service. But at the end of each year, how can we measure achievement of our most cherished goals? If these goals are such nebulous things as truth or knowledge for the sake of knowledge, we are in deep trouble. For all we know, there may be less truth and less relevant or useful knowledge around this year than last, and we should close down. We would like to believe the opposite, but we can never be sure. And so we come back to the infinite resource question. Because we can never measure our most cherished goals, we always need more inputs (money) to make sure that we are at least moving in the right direction. If one philosophy professor seeks truth, surely five will find more truth, and five million are better yet. And so we can find ourselves pouring resources into a bottomless pit, where anything is permitted because no one knows what is happening—no one seems able to evaluate the operation.

It is relatively easy to set out various righteous statements about what universities and colleges are trying to do or should be doing. But to the extent the goals are real, then dollars are allocated to achieve them, and someone, somehow, has to decide which goals are relevant and which are not. One of the hardest parts of the goal process is to figure out what the goal priorities should be. Evaluation of goal achievement is equally difficult, and equally important.

William Baumol (1967), a distinguished economist, has focused in several of his papers on key issues related to the probability that universities and colleges will continue to operate almost as they have been for the past thirty years or so. He did this even before higher education ran into its current serious financial difficulties.

Baumol's basic argument is that no component part of the whole can continue to increase indefinitely faster than the whole. Otherwise, it becomes the whole, sooner or later. Thus, if university budgets increase at 10 percent per year, while total national income is increasing at 4 percent per year, sooner or later the university budget will become the total national income (a patient impossibility).

This leads directly to the second part of the Baumol crunch. He divides the economy into two parts: the portion that has efficiency and therefore increases as fast or faster than total income growth (in terms of output per man-hour); and the part that, for structural and other reasons, cannot increase productivity as rapidly as total income growth. Thus, mass production industries are able—through automation and better management—to increase manpower efficiency by amounts greater than average income growth, which in recent times has averaged about 4 percent per year. But string quartets, education, baseball teams, and other personal services either increase efficiency much more slowly or not at all. The limit is reached by a string quartet, which today requires exactly the same number of man hours to produce its service as it did in 1750. Its efficiency does not increase at all.

Now, if there is a continuing increase in the demand for a sector whose efficiency does not increase, costs for this industry will increase very rapidly. Not only will staff typically obtain annual wage increases about as large as those received by persons in productive industries (or even more, if the skill is in short supply), but the large demand will require additional staff to serve the growing clientele. This, of course, is the university situation. A professor who taught economic theory to thirty students in 1958 still teaches thirty in 1974—but he gets two to four times as much money income for doing it. And other economists must be hired to handle the extra sections of this course required by increased enrollment. The professor's efficiency may not have changed, but costs per student have doubled or tripled.

The lack of efficiency gain was hidden for many years, as universities became more important to society and the national economy also grew. States in particular have been willing to expand university budgets very rapidly, reflecting their popularity with taxpayers and voters, and also the growing realization that a good university system is related to industrial location and growth.

But now it appears that game might be up. From here on

out, most universities will be hard pressed to increase the efficiency of their personnel, whether or not the personnel like it. Clearly there will always be some exceptions, such as well-endowed private schools, but even some of the prestigious Ivy League schools must now tighten their belts. Most American faculty may well spend much of the remainder of their professional lives working with more students, in less desirable physical environments, and quite possibly with less job security. At the very best, we may have five to ten years before the roof falls in. It might be worthwhile to ponder what to do in the short time remaining. And academic managers should take the lead, both in thought and action. This involves the institution's goal system more than anything else.

Experience now suggests that many universities and colleges will not have even a few more years without solutions being imposed on them from the outside. Budgets in most cases are not keeping pace with inflation; professorial salary increases are lagging behind price inflation, so real income is declining; and many if not most institutions are facing serious budgetary problems. Enrollments of students of traditional college age are still increasing, but the rate of increase has slowed quite sharply, and there is no concrete evidence that it will not continue to slow down. The crunch has come, and few institutions seem to be prepared for it.

Probably the best and most meaningful way to get at the problem of what to do is to consider what we are doing and trying to do with our universities and colleges, and this means goal system analysis. Too many academic institutions attempt to emulate the more prestigious ones and to be all things to all men, perhaps because up to now many of them have been able to get away with it. Historically, universities were relatively unimportant, both as users of funds and as educators of a very small elite. Hence they could do just about as they pleased. Now, universities still do, or at least strive to do, about as they please. But the costs of doing so are getting so high that thet sponsors are beginning to critically question what the game is for. Moreover, all of a university's clienteles have at least some ideas of what they want from the university, and there may be a real danger that goals will be dictated increasingly from the outside. If so, professors are in for some traumatic shocks. If the game is to be changed, it is desirable and useful for the players to help figure out the new rules. But, before this is done we must consider the kinds of goal systems universities and colleges seem to have and actually pursue. Consideration will also be given to what the goal systems should be, and the types of changes that are needed.

Gross and Grambsch Study

Before presenting our own conception of university and college goal systems, it is useful to comment on and interpret the more important goal system studies undertaken by others, and in particular a few significant ones that we draw on in this book.

Gross and Grambsch (1968, and Gross, 1971) did a major study on perceived and preferred goals at sixty-eight universities in the mid-1960s and an additional study (1974) focusing on the 1964–1971 period. They sent questionnaires to administrators and a sample of the faculty at the same universities in 1964 and in 1971. The questionnaires contained a list of forty-seven goals, including four categories of output goals (student-expressive, student-instrumental, research, and direct service) and four categories of support goals (adaptation, management, motivation, and position). Each respondent was asked to state the relative degree to which each goal on the list was important (strongly emphasized) at his or her institution, and perceived goal rankings were derived from their responses. Respondents were also asked the relative degree to which they thought a goal should be important, and perferred goal rankings were derived from these responses.

In the 1964 survey, protecting academic freedom distinctly ranked as the first perceived and preferred goal. Only one directly student-related goal ranked in the top seven as both a perceived and preferred goal, "train students for scholarship, research, or both." The relatively low ranking of almost all student-related goals—including emphasis on undergraduate education at the expense of graduate instruction, involvement of students in university governance, protection of students' rights of action, development of students' characters, cultivation of student tastes, provision for student activities, provision of education to the utmost for all high school graduates who meet the basic legal requirements for admission, preparation of students for status and leadership roles, and preparation of students for useful careers—clearly suggests at least one reason for the tremendous amount of student unrest and discontent in the late sixties and at the outset of the seventies. Even more depressing, preferred goals involving students did not differ markedly in most cases from the perceived goal rankings, and often the preferred ranked lower.

The 1964 study is also not encouraging with regard to the preferences and interests of external constituencies, especially actual and potential financial contributors. Providing special adult training, assisting citizens through extension programs, and orienting the institution to satisfy the special needs of the geographic area all ranked low as both perceived and preferred goals. Providing community cultural leadership ranked 16 as a perceived goal, but 28 as a preferred objective. Keeping costs down ranked 24 and 35 respectively. Trying to ensure the continued confidence and hence support of major financial and other resource contributors of the university ranked 4 as a perceived goal but 26 as a preferred objective. Ensuring the favor of external validating bodies with regard to program quality ranked 9 as a perceived goal but 34 as a preferred one. Pure research ranked 7 and 2 respectively, while applied research ranked 12 as a perceived goal, but only 30 as a preferred one. It is not surprising that so many outsiders have become disenchanted with universities. And if faculty and administrator attitudes toward goals and priorities do not change significantly, many academic institutions are probably in for increased problems and conflicts with external groups and constituencies.

Maintaining top quality in those programs the administration and faculty feel to be most important and maintaining top quality in all programs ranked high as both perceived and preferred goals in 1964. But these goals are likely to be rather inconsistent and unrealistic, especially for schools that are not wealthy and that offer many diverse programs in an attempt to emulate wealthier, more prestigious, and larger universities. However, the low ranking for maintaining a balanced level of quality across the whole range of programs engaged in suggests a strong tendency toward suboptimization in this area.

Involving the faculty in university governance, letting the will of the faculty prevail on all important issues (not only academic), and running the university democratically all were ranked rather low. This finding is not surprising since the study was conducted at a time when universities and colleges had relatively abundant resources. There was also a good mesh between the goal preferences and priorities of faculty and administrators. However, as resources now become significantly more scarce, conflicts among groups will tend to increase, and the issue of power and participation in university governance will become important.

Gross and Grambsch's 1964 study clearly suggests why so many private universities and colleges in particular are in serious trouble today. They found that private schools emphasize preserving institutional character, conducting pure research, protecting academic freedom, providing faculty with maximum opportunity to pursue their careers in a manner satisfactory to them, gaining institutional prestige, accommodating only students of high potential, and other elitist goals more than public universities do. Public institutions give more emphasis to preparation of students for useful careers, applied research, extension and special adult training programs, cultural leadership in the community, local needs and problems, acceptance of all qualified high school graduates, student government and activities, undergraduate education, external validating bodies, faculty contributions to the institution (not only to fields or disciplines), harmony among different parts of the university, and low costs (though this was ranked low). However, the most prestigious public universities often take on some of the goals of private universities, and some of the less prestigious private schools resemble public universities with regard to goals and priorities. There tends to be less conflict between the perceived and preferred goals of the public than the private schools, however.

Gross and Grambsch also found few significant relationships between the size and location of universities and their goal systems. The few differences that exist pertain mostly to urban versus rural locations.

In comparing important aspects of Gross and Grambsch's 1971 goal rankings with their 1964 findings, we do not find much overall change in the goal rank orders. There is a trend toward congruence within the universities on perceived and preferred goals. However, the top goals continue to relate primarily to faculty interests and career betterment. The two most marked changes were in involving the faculty in university governance, which moved up from twenty-fifth to ninth place as a perceived goal, and from nineteenth to twelfth as a preferred goal; and involving students in university governance, which moved up from forty-fifth to thirtieth and forty-sixth to thirty-ninth respectively. However, encouraging graduate work fell from 18 to 25 as a perceived goal, and from 27 to 42 as a preferred goal. Assisting citizens through extension programs dropped from 31 to 36 as a perceived goal, but increased from 36 to 32 as a preferred goal, while providing special adult training dropped from 37 to 39 as a perceived goal, but increased from 38 to 33 as a preferred goal. Protecting academic freedom remained in first place in both categories.

Private universities—already differing from public universities in 1964—were more distinctive in goals in 1971, and the prestigious schools were even more distinctive than the others. In essence, distinct "leagues" were being carved out, suggesting decreasing competition. This is basically a healthy trend. Private universities have also been surrendering some of their functions to other higher educational institutions like community and experimental colleges and new state colleges and universities.

In both their surveys, Gross and Grambsch found that faculty and administrators tend to see eye to eye to a much greater extent on both perceived and preferred goals than commonly has been supposed. If anything, the administrators and faculty were closer in 1971 than in 1964. Gross and Grambsch conclude that the greater power of the administrators as compared with the faculty is not necessarily regarded as inimical to the faculty. In our view, given the increased financial problems confronting many academic institutions, it is likely that faculty members and administrators now no longer see eye to eye nearly so much, and power conflicts and possibly also differences in goal preferences between them have likely increased considerably in many cases since the 1971 study.

The Gross and Grambsch studies also document the goal preferences of other constituencies perceived to have or exert power. We say more about these findings in later chapters, but some comments about how they relate to goals are in order here. In general, the internal constituencies (faculty, administrators, students) had more similar goal orientations than did the outsiders (regents, governments, general public) in 1971 compared with 1964. This finding suggests fewer internal divisions and a joining together of insiders to face the opposition from outside power holders; Gross and Grambsch indicate that by 1971 the ominous cleavages that had developed between outside power holders and insiders had significantly affected the goals of universities. In general, they found two distinct clusters—one an inside cluster comprising deans, department chairmen, and faculty; the other an outside cluster including regents, state and federal government, and parents.

They point out that where external power groups have greater power than deans, chairmen, and the faculty, one is likely to find more emphasis on practical and service goals—making students wise consumers, keeping costs down, and catering to the educational desires of adults and part-time students. There is deemphasis on research and graduate work, as well as reduced concern for facilitating faculty interests and careers. Where the reverse is the case, one is likely to find more emphasis on goals associated with the classical ideas of liberal education, along with concern for ensuring that students have freedom to pursue their own interests and that faculty have the same rights, even when they may be opposed to the interests of their universities. There is also more concern for pure research, students' intellects, currency of ideas, prestige, dissemination of new ideas, faculty advancement in careers, and quality and elitism in admission policies. There is a deemphasis on preparing students for practical careers and on undergraduate instruction.

Gross and Grambsch conclude from their 1971 study that a shift in the power of external power holders is more likely to have a greater effect on university goals than would a corresponding shift in the power of internal power holders. In our view, the goal preferences of major external constituents have probably generally not changed significantly since 1971, but the power structure seems to have been shifting in their favor at many universities and colleges, and this shift is likely to continue.

Baldridge Study

New York University ran into some dramatic financial problems in recent years. It closed down some major programs, reduced the size of faculty and staff, and consolidated its campus operations.

J. Victor Baldridge has focused on NYU in the development of his political model of university governance (Baldridge, 1971a and 1971b). He has also presented and analyzed the results of a 1959 NYU faculty senate survey on that university's goals (Baldridge, 1971a, pp. 118–123). That survey suggests some of the historical reasons for the serious problems that have emerged at NYU.

The above survey, which included 569 faculty respondents, asked the faculty to rank the importance of nine university goals. All the goals were ranked fairly high—the scores ranged from a high of 8.3 to a low of 5.6—indicating no clear sense of priorities. The goal rankings were as follows: (1) teaching graduate students; (2) teaching undergraduates; (3) research; (4) maintenance of university conditions attractive to excellent scholars; (5) enhancement of the reputation of the university; (6) maintenance of a scholarly atmosphere; (7) preservation of the cultural heritage; (8) application of knowledge to life situations; and (9) solution of problems of great national and international concern. These goals are stated in a very general way, and most of them are very difficult if not impossible to quantify. In this faculty survey very little attention was given to the student's intellectual or personal development or preparing students for useful careers. Very little attention was given to the desires, needs, or interests of financial supporters, the local community, or the outside world generally. And no attention was given to university governance or management.

Baldridge and others have analyzed some of the above goals and the faculty subcultures that grow up around them. First, there is the split between teaching and research. Within the teaching and research roles there are additional subgoals. Teaching splits into working with graduates or undergraduates, in professional or vocational programs or in liberal arts or other units, with full-time students or part-time adult education, either for credit or noncredit, and so forth. Research can be pure or applied, and it can involve an endless array of topics, fields, methodologies, projects, and approaches. There is also the general rift between pure and applied or theoretical and practical orientations. Even two people in the same field, such as psychology, or medicine, or economics, often have different preferences and orientations. And there are rifts involving the humanistic versus the deterministic emphasis. These distinctions often break along school or departmental boundaries within the university, although this does not always hold true, and within each school there are often variations. Disciplinary specialization also promotes the growth of faculty subcultures with regard to goal systems. And there are the cosmopolitans (who identify with external reference groups in the discipline rather than with local groups within the university, and tend to have low institutional loyalty) and the locals (who have opposite orientations).

All of the above subcultures contribute to many of the goal and other conflicts that arise in universities. And such conflicts tend to increase as resources get scarcer and priority choices must be made. Then power typically becomes an issue of utmost importance. Here the numbers and averages reflected in the goal system studies considered in this chapter can become particularly critical.

If a significant majority of faculty members and administrators—and especially many of those who are highly influential for various reasons—in a given institution favor, say, a liberal arts orientation over a career or practical training orientation, they are likely to win. The business or engineering school might be expanded somewhat if this is clearly essential to institutional viability, but significantly more practical or applied training is not likely to occur in programs dominated by individuals who have strong liberal arts preferences. In fact, even the expansion of the business or engineering school may often be thwarted, even though there may be considerable external demand and need for such an expansion. Similarly, if a majority of the faculty is strongly against the creation or expansion of various kinds of part-time or extension programs for adults, such programs are likely to be thwarted, even though they would serve an important community need and desire.

In such cases, truly effective management and leadership is required to develop and implement programs that are beneficial to both the institution's viability and success and to its external market potential. The expansion or creation of such programs can often, in fact, do much to subsidize the weaker parts of the university and help minimize cutbacks over time.

Peterson Study

Peterson's study (1973) of the goals of 116 higher educational institutions in California is the most comprehensive survey of its type available to date, as noted in Chapter One. The latest

Peterson study was carried out in the early 1970s. The study focused on twenty institutional goals, thirteen of which are referred to as output goals, and seven as process goals. Quite a few of these goals are similar to those dealt with in the Gross and Grambsch and Baldridge studies, and also to those we deal with later in our conception of goal systems. Peterson actually made use of ninety goal statements. For each goal statement, the respondents, using a five-point scale, gave two judgments: (1) how important *is* the goal, presently, at the institution; and (2) how important *should* the goal be. Protecting the faculty or administrators was not one of the twenty goals ranked his way; neither were some of the other faculty or administrative inducement, reward, and special interest goals included in the Gross and Grambsch study and in our conception of goal systems.

Among the most significant is-should gaps revealed by Peterson's study were the following: (1) Students on individual personal and academic development. (2) The faculty on accountability and efficiency (they generally thought there should be substantially less); however, they attached high importance to the creation of a better intellectual and aesthetic environment. (3) Community people on vocational preparation (except for the junior colleges) and individual personal development (they wanted significantly more emphasis); however, they felt that there should be significantly less emphasis on freedom, including off-campus political activities by faculty and students, faculty presentation of unpopular or controversial ideas in the classroom, faculty and student life styles, and talks by highly controversial speakers on campus (4) Administrators on freedom (they felt there should be more).

Among the sharpest discrepancies among different constituencies—suggesting significant conflicts of interest and potential trouble spots—were the following: Students at the uc campuses generally felt there should be significantly more emphasis on individual personal development and on academic innovation and change than did the faculty. Students at the state colleges and private schools desired more emphasis on vocational preparation than did the faculty. Students desired more stress on democratic governance than did trustees generally. And faculty rated the importance of accountability and efficiency considerably lower than did board members generally.

The only perfect correlation in the survey involved community college presidents and other administrators who gave identical "should be" rank orderings for the twenty goals. The correlations were generally higher among the community college and private institution constituencies than they were in the UC and state college systems. The most significant discrepancies at the junior colleges and private schools involved trustees and students. The greatest diversity regarding goal systems was in the private institutions, as is to be expected. For both the UC regents and the state college trustees the wide variations in some of the correlations is significant. In the UC system regents have the biggest discrepancies with undergraduates. In the state colleges trustee goals conflict with those of both the faculty and undergraduates.

The above findings suggest some of the major reasons why the public junior colleges are generally in relatively good shape and the state colleges in relatively poor shape in California. The UC system falls somewhere in the middle.

While accountability and efficiency ranked relatively low as a "should be" goal by both faculty and students in all groups, it ranked higher at the junior colleges and in the private sector than at the UC and state college campuses. Vocational preparation was rated considerably higher at the community colleges than anywhere else, and social egalitarianism also ranked higher. Meeting local area needs ranked considerably higher as both an "is" and "should be" goal at the junior colleges than anywhere else. Students desired considerably more emphasis on vocational preparation at the private schools and state colleges, which suggests why so many of these institutions, especially the higher cost private schools, are having trouble attracting enough students. There were other significant symptoms of student discontent, although they were generally less significant at the junior colleges.

Peterson also obtained responses from 110 chief executives —out of 177 asked to participate—about their goal beliefs. They tended to record significantly higher "is" scores and somewhat higher "should be" scores than did their other constituencies, although their responses no doubt reflect a desire to present their institutions in the best light.

The presidents of the private institutions rated local area

needs lower than did any other constituency, with the biggest difference between them and the community people. This finding probably has significant implications for external financial support. On
social egalitarianism, the private institution presidents were significantly lower than other constituencies; the community college presidents were higher than other constituencies; the state college presidents were lower than all the other on-campus groups except the
trustees; while the UC chancellors were also higher than the regents,
but close to their own campus constituencies. On the freedom goal,
the chief executives tended to be way above the other groups on
"is," similar to on-campus groups on "should be," but higher than
the trustees and community people on "should be."

As for democratic governance, the UC chancellors had the
lowest is-should gap of all the chief executives and were also closer
to the other constituencies generally. The greatest differences on "is"
involved the state college presidents and all their constituencies—
a strong trouble symptom, no doubt—and they also had small is-
should gaps regarding democratic governance.

With regard to innovation as a goal, the chief executives
were generally higher than the other groups. The state college
presidents had the biggest "is" gap vis-à-vis other groups—another
trouble symptom, as is the fact that private school presidents rated
innovation the lowest of all the chief executives. The UC and junior
college chief executives rated innovation the highest "should be,"
and they were higher than their constituencies on this, especially
their trustees.

On accountability and efficiency the chief executives were
well above their faculties, students, and administrators on "is," and
close to their trustees. On "should be," the UC presidents were the
highest of the chief executives and much higher than their on-
campus constituencies. The chief executives of the state and community colleges and the private schools were close to their trustees
on "should be," and much higher than their faculties. All these
findings have significant implications for potential conflicts.

Peterson considered the issue of tenure in his study, but not
as part of the twenty goals which were ranked. Not surprisingly, the
faculty was clearly the most protective about tenure generally, espe-

cially in the UC system. They tended to be somewhat less protective in the private sector. In the private sector and community colleges, the trustees, community people, and students strongly favored changes in the tenure system. Administrators generally took a middle position, but were most strongly in favor of changes in the private sector—no doubt in large part because of their financial crises.

Peterson's study reveals considerably more agreement among the institutions and constituencies surveyed on "should be" goals than on "is" goals. This could be a legitimate basis for cautious optimism about the future. However, highly rated "should be" consensus goals are typically very general and rather abstract—for example, student intellectual orientation and creating a sense of community and healthy climate on each campus. Nevertheless, this does suggest that even external constituencies and financial supporters recognize the importance of some of the ultimate or basic purposes and aspirations of higher education. But getting from "is" to "should be" is far easier said than done.

If relatively high consensus "should be" goals are to be pursued in an effective and efficient manner, they have to be operationalized, evaluated, measured, and verified in concrete ways. This, in turn, necessitates establishment and verification of various related subgoals for each basic goal that can be expressed and evaluated in concrete ways. These subgoals would involve both output and process.

Restructuring and operationalizing goal systems and priorities, and getting from perceived goals to "should be" goals, requires truly effective, creative and often courageous institutional leadership and management. The faculty is not going to do this on its own; nor is any other constituency. Top management must somehow get enough of a consensus among key constituencies and external fund and other resource providers to do this. Much genuine innovation and change is likely to be required, as well as serious and sound planning and control, effective information systems, proper staffing and organizational design, and finally relatively effective and efficient implementation of the desired changes related to the desired goals. Considerable faculty resistance must be overcome, particularly at schools faced with acute financial problems, and where the faculty is preoccupied with protecting their personal interests, jobs, benefits, incomes, and rights. Faculty must be made to realize that reordering certain priorities, operationalizing the goal system, and pursuing some new kinds of goals is in both their own and the institution's enlightened self-interest. This persuasion also requires much managerial and leadership ability.

The Peterson study found that the "should be" goal pressures were generally in the direction of greater homogeneity, and this is a danger signal. And these pressures came not only from faculties but also from administrators, especially at the state colleges. We agree strongly with Peterson's conclusion that homogeneity— or similarity of institutions—is not in the interest of students (or others) in a diverse, pluralistic society, nor is it probably in the interests of economy and efficiency. Institutional diversity—including planned diversity, and program specialization—is a much sounder and more viable approach. And this involves the development of a relatively distinct place in higher education, serving effectively only a limited portion of the overall higher educational market. There can be many bases for institutional diversity, far beyond the traditional ones. Only a limited number of the larger highly prestigious private schools and first-rate large public campuses might be able to afford to pursue a broad range of goals and priorities and to do so in a reasonably effective, balanced, and viable way. The tendency among universities and colleges to try to emulate those that are viewed as more prestigious, wealthier, and successful is far too often unsound and dangerous. The recent March and Cohen study (1974) provides some additional suggestive evidence of this emulation tendency.

Finally, the Peterson study has revealed that various off-campus groups, and especially the local citizenry, are clearly out of sympathy with what they perceive quite a few campuses to be doing. This attitude was found to be most serious with regard to such process goals as freedom, participation, and other related aspects of on-campus life. Peterson contends that lay people can understand and will accept institutional goals if campus officials will make an effort to communicate. We would also add that off-campus constituencies, individuals, and actual and potential financial supporters will be much more likely to accept and support an institution with enthusiasm if they see its goals and priorities are sufficiently operational, reasonably clear and verifiable, adequately meaningful to them, and also in substantial part (if not entirely) relevant to them.

Cohen and March Study

As part of their study (1974, Chap. 4), Cohen and March obtained personal opinions from thirty-one university and college presidents. These respondents were asked to name the one individual they considered to be a clearly successful current president. Twenty-three different presidents were mentioned. Only three were multiple nominees, with Brewster of Yale getting the most mentions—five. The goal systems at the institutions headed by the twenty-three named chief executives were not viewed as significant in determining presidential success. This is not surprising, because a major finding of the overall study is that university and college goal systems are ambiguous.

There was, however, a very clear pattern—respondents named chief executives of institutions that are larger and wealthier institutions than their own. This suggests that many chief executives want their own institutions to emulate those they feel are more prestigious, larger, and hence successful.

There was considerable regionalism in the choices of successful presidents. There was also a bias towards prestigious private universities. The specific criteria mentioned most with regard to presidential and institutional success included the following, ranked in order of response frequency: (1) quiet campuses; (2) growth; (3) quality of the faculty; (4) educational programs; (5) respect of faculty; (6) respect of the community; (7) respect of students; (8) financial positions; and (9) quality of students.

Chief academic officers questioned by Cohen and March nominated as successful presidents individuals who are closer to home in terms of the type, wealth, and size of their institutions. They stressed educational program and fiscal matters more strongly than the presidents did, and were not as concerned about campus quiet. Assistants to the president were generally similar to presidents in their choices, although their criteria for success more strongly emphasized the crisis areas of fiscal policy and campus quiet, which tend to be their special concerns. Key business and financial officers made consistently greater reference than other groups questioned to the presidents of larger and public schools and relied on growth and fiscal criteria of success to a greater extent. They also leaned toward an entrepreneurial view of the presidency, while the academic officers leaned toward an administrative-functional view, and the presidents leaned toward a constituency and political orientation. The criteria used in determining presidential success were the most diverse among student respondents, followed by trustees.

The Cohen and March study concludes that there does not seem to be a clear core of objectives that presidents should pursue and, consequently, no clear set of attributes that will assure success. Our position is that an operational institutional goal system and related priorities are essential for a useful evaluation of both presidential and institutional success. If the goals and priorities are achieved to a sufficient degree, and if the institution is also viable, has adequate resources, and has adequate external as well as internal support and cooperation, these factors would clearly imply both presidential and institutional success. Success here is a relative not an optimum concept, because it is impossible to define what optimum is in this context.

Conception and Analysis of Goal Systems

Our interest here is in the goals and priorities that universities and colleges actually pursue, strive to attain, and desire to achieve—what they actually do and would do if they could. The administration (especially the top level and other key managers or administrators) and the faculty (especially the more influential and active faculty members) typically tend to be the most important constituents in this regard. The goals that are most strongly pursued frequently are a mixture of the perceived, or "is," goals given high priority by academic institutions and the "should be" goal preferences that they really place high priority on. "Should be" goals that are actually strongly pursued and highly desired often seem to be considerably more important in reality than "should be" goal responses given on questionnaires.

In numerous if not most cases, the faculty tends to be even more important with regard to the real goal system than the administration is. There are several reasons for this. First, the administration needs adequate or at least workable faculty support to remain in office and get things done. Second, most administrators have been faculty members. Third, most administrators assume that they may well become full-time faculty members again sometime in the future. And fourth, many administrators consider themselves to be faculty members as well as administrators.

However, when the institution runs into serious trouble, such as a financial crunch, a key administrator is likely to find himself in role conflicts. For example, the trustees may be on his back to do things that the faculty does not like; the same might be true of legislators, politicians, the media, private donors, students, and other influential constituencies. But the administration and faculty still generally seem to be the most important constituencies with regard to the goals and priorities actually pursued and strived for at most schools. This is frequently a major reason why they run into serious problems with other constituencies, have trouble getting enough financial resources, and cannot attract enough students of the kinds they want.

Examination of pursued goals and priorities—whether or not they are achieved—reveals much about the troubles and conflicts in which many institutions find themselves. It can also serve as a very useful basis for prediction and prescription. Our conception of goals and priorities commonly pursued by higher educational institutions generally, and also with regard to various types of institutions, is still largely in the hypothesis stage and admittedly needs much more empirical verification. However, even in this hypothesis stage much fruitful and meaningful explanation of problems and conflicts can be derived that can be quite effectively supported and defended by logic, observation, and considerable available evidence.

There are a number of bases for our conception of goal systems and priorities. First, there are the other goal studies cited in this chapter, as well as numerous other sources of many types. Perceived goals are often not the same as goals actually pursued, but they do shed much light on pursued goals. Second, we have had personal discussions over the years with many people at and interested in various universities and colleges. Third, we have our personal experiences, observations, and impressions at a limited number of institutions of different types.

A number of factors can be used to make a meaningful assessment of goals and priorities actually pursued. From an institution's overall budgets and subsystem budgets of the recent past, the present, and those projected into the future one can frequently deduce quite a bit about what the institution's goals and priorities really are. If budgets rise fast enough to enable everyone to enjoy a reasonable share of the system's expenditures, then everyone can do what he has been doing and more or less what he wants to do, without much concern for ultimate goals or priorities. But this is now rarely the situation at universities and colleges. The administration and faculty must determine priorities. Observing what institutions do in such situations gives one some idea of what the goals really are and what is important, regardless of what is said at commencements or testimonial dinners.

Which departments, programs, schools get the most money and best facilities? Who is subsidizing whom? (That is, which units generate more revenues than they spend and vice versa?) Which units have the highest and lowest student-faculty ratios and levels of support services? Which are hiring the most and cutting back the most? Who is getting salary increases, fringe benefits, and promotions? What new programs are being funded and which are being cut back or terminated? What innovations and changes are being introduced and with what resources? How much money is available for research and where is it going? What is happening to the library, the university press and other publications, student services and activities, travel funds, computer budgets, fellowships and student financial aid, public relations, student placement and recruitment, faculty recruiting and other personnel recruitment?

The budget provides answers to all of these questions, if it is done properly. However, the budget is not necessarily based on well thought out institutional goals and priorities, even though it is one reflection of them. Nor is it necessarily good or sound in terms of institutional viability and success. Nevertheless, the budget sets constraints on goal attainment and provides a number of constraint type goals.

However, the approved budget frequently does not indicate quite a few very important things about the goals and priorities actually pursued, strived for, and strongly desired by the institution as represented by the faculty and the administration. What do they really fight for? What do they really care most about? What do they actually spend much of their time, attention, and energy on? What are the most time-consuming committees and meetings really about? What are their real intentions, aims, aspirations, and personal goals, and not only their readily observable activities? The approved budget does not clearly reflect much of this, because trustees, legislators, politicians, private donors, and at times other groups have a major say in the final budget. There is often much conflict as a result; and the goals and priorities actually pursued and desired by the faculty and key administrators are typically a major reason for this conflict.

The faculty and the administration strive to keep layoffs to a minimum, even and very often especially when the institution is in deep financial trouble. They want higher pay, more benefits of various types, job security, more freedom, more power, more support services, and better facilities. However, if the external resource providers and the students who generate revenues for the institution believe that the goals and priorities that they feel strongly about are not being adequately achieved, they are not likely to sympathize with the faculty or the administration.

Many innovations and changes that could prove beneficial are opposed and resisted by the faculty and the administration. Some traditional programs are strongly protected at the expense of other programs that could and should be created or expanded because there is a market for them. Part-time programs and various kinds of adult educational and training programs are opposed. Serving the needs and interests of the local community better, public service, taking in sizable numbers of elitist students, and preparing students for jobs and useful careers are also opposed. Keeping costs down, operating efficiently, and being accountable with regard to goal attainment are similarly regarded as inappropriate and unimportant activities for an academic institution. Little effort is made to fill most of the administrative jobs with truly efficient and effective managers. And even when an attempt is made to do this, the job holders are frequently frustrated because of the highly ambiguous institutional goal system they must work with.

Below is a list of thirty-one common goals pursued by higher educational institutions, arranged into five basic categories. We do not differentiate between outcome or process goals. Instead, we treat them all as results, outcomes, or outputs of institutions. Some are essentially deterministic, others are basically constraint goals. Many of them are related, often in a means-end fashion. All of them are of at least some importance at universities and colleges generally, although a specific goal may not apply to a particular institution. The numbers in parentheses are our rankings of these goals for American colleges and universities in general, but before we discuss this suggested rank ordering, a detailed definition of each goal is warranted.

A. *Program Goals*

1. *Undergraduate education* (2) Most universities and colleges have undergraduate programs, although the importance of undergraduate education as a goal often varies dramatically from one institution to another and the quality desired is often obscure. Content, approaches, and emphases also can vary markedly. One can measure this goal by counting students, but many of the qualitative aspects of the problems have eluded scholars and men of affairs for many centuries.

2. *Graduate education* (5). This can be subdivided into advanced general learning and professional education. The appeal of turning out professionals for various purposes seems to be gaining (and one could verify this point by studying graduate professional school trends and budgets), but general education still has probably more fervent supporters among academics. Professional education tends to have the advantage of more verifiable—though still by no means very precise—quality control.

3. *Part-time and continuing education* (26). This includes both degree and nondegree programs, usually for adults. Extension and correspondence programs, open university concepts, special courses, and conferences of varying lengths and covering various topics, career training, general education, leisure and hobby courses, and current issue seminars all come under this category. Many of these programs may not even be conducted on the main campus.

4. *Research* (6). This can be roughly subdivided into basic, applied, theoretical, and practical research. Applied research can

typically be precisely evaluated; theoretical or pure research work is likely to defy cost-benefit analysis. The payoff of pure research is at times great, but this may take many years to realize. And very often the payoff is not very useful to society or to anyone except those who have benefited in various ways from working on the project.

5. *Athletics* (7). Produce athletic teams that win. Not a few of the academic institution's clientele still seem to think that this is what universities and colleges are largely for. This is one of the easier goals to quantify—you either win or you do not.

B.   *Student Impact Goals*

6. *Intellectual development* (11). Cultivate student intellect by imparting knowledge to students in ways that will prove durable and hopefully useful to them in the future. Develop in students the ability to define and solve problems and the ability to synthesize knowledge from a variety of sources.

7. *Student scholarship, scientific research, and creative endeavor* (12). Train students in methods of scholarship or scholarly inquiry, scientific research, and creative endeavors. This is seen as desirable regardless of a given student's particular field or major. Some institutions or programs place greatest emphasis on creativity, others on scholarship, and still others on scientific research. However, it is common for all of these aspects of education to be given at least some attention.

8. *Jobs, careers, and status* (22). Students come to college for knowledge, but they also typically come to prepare themselves for useful careers, reasonably satifying jobs, and a better position in society. In a mass or universal higher educational system, they also come to increase their incomes and raise their social status.

9. *Individual personal development* (15). Produce well-rounded students of sound character who will be objective and constructive in the changing and often confusing and difficult world that will confront them when they graduate. Develop their capabilities for lifelong learning.

10. *Student activities and rights* (19). Each student has the right to pursue his own lifestyle and interests on campus and enhance his own personal satisfaction, growth, and development, as long as this is not destructive to others or to the institution. This goal includes student leadership and involvement in extracurricular activities, student par-

ticipation in various kinds of university decisions, and student rights to criticize and inquire, and to participate in social and political action.

11. *Cultural and religious assimilation* (18). Many institutions with church or religious affiliations place high priority on educating students in a particular religious heritage. Many are largely nondenominational or nonsectarian in their student enrollments, but religion is often an important part of the curriculum—even though church attendance may not be compulsory. In general, the humanities and liberal arts curriculum is usually expected to play a major role in cultural and religious assimilation. In addition, just being around a university can be a major cultural or social assimilation process for many students.

C. *Faculty Oriented Goals*

12. *Protect the faculty* (1). This is most commonly discussed in terms of academic freedom as a faculty right. However, the concept of academic freedom is often used in efforts to achieve other kinds of protection and rights for the faculty, especially tenure, job security, prestige, and relatively high incomes. Most professors, protestations to the contrary, are quite concerned about job and economic security. They also usually like students, folklore to the contrary, particularly as individuals and in small groups. However, a very real high-priority goal for faculty members is the protection and optimization of their positions. One can note that the AAUP to date is almost exclusively concerned with this goal, to the virtual exclusion of all others. If professors unionize formally on a broad scale, they may gain protection or rights—especially in the economic sphere—but they are likely to lose out in many ways that are more central to the educational process.

13. *Faculty governance* (14). This relates to faculty participation in important institutional decisions, as well as the right to make various kinds of decisions, especially with regard to academic and faculty matters. All of this is usually done within a framework of budgetary constraints, but the faculty may have the right to participate in the formulation of the budget through some kind of representation. Some institutions have a general policy, if not a goal, that the will of the faculty should prevail on all important matters.

14. *Faculty benefits and privileges* (4). Faculty members are interested in status, prestige, various perquisites, fringe benefits, particular kinds of teaching assignments, and wide latitude to pursue their

careers in a manner satisfactory to them by their own criteria. They are also typically interested in promotions, merit increases, cost-of-living increases, the number and sizes of classes they must teach, and the types of offices, other facilities, services, and logistic support they have. And they—as well as the administration—often spend considerable time and effort trying to secure these things. This relates in part to the goals of protecting the faculty and faculty governance. The personal prestige of a faculty member typically relates to his reputation in his field or discipline and not to what he does for his institution. However, the personal prestige of faculty members is an important ingredient of institutional prestige.

D. Institution and Administration Goals

15. *Seek truth* (16). This includes scholarly inquiry, regardless of where it may lead, and knowledge for the sake of knowledge. Truth-seeking is traditionally the purpose of universities, and many still seem to try to do it, although this is the hardest goal of all to quantify. Who really knows whether there is more truth around this year than last? And who knows what kinds of truth or inquiry may prove useful in the end?

16. *Admit students of high potential* (13). This relates to high potential in the specific strengths and emphasis the university or college feels it has and wants to maintain. Therefore, high grades may not be a necessary condition, although most institutions prefer students with good academic records.

17. *Social egalitarianism* (24). This is a policy or goal of essentially open admissions and development of meaningful educational experiences for all who are admitted. This may include admitting more minority group students, women, the poor or underpriviledged, the handicapped, and all high school graduates who meet the basic minimum legal requirements for admission. Special developmental and remedial programs in basic skills like reading, writing and mathematics may be required to bring such students up to minimum college standards. Social egalitarianism also relates to staffing policies for both academic and nonacademic jobs.

18. *Innovation* (21). Academic programs must be kept responsive to the changing needs, problems, and requirements of society. This goal involves building a climate on campus in which continuous educational innovation is accepted as an institutional way of life. It includes experiments and innovations in teaching or instruction, curriculum,

evaluating and grading students, faculty and nonfaculty personnel evaluation, research approaches, and goal evaluation.

19. *High institutional prestige and pride, good facilities, and a healthy climate* (9). This involves all major constituencies of the institution. The administration has the ultimate responsibility for achieving this overall goal.

20. *Maintain high quality in a balanced way in all programs, taking into account institutional priorities* (28). Here, too, the administration has the ultimate responsibility. If priorities are lacking or are ambiguous, there is likely to be considerable suboptimization, as well as much waste and inefficiency in the system. The aim is to strive for an adequate balance without threatening high-priority programs.

21. *Maintain top quality in most important programs* (10). The quality of particular programs is emphasized, often in ways that are detrimental to an adequate or desired minimum quality in other programs. This is a form of suboptimization. And those programs that get the greatest quality emphasis may not necessarily be those for which there is the greatest student demand, or those that the larger society is most interested in or in need of. In such cases, the preferences of influential faculty members take precedence over the interests of students, other groups, and society at large.

22. *Effective and efficient staffing of managerial and support staff positions* (22). Ensure that managerial or administrative and non-academic staff and service jobs are filled by individuals according to their ability to attain the goals of the institution in the most efficient manner. In turn this requires effective management and leadership, and often considerable entrepreneurship. If the goals and priorities of the institution are highly ambiguous, it is not likely that staffing will be effective and efficient. This relates to the question, management for or toward what?

23. *Income, perquisites, prestige, and job protection for administrative personnel* (7). Providing good salaries and various perquisites and protecting the jobs of administrators form an important goal at most academic institutions, even though they may not do a good job in balancing contributions and inducements. This goal is particularly important with regard to key administrators or managers, including the chief executive.

24. *Democratic governance* (20). Create an overall system of campus governance—involving all major constituents within the university or college—that is genuinely responsive to the concerns of all people at the institution. It involves assuring individuals the right to

participate or be represented in significant decisions that affect them.

25. *Operating efficiency* (30). Keep costs as low as possible, without hindering the attainment of institutional goals and institution efficiency. Again, if the goals and priorities are unknown or unclear, efficiency is likely to be low. Cost criteria should be applied in deciding among alternative academic and nonacademic programs and, where possible, some type of cost-benefit analysis should also be undertaken. Efficiency also relates to the utilization of space and time, reduction of course duplication, resource allocation, and all other input-output relationships and resource use.

E. Goals Related to the Outside World

26. *Public service* (23). This includes public service both in the local community and beyond. Quite a few universities and colleges do all sorts of tasks for various public bodies, often for nothing. Faculty members are typically the most heavily involved in such activities, and they often get paid something or get some other benefits from their service—pure altruism is often not the only motive. Administrators and nonacademic staff may also be involved in public service activities. At a growing number of schools, more students now also engage in various kinds of public service. In general, public service activities are frequently important, but it is often quite difficult to quantify what they are worth. Nevertheless, they can do much to build a favorable reputation for the institution externally.

27. *Serve as a major cultural and information center for the community* (25). The institution can often improve its external image if it offers a variety of cultural events and activities for the public, lets outsiders make use of its libraries and other facilities, and disseminates various kinds of useful or interesting information to the public.

28. *Social criticism and activism* (29). Provide critical evaluations of prevailing values and practices in society, and serve as a source of ideas and recommendations for changing social institutions judged to be unjust or otherwise defective. Engage, as an institution, in working for changes in American society.

29. *Outside validation of programs* (8). Ensure the favorable appraisal of those who validate the quality of programs offered by the institution. Validating groups include accrediting bodies, professional societies, scholarly peers at other schools, and respected professional practitioners.

30. *Ensure desired funds and other resources from external*

sources (3). Administrators at most universities and colleges spend considerable time these days trying to get what they feel is at least adequate financial and other resource support for their institutions from outsiders—for example, governments, legislators, private donors, and foundations. The institution must adequately verify how efficiently and effectively it is performing in relation to its goals and priorities. In turn, inadequate verification is typically the result of ambiguous and unoperational goals and priorities. All of this relates directly to the next and final goal of accountability.

31. *Accountability and goal attainment verification* (27). Regularly provide concrete evidence to interested outsiders, as well as insiders, that the institution is actually achieving its goals and priorities. The institution must also be accountable to external funding sources of all types with regard to the effectiveness of funded programs. Ensure the continued confidence and hence support of those who contribute significantly to the financial and other resource needs of the institution through accountability that includes concrete data verifying goal attainment.

Rank Orderings, Priorities, and Institutional Typologies

Based on the empirical research of other scholars and our own experience, we hypothesize that, as indicated by the figures in parentheses in the above list, the pursued goals of American universities and colleges fall into this rank order:

1. Protect the faculty
2. Undergraduate education
3. Financial support and resources
4. Faculty benefits and privileges
5. Graduate education
6. Research
7. Income, perquisites, prestige, and job protection for administrators
8. Outside validation of programs
9. High institutional prestige and pride, good facilities, and healthy climate
10. Top quality in most important programs
11. Student intellectual development
12. Student scholarship, scientific research, and/or creative endeavor
13. Admission of students of high potential
14. Faculty governance

15. Student personal development
16. Truth
17. Athletics
18. Cultural and religious assimilation
19. Student activities and rights
20. Democratic governance
21. Innovation
22. Preparation of students for useful careers, jobs, and status in society
23. Public service
24. Social egalitarianism
25. Provision of culture and information to community
26. Part-time and continuing education
27. Accountability and goal-attainment verification
28. High quality in all programs in a balanced way
29. Social criticism and activism
30. Operating efficiency
31. Effective and efficient staffing of management and support positions

This rank ordering is necessarily hypothetical, but if it is generally correct, it may explain a great deal about the problems confronting so many universities and colleges. Faculty and administration may give low priority to many of the goals viewed as being of considerable importance to financial and other resource providers, the community, other outside groups and individuals, and numerous, if not most, students. Conversely, many of the goals that are strongly pursued and highly desired by faculty and administrators may not be of high priority to most if not all the other constituencies.

One problem with both actual and pursued institutional goal systems is that different constituencies may want different things, and often they have the political, legal, or economic power to impose their wishes. Another problem is that not every administrator or professor wants the goal system or the various goals that the institution seems to be following, although there do seem to be dominant patterns involving the goals and priorities that are pursued and how strongly they are pursued generally by the institution. Hence, much tugging and pulling occurs within the system and among different groups and individuals. Indeed, this is what most of the struggle and conflict is really about. The result may be great debate, considerable confusion, and in the end, some compromise that achieves nothing useful. This is even more likely to be true when the goal system is ambiguous and there is no real sense of priorities. It may be very difficult if not impossible to quantify precisely what a particular goal might or should be, and when it is reached, but it is usually possible to make some kind of useful evaluation. Table 5 presents our rankings of pursued goals for six types of institutions.

We invite the reader to consider what he feels the goal system really is at his own institution. Which goals are the most vigorously pursued and the most desired in reality? How do others perceive the goal system and why? How would you shift the goal system and priorities and why? What should and could your institution do about its goal system and why?

Examination of Table 5 shows that protecting the faculty (12) ranks first for all but one category of institutions. Faculty benefits (14) ranks relatively high in all cases, and benefits for administrators (23) ranks pretty high in most cases. This may seem unkind or cynical, because professionals typically do not admit that they are trying to optimize for themselves, even when they really are. But realistic observations of academic institutions, as well as other kinds of organizations, suggest that when the chips are down, the personal angles come out first. And these groups or individuals who wield the most power and influence come out better in terms of their most highly desired goals. There is generally nothing wrong or immoral about this humans tend to behave this way. But there may be much wrong with fervently trying to deny it, especially when outsiders see that many if not most of the institutional goals that they place high priority on are being ignored.

Various influential and possibly powerful off-campus constituents and outsiders may care very much about such goals as job preparation for students (8), part-time education (3), community service (27), social egalitarianism (17), public service (26), operating efficiency (25), effective and efficient staffing of managerial and service jobs (22), and accountability with regard to goal attainment (31). Yet these goals are ranked quite low generally. Interestingly, however, most of them are ranked higher for the junior college segment, and this segment is generally in the least trouble. Many of the state colleges and the less prestigious private schools are in the most trouble, as are quite a few of the religious-

Barry M. Richman, Richard N. Farmer

Table 5.

SUGGESTED GOAL RANKINGS FOR DIFFERENT TYPES OF
UNIVERSITIES AND COLLEGES

State Multiversities	Other State Universities and Colleges	Junior Colleges[a]	High Prestige Private Schools	Less Prestigious Private Schools	Religion-Sponsored and Affiliated Schools
12[b]	12	12	12	12	11
4	1	1	4	1	12
2	30	8	14	30	1
14	2	30	2	2	9
21	6	9	21	14	30
30	14	14	23	6	14
23	29	29	7	9	5
1	29	3	6	23	6
15	21	27	19	29	21
7	9	23	16	7	29
6	11	6	1	21	19
29	7	17	9	19	23
19	13	21	30	16	16
16	17	18	15	13	27
13	15	26	13	11	10
24	16	20	24	14	17
18	8	11	18	5	26
10	26	24	26	15	15
17	19	31	10	10	7
9	10	13	11	18	8
8	24	25	29	24	13
5	5	22	20	26	24
27	3	16	8	8	18
3	27	19	27	17	31
26	18	10	31	3	2
11	24	7	17	20	20
31	28	15	3	27	3
20	31	5	28	28	4
28	25	4	5	31	28
25	20	28	22	22	12
22	22		25	25	25

[a] There are no graduate programs at junior colleges.
[b] Goal numbers are those listed with the description of goals earlier in this chapter; 12, for example, is "protect the faculty."

affiliated institutions. Some of the latter, however, have created a viable niche because of their stress on religious and cultural assimilation (11). But the most successful ones in this category typically do considerably more than provide such assimilation, and they attain other goals quite effectively.

The prestigious and successful private schools as well as the prestigious, large, and successful state multiversities do the high-priority things well enough and also can often afford to pursue more priorities effectively, so they are not usually wanting for enough students or financial support. Because of their reputations, most of their graduates are also usually assured of at least reasonably good jobs or careers and status in society, regardless of the programs or courses they have taken. This is frequently not true, however, of graduates of the other institutions.

Table 5 also suggests some of the reasons why so many students, particularly undergraduates, are at least somewhat disenchanted at so many schools, even though undergraduate education (1), at least in terms of quantity of students, is often a relatively important goal. At many institutions, students are not really considered very important by the faculty, the administration, or the institution. As a result, they get the short end of the resource stick, and frequently face huge classes, indifferent, inferior teachers who cannot do valuable research, and teaching assistants rather than the really good faulty members who are too busy doing other things.

Various other student impact goals also are not ranked very high in Table 5. Student activities and rights (10), for example, does not rank very high generally, though it is somewhat higher in some sectors than others. However, the types of student activities available (such as religious services) may not really turn many students on. Many schools do put teaching ahead of research (4). Religious schools, state colleges, and less prestigious private schools often place considerable emphasis on the student's personal development (9), but frequently do not achieve this goal very effectively, or in a very broad or durable way. The same is often true of the student's intellectual development (6) and student scholarship, scientific research and creativity (7), even at quite a few institutions in the other sectors. As noted earlier, junior colleges are much more interested in job-oriented training than the other institutions.

Innovation (18) is not a high priority pursued goal in any sector. It is ranked lowest for the state colleges, followed by the religious schools, and then the less prestigious private institutions—and these are the sectors that generally seem to be in the deepest trouble.

Within institutions, the goal rankings presented in Table 5 typically do not hold across the board, although there seem to be dominant and common overall institutional patterns. For example, a business or management school even in a private or public prestigious university may have an internal goal system resembling other state universities, or perhaps even various junior colleges, more than its own liberal arts school or college. Various other professional schools may also have similar attitudes and goal systems.

Universities and colleges tend to be primarily for faculties and administrators, but there are also orders of priorities between classes of institutions, as commonly perceived by administrations and professors. This has already been discussed in connection with the Cohen and March study (1974). The following is a rank ordering, with regard to respect and prestige, of different types of academic institutions in the United States: (1) Ivy League, (2) state multiversities, (3) private, (4) other state universities and colleges, (5) religion sponsored schools, and (6) junior colleges.

The Ivy League type schools stand supreme. Their standing suggests why many other types of institutions try to emulate the Ivy League colleges, although trying to be like Harvard is usually unwise. Institutions at each prestige level can make their own important kinds of valuable, useful, needed, and desired contributions to society, and both they and society are best served if they stick to what they can and should do best.

For example, the president of a southern state university in the 1960s tried to turn his institution into a prestigious scholarly university. Athletics were deemphasized in the process, even though much of the external support and prestige that the university had in the region was related to its excellent athletic record, especially in football. The president lasted through only a few losing seasons. Then the institution hired the "right" coach again, and the president was forced to resign.

A vocational school focusing on the nuts and bolts of foreign trade and international business gained a good reputation for what it was doing. It filled a valuable, specialized, and solid niche in higher education quite effectively and successfully. A new president however has given it a more prestigious sounding name and has been trying to give it a scholarly image and to make it academically respectable. Before it was a good trade school giving high priority to preparing students for and helping them get jobs. Now it seems to be becoming an expensive MBA operation. But what competitive advantages will it have over other MBA programs, especially those good at international business? If the answer turns out to be none, or close to it, the institution is likely to run into serious difficulties. Here is a good example of a president—either with board approval or on his own initiative—who has been shifting the goal system and priorities quite dramatically and in ways that could turn out poorly. Emulation is often not a wise path to follow.

Critical Problems and Alternatives

When confronted with the complexity and ambiguity that are in large part inherent in the goal systems of academic institutions, most administrators (and others) feel and act as though they simply cannot meaningfully discuss or deal with a specific problem. Complicating their attempts at analysis are the many intangible, unquantifiable problems relating to the operationalization of goal systems. For example, few people feel competent to judge precisely or are willing to try to judge objectively whether a paper on a seventeenth-century German author is better or worse than a paper on marketing systems in Virginia, but this is the kind of judgments that may have to be made in deciding whether certain goals are achieved.

Since so many goals, subgoals, or parts of them are difficult to quantify in a precise way, we tend, first, to count the things that can be counted and hope this tally measures something useful, and, second, to resort to process—that is, to follow procedures rather than to question goals or end results.

Thus, in the first instance, we tend to count publications when evaluating a scholar or researcher, but often make little effort to determine how good or bad the stuff really is. We note that a certain faculty member obtained X dollars in research grants, but make little effort to assess how well these funds were used. We count enrolled students and graduates without trying to decide how good their education is or might have been. We look at the number of students a given instructor teaches and advises, often without doing an assessment of how effective the faculty member is as a teacher or advisor.

We see on Professor X's biography that he has done some administrative duties and serves on four committees, without really trying to decide whether he was effective or what he accomplished. And we note with pleasure (or disdain) that Professor Y was elected to the local school board, without trying to decide whether or not he was a valuable member. We also may count such things as salary increases, promotions, terminations, number of new recruits, fringe benefits, dollars spent on support services and facilities, student-faculty ratios, and class sizes without making an in-depth evaluation about what these numbers mean in terms of institutional goals and priorities.

We also resort to process, and become absorbed in doing the job, without asking whether the job is really meaningful in terms of goals and priorities. A good man can spend a lifetime trying to teach a single course better, without asking (or being asked) whether or not the course is really relevant. He can spend endless hours revising a paper, without questioning whether or not the subject amounts to anything. He can also spend endless hours in meetings, without any assessment of the value of this activity. He can endlessly politic for university reform, without questioning whether or not the given reform will really change anything important. The overall result is that we tend to drift from one false or innocuous measure to another.

Of course, reversion to process is often convenient, especially if professors do not really have budgetary control. The allocators determine basic goals and policy as best they can, in an administrative vacuum, since the potential helpers have not shown any serious interest in assisting them.

All of this was quite workable until recently, and in quite a few kinds of situations it may still be workable—but only where budgets rise fast enough so that everyone can do more or less what he has been doing or wants to do, without much concern about institutional goals and priorities. However, this particular game is about to end. The available resources are simply not large enough to allow all kinds of implicit as well as any explicit goals to be achieved simultaneously. Some rather drastic changes will have to occur, and the allocators of resources will have to make them. What criteria can they use?

Any criteria will be painful to faculty and students alike, as well as many administrators. Consider some very likely alternatives, particularly if chief executives and their administrators do not take the lead and exert much more effective and creative managerial ability than most of them have until now, and if the faculty continues to behave and act as they typically have been. (1) Lacking the ability to do everything, fund providers and powerful administrators will simply demand from the university or college what they feel is needed most. The first demand is for the kinds of manpower or student outputs that the fund providers in particular think is important. One can examine the needs of most communities and states and quite easily deduce what follows: more lower-level and semi-professional technicians, more medical doctors, and more professional personnel of various types. What happens to the budgets of the arts college and humanities? The students are also fund providers in a very real sense, and they too will vote by deciding where to go and what courses to take. (2) If the institution can do research, what kinds are seen as relevant? The fund providers will inform us. It will undoubtedly be largely practical, applied work, relevant to a variety of relatively short-term needs. What happens to artistic and more basic theoretical research if the piper calls the tune?

It seems useful to get university and college administrators and faculty into this argument, because they are the ones who will be most directly affected by such changes. And it would be useful to ponder what other alternatives exist before someone else calls the tune. The reasoning and inferences of respected and very able scholars like Cohen and March (1974), that the goal systems of academic institutions are not only ambiguous but are destined to remain so, and that this is beneficial and desirable in many ways—as is a good deal of sensible foolishness and playfulness in organizations—do not provide much help or solace to institutions faced with very critical financial problems. And the viability and survival of many are already or soon will be in jeopardy.

Many universities and colleges will continue to stumble from one serious crisis to the next more serious crisis and many will succumb sooner or later. The usual response is that something will turn up to alleviate such crises. So far, this usually has been correct. But given the logic of Baumol and others, time seems to really be running out for many schools. Because faculty members in particular typically show little or no interest in the critical variables, it is quite likely that whatever happens will descend upon them. Scream they will, but it will be far too late for them to take part in the decision process.

However, university and college administrators, and especially the chief executives, will still be held responsible for getting the job done—if they and their vociferous advisors and the powerful and influential outsiders can somehow figure out what this job is and should be. And much change will have to occur.

A number of fundamental questions seem relevant and crucial, given the foregoing discussion and analysis. What goals are appropriate for a given university or college? In what order of priority should they be placed? How can the institution's goal system be adequately operationalized? The choice of suitable goals and related priorities is at least as important as operationalizing the goal system or trying to quantify the goals. If the first set of questions can be decided in a meaningful way, how can these goals be evaluated, measured, and verified? That is, if we do something, how do we know that we have achieved to an adequate degree and extent the goals we set out to achieve? What can and should the administration, particularly the chief executive, do with regard to the above problems?

We do not intend to cop out in this book, even though these problems are very complex and there are no easy or simple solutions. We will further address ourselves to them, as best we can, in later chapters, particularly in Chapter Thirteen, and to some extent in several other chapters.

Sound Goal System

Before concluding this chapter, it seems worthwhile to present one case of an academic institution that has a relatively sound, meaningful, and adequately operational and verifiable goal system.

We have selected Berea College for our example. Richman has visited Berea. It is an institution that is not wealthy and does not have much prestige on a national scale—have you ever heard of it? However, it serves a very critical role in its region and has proved itself to be both viable and successful over the years. It has also achieved a solid and important place in American higher education. And Berea's future seems to be assured.

Berea, a private four-year undergraduate liberal arts college, is situated in Appalachia, in a small city in Kentucky of about 7,000 people that bears its name. The college was founded in 1855 and its earliest employees—many of whom came from Oberlin College and Seminary—were against slavery and mostly quite religious Protestants. Berea has emphasized Christian ideals, service to others, individual freedom and responsibility, and interracial brotherhood. Faculty and administrators typically were and still are practical idealists who place great emphasis on translating visions into effective programs. One basic policy has been to attract similar—though not necessarily Protestant—faculty members from good schools. Berea has had an interracial mix of students from the outset, and it has been a coeducational and nonsectarian college devoted to the service of Appalachia. Although it has clearly been viable and successful, it has never really been rich or affluent.

Today Berea has over two thousand students, faculty, other employees, and their families. The student body numbers about fourteen hundred. It is primarily a liberal arts college, but it has considerable applied, practical, and career preparation emphases. The college owns and operates a collection of businesses, a public utility, and some farms and forest lands. It is a self-sufficient, 1400-acre campus community.

Berea charges no fees or tuition for instruction, and all students engage in part time employment which is assured. Work, both mental and manual, is seen as good, as having dignity, and as often bringing spiritual balance. A central goal is to admit students from the region who cannot afford to go elsewhere. There is a strong tradition of self-support, self-help, and self-respect. Work is viewed as a valuable part of the student's educational and personal development. Moral character-building is also considered important. Education is viewed not only as an end, but also as a basic means for fulfilling other personal needs and goals after graduation. The institution stresses that if the weakenesses of society are to be remedied, people of knowledge, conviction, and energy must remedy them.

Some four hundred freshmen are admitted each year. Around 70 percent of them are from families with incomes in the lower half of their counties' income distribution. About 39 percent of the students are from farms and 41 percent from small towns in the region. Berea also admits a limited number of students from other parts of the nation, as well as some foreign students, in order to achieve greater diversity and balance in its student population. In recent years there have been about seventy foreign students from forty or so countries. Students serve on most college committees, and the institution's governance appears to be democratic and participative.

About 57 percent of the graduates go on to graduate studies, many of them to leading schools. Of Berea's graduates, 45 percent return eventually to the Appalachia area to work in service jobs as teachers, doctors, lawyers, county agents, ministers, social workers, in business, or in some other occupation. The primary reason that even more do not return is that there still are not enough adequate jobs available. A recent study reported on the collegiate origins of younger American scholars by giving the percentage of graduates from 377 institutions who later achieved scholarly distinction. In this study Berea ranked 32nd—or in the top 9 percent—in the nation and was 17th in the field of the natural sciences.

As regional and educational conditions have shifted, so have Berea's programs and emphases. For example, the college's dairy was eliminated and a new ceramics industry is being developed. Nursing and public health as well as industrial arts and business education are being expanded. Berea's faculty members are in demand for teaching and administrative assignments abroad and many, including current President Willis Weatherford, have lived and worked overseas. Many students earn summer scholarships for study abroad. The college's Country Dancers have performed in many places in the United States and abroad.

A number of new units have been added to the campus, which has long served as a major cultural, information, service, and tourist center for the region. An Appalachian center has recently been established, one purpose of which is to provide detailed and reliable information about the Appalachian region. A speaker's bureau has been set up to respond to invitations for lecturers and teachers qualified to discuss cultural matters and contemporary problems and possible solutions. A new Appalachian museum at Berea College has recently been opened to the public. The college library is continually being expanded and is one of the most important and publicly used in the entire region. Berea College has done a great deal to make the federal government and the people of America aware of the needs, problems, and conditions of Appalachia.

Because Berea charges no tuition, its existence, its work, and its success depend largely on gifts from donors, income from the accumulated endowments, and the revenues it generates from its various businesses and other activities. The college is presently involved in a $35 million development program. Given its past accomplishments and its importance to the future, Berea is likely to achieve this target.

Although Berea College clearly has a much more distinctive character, a clearer mission, and a more visible and stronger sense of purpose than most universities and colleges, it does not just rest on its laurels or past accomplishments. It also has a more operational, clearer, verifiable, and meaningful goal system than most academic institutions. This, in turn, enables it to shift emphases and change directions quite effectively in response to changing external conditions, needs, and requirements.

Berea has seven basic goals to which it gives highest priority. These goals are central to the educational process and to service to the region. Let us discuss and illustrate each of them briefly.

1. *To provide an educational opportunity for students primarily from Appalachia who have high ability but limited economic resources.* Berea has a policy of accepting 80 percent of its students from Appalachia. Quite a few are given special assistance, such as remedial training in basic subjects, to bring them up to par. The student output success rate is impressive.

2. *To provide an education of high quality with a liberal arts foundation and outlook.* The overall educational program has a liberal arts foundation or core, since this is seen as essential to serving the needs of the region. A liberal arts orientation or phi-

losophy pervades the entire curriculum. However, the college also offers courses leading to BS degrees in agriculture, business, industrial arts, nursing, and home economics, all fields of major importance to the region. There is a teacher education program, a program in Black studies and one in Appalachia studies, and an issue and values course. There is a periodic review and updating of all programs and courses. The curriculum has become substantially more interdisciplinary in content and orientation over the years, as has the faculty.

3. *To stimulate understanding of the Christian faith and to emphasize the Christian ethic and motive of service to mankind.* Although Berea has always been a nondenominational school, its founders were deeply religious spiritually and committed to exemplifying Christian beliefs in constructive social action. This tradition has persisted over the years. The school's religious program is developed in terms of contemporary relevance and social concerns. A basic aim is the acceptance of Christian standards, as well as standards of academic freedom and respect for the convictions of others. The attainment of this goal is reflected in many of the things students do both while at Berea and after they leave.

4. *To demonstrate through the labor program that labor, mental and manual, has dignity as well as utility.* Real-life experience is the cornerstone here. One of Berea's most distinctive characteristics or goals is its labor program, in which all students participate. The aim is threefold: educational development, student self-support, and institutional utility. A wide and varied choice of jobs is available to students. These include institutional, academic, industrial, business, administrative, and agricultural jobs, as well as community service work. There are significant vocational and preprofessional benefits from the students' work, and many students have found their careers from interests developed through their student labor. However, this is by no means the only intent of the labor program. The program is also intended to provide a general experience in work, to develop skills and attributes useful in any work situation, and to help students appreciate the values of labor.

5. *To promote the ideals of brotherhood, equality, and democracy, with particular emphasis on interracial education.* A passion for human freedom led to the founding of Berea, and this

passion persists today, as evidenced by many of the activities and much of the observable behavior. When, in 1904, a Kentucky law prohibited interracial education, the college vigorously, but unsuccessfully, appealed to the United States Supreme Court to declare this statute unconstitutional. This action obviously did not set very well with many influential and powerful people—including potential fund-providers—at that time, but the college adhered to its principles and convictions. In 1950, when Kentucky finally amended this law, Negro students were immediately readmitted in significant numbers. Berea strives to be a truly democratic college, with a philosophy, overall educational program, student economy, and regional outreach that provide living examples for its constituents, region, and country, and also for foreign leaders and students.

6. *To maintain on campus and encourage in the students a way of life characterized by plain living, pride in labor well done, zest for learning, high personal standards, and concern for the welfare of others.* The leaders of Berea College realize that this is perhaps the most difficult goal to measure or quantify. It is unavoidably stronger in its high aspirations than in its specifics of implementation. However, through effective leadership, management, and both faculty and administration demonstration by personal example, continuous effort is given to creating a climate for achieving this goal and for giving appropriate guidance. But in the end the students must learn for themselves—and from each other and there are many indications that most of them do. This may also be in substantial part due to a type of self-selection process by students who go to Berea. Considerable attention and effort is given to the development of appropriate recreational, cultural, athletic, religious, and other nonacademic programs that contribute to improved college life at Berea. And there is also a great deal of student government. The counseling of students is taken seriously. Considerable emphasis is placed on developing a strong sense of justice, a commitment to civic participation and responsible citizenship, a personal sense of noblesse oblige, and good capacities for self-discipline and self-direction. A real effort is given to making students mindful of the strengths of our democratic society and to encouraging them to develop an awareness of the numerous and tragic gaps between some of our society's ideals and current actualities. Students are strongly

encouraged to strive through general influence and appropriate participation to remedy specific shortcomings and eliminate handicaps in the lives of the disadvantaged. Berea's goals are not limited to academic performance to the exclusion of other values.

7. *To serve the Appalachian region through education but also by other appropriate services.* From its earliest years, Berea has been aware of the difficulties and potential of the Appalachian region and has endeavored to assist its people in finding solutions to some of their problems and in attaining better levels of living. However, one academic institution can only do so much. Therefore, education—which is probably the best means of giving men and women greater vision and effectiveness in their personal lives, economic activities, and community leadership—has always been and should continue to be Berea's primary way of serving the region. But Berea College has never limited its efforts on behalf of Appalachia to its own campus and classrooms. It pioneered in agriculture and home economics extension, in the preservation and improvement of traditional handicraft skills, in promoting the establishment of local schools, and in community health and development programs. It has also carried out literacy projects and school library services. Many of these have been pilot projects, initiated according to pressing needs in eastern Kentucky and supported to the extent college resources made possible. The success of these activities and their relevance to basic area needs are shown by the fact that these are now continuing, comprehensive programs operated by public agencies.

In recent years, Berea has effectively conducted rural school improvement programs in several counties. Other important projects have been undertaken to assist young people who are disadvantaged and discouraged in their schoolwork. As a means of assisting some of the most promising students from schools in the area, Berea, along with some other nearby colleges, is engaged in Project Opportunity, a program designed to motivate and prepare these students for college study. Berea students, faculty, administrators, and other college employees are involved in such public service activities. Berea is currently conducting community aid projects in the state through a student group called "Students for Appalachia." These students have no set pattern of directives other than to interest themselves in the community and its people, and to advise and encourage disadvantaged families in meeting their problems and in becoming more self-sufficient. These students are members of the college student labor force and are paid on the same basis as those who work on campus. Berea has every intention of continuing to discover and pioneer new ways to serve its region in the future.

We are not advocating Berea's goal system for every, or even very many, universities and colleges, although at least some parts of it may well be worth considering. The main point is that Berea has shown that it is possible to design and implement a relatively sound, meaningful, operational, verifiable, truly relevant, and adequately comprehensive institutional goal system. Berea College knows both what it wants to do and what it should do with its always limited resources, and it does it quite effectively and efficiently, and in numerous ways that all those who are interested can see, evaluate, and verify. For this fundamental reason Berea will no doubt continue to be both vital and successful in the future. Most universities and colleges, on the other hand, do not seem to have even explicit or very clear goal statements.

Power and Goals

We have taxonomized and interrelated rather crudely the components of the university or college system and its environment in Chapter Three. This is the nature of the system—now, how can it be made to perform better? Chapter Thirteen focuses on significant policy implications and institutional change, but some comments about some of the things that might be done are in order here.

Of course, performance depends on the thing that is being accomplished. Until you know what goals are being reached for, it is rather difficult to determine what should be done to achieve them.

This is precisely where academic institutions tend to get into deep trouble. A goal system was suggested in the output taxonomy in Chapter Three, and suggested values were placed on goals, giving a priority order. But rarely does anyone sit down and systematically attempt to do this. Because this is not done, goals tend to be quite diffuse. And because there is a considerable disagreement about what the goals should be, often there is a tacit attempt to try to do everything at once, rather than set meaningful priorities. Moreover, virtually every subsystem administrator has quite strong feelings about what should be put first. Hence, it is typically not clear which parts of the system are significant. The reader is again invited to change the goal values or add new goals, work back through Tables 3 and 4 in Chapter Three with the new values, and see what changes. These changes not only reflect power shifts but also show top managers what is important. Until the goal question is resolved, it is impossible to say what is really important, and hence where time, effort, and money should be put.

Administrators do the best they can. Then try to figure out (intuitively or objectively) what goals are significant; then they pay attention to subsystems that handle the critical interfaces around these goals, and they perhaps also try to compromise between various vociferous constituencies (inside and outside) who may disagree with these priorities. The results of such management are quite familiar. The system functions, in that its major goals are at least partially achieved. But many components are somewhat out of phase with what is being done. And as the critical problems shift through time, this outphasing becomes critical. If the outphasing becomes too critical, the system is disrupted—as happened at Columbia, Parsons, San Francisco State, and the university discussed in Chapter Two. It is quite possible that this sort of administration is highly inefficient, in that it results in too much input for the given outputs. Too much time, money, and talent is spent in doing the insignificant, rather than the significant.

This point might be checked, by using the weights and scores developed in the preceding tables for various subsystems and other items. How many of these subsystems, at a given university, are given anything like the attention they merit? For any number of reasons, some subsystems get far too much money, manpower, attention, material, and what not, while others, perhaps even more important, get relatively little of these inputs or attention. It is easy in retrospect to see what went wrong, but good managers should be able to forecast such things. They cannot because there is rarely agreement or goals, and the intuitive or implicit assumptions about relative importance or power may prove wrong for any number of subsystems, inputs, or environmental factors. But what are the right numbers, or order of priorities, for goals? Until we can figure this out, we will constantly be having trouble with university and college systems. So, what might an administrator or manager do, given these problems? The pattern might go something like this.

1. Figure out what the goal system really is, and what the priorities within it really are. Then figure out what goal system and related priorities seem to be the most desirable for the institution. This is not necessarily the best of all worlds, but it has to represent some kind of working compromise among the goal preferences of many active and influential critics. If top management really understands the overall system and its more critical interrelationships, has adequate formal authority, and has really effective managerial skills and leadership ability, it will usually be able to do much more than is commonly considered possible to shape the institution's goal system and priorities and bring about positive institutional changes. The absolute constraints here are usually clear enough: (a) The goals selected must not cause critical withdrawals of too many clients, supporters, students, or professors. (b) Whatever the goals are, they must not cause violent rejection by significant groups. (c) Given the complex structure of a university, goals are almost always compromises—but compromise must not cause either (a) or (b) above. On the other hand, they must not be watered down until they are ineffective or inoperative.

This is much easier said than done, but if it can be accomplished—and more will be said about this in later chapters, especially Chapter Thirteen—the administrator is perhaps 90 percent done with his job. The rest is downhill.

2. Given goals and priorities, the next step is to taxonomize the elements in the system and analyze power. This was done earlier in this chapter, but some other taxonomies may prove more useful, particularly in combining or disaggregating categories to meet relevant needs.

3. The critical interfaces are identified and those dealing with them also are identified. As mentioned earlier, what is really critical at any given moment depends on circumstances; the manager or administrator should be able not only to see what is important now, but what will be important tomorrow.

4. The critical interfaces will be handled by some subsystem.

This is where the talent and money goes. How any critical interface is handled depends more on how the problem is identified and who works on it than on anything else, so the administrator has to find his talent. Fortunately, universities are full of high-talent manpower who can do very well with problem-solving, once the problem is defined.

5. Identification of really critical interfaces typically depends largely on data passing through the system. All or even a majority of the critical interfaces noted in Tables 3 and 4 will not normally be at a crisis stage all at once—if they are, it is very likely that the system will collapse. Rather, a limited number are showing signs of deviation that indicate that something horrible will happen if nothing is done to correct the deviation. (When this is happening with a sizable number of interfaces and top management is ineffective, you get the kind of crisis described in Chapter Two).

This point suggests the extreme importance of data and information in the university or college system. If a critical interface shows signs of blowing up, the administrator must be aware of problems before he can act. Far too often, the information systems of an academic institution are not designed to give such information. Such feedback is critical, and administrators should try to design systems that provide useful, adequate information to the relevant places on time and in proper order.

6. The administrator decentralizes what is not important, and centralizes what is. This, of course, is very directly related to the identification of such problems. What is important? The tables presented in Chapter Three suggest possibilities, but these will change with time, place, and institutions. Here is where the art comes in. No schema or theory can really tell anyone what is important, particularly because so much of what occurs in a university is judgmental, emotional, and behavioral. But the insensitive administrator will not last long if he fails on this point. Perhaps the rapidity of change explains why so many university and college administrators in so many schools get into real trouble. What was valid and useful five years ago may have changed completely. Yet relatively few men can change their own perceptions this fast, particularly if such changes involve some basic value changes.

We return to goal systems at appropriate points later in the book and especially in Chapter Thirteen, which deals with significant policy implications. Now that we have explored the outputs of academic institutions, we turn our attention to the inputs. Then we focus on power, internal system interrelationships, environmental constraints, and other issues central to academic management and mismanagement.

Chapter V

Inputs

What goes into the university depends on what is wanted from it. If one key goal is to produce highly intelligent, well-trained undergraduates, then student input at the freshman level should be the most intelligent persons who can be recruited. If winning basketball games is another goal, some of these freshmen had better be six feet eight or taller.

Difficulties in defining goal systems quickly create major problems in planning relevant inputs. If we really do not know or care what comes out, then it does not matter too much what goes in. Thus, we must begin any discussion of inputs with some consideration of outputs. The determination of relevant outputs or goals may be the most vexing problem faced by any university.

Input problems are also complicated by the very long time

spans that may be necessary to get full use of an input. Some buildings over a century old are still used by many universities; it takes four years to turn a freshman into a graduate; and giving a faculty member tenure at thirty-five locks in his input for thirty years. Even if the university knew exactly what it wanted in the next five years, it might take over thirty years to get the system completely adjusted to major changes. The implicit forecasting problems involved in such long-term decisions are extremely difficult to handle. But they must be handled well because what is being decided today will still be affecting what happens twenty or thirty years from now.

This chapter relates to the taxonomies developed further in Chapter Three. Necessarily some value judgments are made about goal systems, as we systematically consider problems connected with various kinds of inputs. Any university has two basic inputs, people and things. Dollars are the glue that holds the system together, and they are considered separately.

Budgets

In a money-oriented society, dollars are crucial. Making money available to various subsystems enables them to obtain their own subgoals. But the total amount of money available is never enough to cover all demands. Resources are scarce, and they must be allocated. How? This is the single major strategic question for university management.

People talk a lot, and one can become confused by listening to all the platitudinous statements being made around any campus. One way to find out what goal systems actually are is to examine budgets in detail. If administrators talk about the glorious future for fine arts, but the budgets shows that this department is getting $800 per year for research while the physics department is getting $800,000, then something can be deduced about the goal system. If administrators constantly complain about the shortage of classroom space but the only major building under construction is the new gym, more can be determined.

Even in public institutions, budgetary details are not publicly revealed. Thus, many goal decisions are made *in camera,* by interested deans, trustees, presidents, and others in power. As a result of such secrecy, administrators are often subjected to endless, ill-informed criticism. The more articulate and interested academic critics and participants are, the more likely some real problems will emerge if total secrecy about expenditures is observed. But revealing everything could be much worse. Proper balance here is necessarily judgmental.

If money is to be spent wisely, some method must be evolved to determine how allocations are to be made. One useful tool is cost-benefit analysis. The basic methodology is as follows. First, the university is divided into subsystems related to goals. This breakdown should be as precise as possible, although precision is often difficult. For example, the English department typically serves not only its own undergraduate and graduate majors but most other students at the undergraduate level, and the economics department may serve a similar function for majors in business, engineering, and other fields. The subsystems must be related to outputs. If you know what the relevant output is, you can determine what the inputs should be. Essentially, this is program budgeting.

Second outputs or benefits have to be quantified—a very difficult task. The best measure of quantification is dollars, because inputs are also valued in dollars. This notion horrifies many university people, because so much of what a university is cannot be reduced to dollars! But if this is not done, the whole university system functions aimlessly. Anything goes, and in many universities this is exactly what does happen. No rational resource allocation occurs, because the system is irrational. This difficult step cannot be done as precisely for a university as for a more dollar-oriented system, such as a private business. However, more can be done than is. Some motion of output can be determined, even in value-laden situations.

The third step is to determine potential program costs. This step is more precise than the first two, although the long time-dimension of decisions precludes accurate assessment of many costs and benefits in the short run. But most inputs can be reduced to dollar figures, and these figures are assigned to the relevant programs. The fourth step is to allocate resources on the basis of information gathered during the preceding steps. The basic decision-rule is to put dollars into the programs where benefits exceed costs by the largest margin. If one can obtain $5.3 millions of benefits for

$1.3 millions of costs, it seems worthwhile to allocate this way, particularly if the next best payoff for the $1.3 millions is only $900,000.

This technique works best in determining where the greatest payoffs are likely to occur with given amounts of inputs. Given a going operation, if some additional dollars are made available, where should these dollars be put? Many traditional or necessary expenditures cannot be sharply cut, but new money can be placed strategically.

Examination of many requests for additional funds reveals how seldom this decision-making process is used. Every viable subsystem will give many reasons why its new or expanded program will pay off. But the statements of such payoffs are too often obscure, and do not reflect efforts to measure actual results. Prestige, favorable outside reactions, and even publicly are cited as payoffs. When the payoffs are not precisely defined, the administrator has to decide who gets what.

Such suggestions are not warmly received by subsystem participants whose main interest is in their own subsystem. Many claimants for new funds really have no idea what short-term or long-term payoffs they may achieve. Lacking this knowledge, they cannot respond rationally to questions.

Another potential weakness of this system is that it may favor those programs or goals where outputs can be quantified. If the medical school can point to high dollar values for each graduate, it may be able to prevail over the arguments of the English literature group. If the engineering school can show large gains in state or regional productivity as a result of its new program, philosophy may suffer.

But what better approach is there? Demands for funds are always greater than supply, and someone must allocate. Allocations made without rational decision-making are accidents of history, personalities, or pressures. This cost-benefit allocation system can also be used as a defensive mechanism for harrassed administrators. If critics question what is going on, administrators can always cite detailed studies (which few ever read) suggesting that the allocations meet rational criteria. Many university critics are deterred by hard statistical data, no matter how they are derived. A very large bibliography of cost-benefit materials and analysis is available in economics, business, and public administration, although university and college managers have not used them extensively. But without rational allocation decisions, everything else falls apart.

People

By far the largest university operating cost is for personnel. If the opportunity costs of students' time (what they could be earning if they were not in school), were also considered labor costs would be huge.

Professional Staff. Given dollars and goals, the relevant questions are: What kinds of professionals are needed to achieve the goals? And at what cost? This consideration leads quickly back to cost-benefit analysis. We must each decide on our goals and priorities, determine what cash is available, and then decide what kinds of staff to utilize.

Professors tend to overtrain themselves and their students. Professing implies extensive competence, and since one major goal of any profession is to guard against incompetents, there tends to be a bias toward overqualification for any given job. Excess reliance on credentials such as terminal degrees is one expression of this bias, and often leads to overqualified people in university and college jobs. They may be overpaid as well.

Often a good decision rule is to make sure that the *minimally* competent and effective person holds a position. This rule is contrary to most professors' feelings, but it reduces the costs and friction of traditional staffing. A minimally competent person struggling with his job is much less likely to get into trouble than an overqualified person, and he is also likely to get more intensive job satisfaction.

Professors do four things: teach, research, perform public services of every sort, and administer, usually in unstructured ways. But the administrator should be utilizing high-level manpower so that benefits exceed costs by the largest possible margin for each man. It is common to find a great teacher in the laboratory, or a capable administrator trying to get some research done, or a good graduate student handling freshman classes. Even junior professors now cost more than $20,000 per year (including fringe costs, office space, and secretaries), and this waste quickly becomes burdensome.

Few universities seem to know enough about their professors to put them in relevant roles, and conventional departmentalization may lock capable people into jobs that do not make full use of their abilities. Modest improvements in professional time allocations can have big payoffs, and modern data-processing systems can be used to develop better information than is now available.

People are hard to handle in complicated situations, and highly articulate and intelligent professors are more difficult to handle than most people. Many academic institutions are always in trouble on this score. If a faculty holds deep-rooted grudges against the administration, productivity is only a fraction of what it might be. One result is that some professors are the most gifted gold-brickers to be found anywhere. Another is that some are very inquisitive, looking into matters which really do not concern them. Some professors believe they know more about operating a university than the administration, and many try to do it. Professors have time to ponder all issues, relevant and irrelevant, that surround the university. They are a petition-signing, highly articulate group of critics. In short, they are a very difficult work force to operate with. But a university cannot function without them, and they give the university its unique flavor. The administrator can do some things to keep the static down. Here are some suggestions:

First, professors like to think that they run the place. They often do, both at the top and middle levels. One way of getting a noisy professor in harness is to give him some administrative responsibility. The rule of minimal competence applies, but often administrative responsibility can calm even very agitated individuals.

Second, most professors' attitudes and reactions are quite directly related to their next best job option. Professors with good alternatives are more self-confident than those with poor options, and this self-esteem shows up in job performance. It also shows up in attitudes toward administrators. If they give a man with good options a bad time, he will not be around long. But if the man with poor options has trouble he will complain about it in whatever ways he can. Potential inside options include union activities, petition signing, subtle or overt sabotage, and goldbricking. With no place to go, the professor may well spend his time scheming to rectify real or imaginary injustices.

Third, the larger the faculty, the more likely that it will be proletarianized. If the administration is tightly structured, the problem is compounded: faculty members may feel hopeless, unable to contact those in command, and unable to get anything done without violent upheaval.

The combination of a large proletarianized faculty with poor job options can create a particularly nasty situation. The worst of all possible academic worlds is a huge faculty in an undistinguished institution with few options open to them elsewhere: such a situation means that trouble is certain and that the institution is ripe for trade unionism. Conversely, a school with a small faculty with good options rarely has faculty problems. During the second half of the 1970s and beyond, most faculty members will have fewer and poorer options. As this situation develops, union territory is bound to expand.

Fourth and finally, Gresham's law applies to professors as well as money (the bad drives out the good). Moreover, the time span of a career is so long that a few bad apples can kill a department, school, or even a whole university for decades. One only has to look around to see situations where this has happened. Many administrators are slow to get rid of disruptive or incompetent persons. Tenure rules are good excuses, but it is possible, when necessary, to remove an inadequate faculty member. Every university has some Siberia to which hacks and incompetents can be dispatched. And the man who never receives a raise is eventually so far behind financially that he may have to leave. Few administrators make serious efforts to evaluate professors because information systems are so inadequate. Most such systems were built and are operated by professors. And virtually no one makes any effort to find out what is wrong with an incompetent, or any effort to help him become a productive citizen. Most incompetent faculty members were once creative people. What happened along the way? Is it possible that the university is to blame for their decline? No one knows or cares. Caution is necessary, because it is easy to misjudge a man, and the resulting morale problems can be serious. Often overlooked is the morale-building value of putting hacks out to pasture, leaving the way open for competent men to advance. Administrators bogged down with many problems often have defaulted on their obligations to the best (and worst) professionals. It is too easy to argue that the tenure system and the inability to evaluate a specialist make it difficult to reward men properly. But this is not true. Keen and fair evaluations are quite easily made by faculty all the time. Given that the heart of a university is its professionals, it is strange that administrators lack courage to make and act on personnel evaluations in the best interests of the organization. A major reason (which any manager or administrator knows all too well) is that it is painful to fire anyone. But if no one is ever fired, a faculty may become mediocre, full of artful goldbrickers, hacks, or worse. No university is so good that it does not have a few such people, and some have far too many. The ability to fire a truly incompetent—and not only an immoral—faculty member may be necessary in any successful administrator.

Other Manpower. Universities are major users of skilled and unskilled manpower. Most of this utilization just happens because universities rarely analyze their personnel needs for the next few years. One result is that much labor is poorly utilized. As long as the phones work, the air-conditioning systems function, and the letters get typed on time, few persons care about nonprofessional labor. Only in crisis situations, such as strikes, is attention focused on this group. This labor utilization is more amenable to systematic efficiency evaluation than are most university activities, and careful analysis can prove rewarding for financially hard-pressed administrations. In rare cases some administrator may have laid out job tasks and work measurement programs, and these can be used in evaluating nonprofessional labor.

Budgets for such labor are prepared by subordinates within schools, departments, or other functional areas. Because this item may not be large, it is not examined as closely as more significant items. An aggressive subordinate, anxious to make his professional's tasks easier, may constantly press for more than his share of work and get it. In ten years, deviations can grow. We know of a university where the ratios of secretaries to professors range from one-to-two to one-to-twenty, depending on the functional area.

Job analysis has been covered extensively in personnel literature. The administrator specifies the job to be done. Quite often this is a fairly precise type of measure—so many letters per day or so many acres of lawn mowed per week. Then reasonable standards are set and actual performance is measured against standards. If significant deviations occur, a closer look is needed to see what the problem is. This is simple to state but quite complicated in practice. It takes skilled professionals to develop rational work standards, and many booby traps—such as trade unions, worker suspicion of any standard setting, and measurement difficulties lie in the path. But even crude attempts can have considerable payoff, if the job is done by specialized professionals. Normally this is not a task for the top members of the administration.

Many employees feel that universities are attractive places to work. Maintenance technicians find good pay and steady employment; many skilled subprofessionals may be attracted by the intellectual excitement; secretaries may find that some professionals are interesting and not too demanding bosses; and most of the work is not tough. Administrators should often stress such comparative advantages in their efforts to recruit competent personnel for the institution.

Students. We will discuss students in greater depth in Chapter Twelve, but two comments should be made here. One relates to the use of students as cheap apprentice manpower. Having a teaching assistant handle undergraduate classes cuts costs sharply. Teaching assistants paid less than one fifth of faculty rates, and universities want more doctoral candidates for this reason. If the graduate students teach, then professors are free to do "better" things. One graduate school dean once suggested to us that he would write a paper called "The PhD Program as a Profit Center." He felt that he could prove conclusively that the more doctoral students a school has the lower the schools' costs are.

But this situation could change if jobs for doctoral students continue to be hard to find. If few attractive jobs are available when the degree is finally earned, enrollments could fall off. This is happening already in many fields, and more may be affected soon. One option is to find more foreign students, because they cannot object very much to the pay and working conditions, and they want and need the degrees. An Indian PhD student, earning perhaps $3,000 per year as a teaching assistant, will actually be making as much as he will earn when he goes back to India to become a professor. It is strange to watch the cynical exploitation of such students by faculty who are full of the milk of human kindness, love, and humanitarianism, but it happens on virtually every campus. However, undergraduates may finally rebel at being taught statistics by some one who cannot speak English very well, or at all. This has happened.

The second point is that if you do not have students, you are not in business. Declining enrollments are going to necessitate more and better university and college marketing—including marketing research—in the future. The colleges will have to offer an appealing product if they are to attract students. This can lead to open universities, lifelong learning, and similar experiments. We can expect much more serious work in this area in the 1970s, along with increased use of accepted marketing ideas by colleges.

Fixed Plant

Universities and colleges are big business. Billions of dollars have been poured into facilities, but not nearly as much attention has been paid to this expense as might have been. As with other aspects of university management, the somewhat antibusiness environment of the university has deterred administrators from taking advantage of existing knowledge about fixed investment. Moreover, the lack of clear-cut goals, unclear thinking about what is essential before the construction of new facilities, and difficulties in making rational choices in multiple-goal situations may make the university fixed-plant problem seem more unsolvable than it is.

Goal systems are critical here. Buildings reflect the values of their designers, builders, and operators, and a walk around any university campus suggests how radically these goals have changed in the past fifty years. We are stuck with our history, but anything built next year will still be in use in the year 2020, so we should consider what is relevant in planning new construction. Most campuses contain buildings with all sorts of hidden 1895 assumptions about the quality of students, capabilities of professors, and the desirability of beauty. Some general observations may be useful.

Building costs are going up much faster than other prices, so there are advantages in building quickly. Most cost increases are not in the shell (if you only want barn-like square feet, costs may actually be low), but in the innards—electronics and electricity, communications, heating and cooling, and plumbing. Each new building is much more complicated than the last. What was considered comfortable twenty years ago is now hopelessly outdated.

Any building will be hopelessly obsolete in twenty years, so keep things flexible! Observation of 1950 buildings will suggest how true this point is. Our forecast time is about five years, which is far too short for building planning. Of particular importance are factors that lock in activities. Thus, classroom sizes tend to make class sizes in 1990 readily predictable, unless the buildings can be changed. Bricks and mortar are very permanent. The tangle of new plumbing, ducting, and electrical fittings in basements of old buildings suggests that no matter how much stuff goes into a modern building, more will be in it within a decade, so space should be reserved for these things.

Goals will change, so buildings should be flexible.

American society is using more space than in the past, which suggests that the ratio of land to buildings is changing. Consider, for example, the needs created by our use of the auto, which apparently is here to stay in spite of the energy problem. Autos are a focus of emotions for most people, and this can mean trouble for administrators. Liberal professors can get more upset about parking problems than about the race question, and any university with pre-1960 buildings has many parking problems. Unless administrators are very lucky, or are in a position to force students and faculty to ride buses, auto problems will always get much more attention than they rationally deserve.

Many influential Americans still think that capital is more important than people. Often people are not even considered. This attitude relates to early property rights ideas: You can own a building, but you cannot own a person. Hence, investment in buildings is still often viewed as good and just, while investment in people (as in education) is their own business. This attitude is beginning to change, but one effect is that it is easier to finance buildings than to finance faculty salaries, research, or student aid.

Modern plant and facilities use up manpower at rapid rates. Every kind of high-skilled maintenance technician is needed, as are cleaners and washers. For complicated scientific equipment and computers, service may cost more than the equipment. The new library may be imposing, but it will also require far more trained librarians than the old. Because property is still often valued more than people, it is relatively easy to get money for a computer, an expensive piece of physics equipment, or a library. Once these funds are obtained, more high-skilled manpower is required. Budget-makers and fund allocators may be trapped into providing these. Administrators may also be trapped here too. It is easy to forget that operating costs rise at least as fast as building costs, and a new facility can be underutilized. Thinking ahead can pay big dividends.

It is often hard to figure out whether an item is a critical necessity or an expensive new toy. Computers are the classic case. Because users (including professors) do not pay for computers and expensive lab equipment, they will always want more; and they make good arguments for what they consider critical necessities. The administrator can obtain good outside counsel. Spending a few thousand dollars for advice about the usefulness of a proposed item can save millions in the end. But outside preaudits are rare.

Utilization rates of much university plant and equipment are very low, and any improvements in utilization can save money. This is an attractive notion that often has been carefully considered. If 50,000 square feet of classroom space is being used five hours a day, capacity could be tripled at very low cost by tripling classroom use. But most professors want to teach only from 9:00 A.M. to 3:00 P.M. on Tuesdays and Thursdays, and resistance to late, early, or Saturday classes is certain, intense, and successful. Equally difficult to implement are year-round operation and part-time programs. One possibility has not been tried is extra pay to compensate for the inconvenience of odd hours. Why not pay 5 percent more to the professor who will teach at 4:00 P.M. on Saturday afternoon? If this generates a rush to teach such classes, reduce the increment to 2 percent. Some minor economic incentives might facilitate signi-ficantly improved utilization of existing plant.

The plant and equipment question is complicated and full of implicit value judgments. Many administrators become preoccupied with physical empire-building and forget that buildings are only a means to an end. But how else in a university can you get something named after you, or see your name on the little brass plaque at the door? Campuses are full of the wrong buildings, built in the wrong places; buildings that are too expensive or too cheap; buildings that often operate at less than capacity, because someone forgot to calculate costs involved in operation and maintenance. And much land use has been a disaster for fifty or a hundred years because no one really considered the implications of building location. Experts give good advice, and they should be used. Nowhere in the university are mistakes perpetuated over so long a time. Smith's folly can become Smith's triumph (long after he is gone), if only we think about building implications.

Equipment and Supplies

Universities are big consumers of minor equipment (typewriters, calculators, desks) and supplies. The big multiversity spends millions of dollars every year for erasers and fuel and lawn seed. Responsibility for such purchases normally is delegated to subordinates. In public universities, the usual rules for public purchase apply. Bids are made, evaluated, and accepted. With luck and capable subordinates, purchasing supplies and equipment is rarely a problem. But this does not mean that it is not important. Precise efficiency criteria can be applied to the purchasing of supplies and equipment. It is thus very useful to take full advantage of extensive work that has been done in both public administration and business studies of efficient purchasing. The biggest problem is that purchasing is not seen as important. After exhaustive struggles with a dean about his big budget items, it is easy to resolve the problem by taking two minutes to cut his equipment and supplies request by 10 percent, leaving him the rest to use as he sees fit. One result of this type of allocative procedure is that the clever dean can have a good thing going with supplies and equipment, to the delight of his faculty and employees. While one office gets new electric typewriters every three years (and also gets the best secretaries), in another department someone is still pounding out letters on a 1934 Royal.

One thing that can be done, given that top officials rarely will bother with this problem, is to encourage those responsible to become as professional as they can. Various societies of professional purchasing agents exist—encourage participation. Some faculty members in public and business administration may have considerable expertise in this area—utilize them as consultants. Incentive structures can be set up for those purchasers who do a good job— figure out and utilize good ones. Anyone can cut 10 percent off purchases, if he is willing to try—although this does not mean that flat 10 percent cuts will work. Supplies and equipment purchases are only the means to an end. It is surprising how many cobwebs can accumulate if no one audits the expenditure pattern. It is useful to conduct a fairly thorough inquiry every five years or so. And such audits may save enough money to hire a few new professors or give some more scholarships.

Labor is the key university cost, not supplies and equipment. When economy waves are on, the usual pattern is to cut back on carbon paper and pencils. Supplies do not object, but people do. This sort of nonsense is cost-creating, not cost-saving. The secretary without the carbon paper types lots of letters twice; the professor without a typewriter writes a memo or exam in longhand; and the Xerox machine without paper stands idle, eating up fixed costs. Saving the cost of one skilled employee per year (at a minumum cost of $10,000 to $15,000 per year) can keep everyone in supplies for a long time.

Land

Americans love land speculation, and anyone who can influence land use in a major way will be observed carefully. Universities are major land users, and they influence land use for miles around the campus. So they are land speculators whether they like it or not.

The auto is here to stay, and administrators should take this into account in planning all future land use. It may be difficult to change what is, but certainly we can do better in the future than we have done in the past. Building locations and uses are relevant. So, too, are access roads, parking lots, parks, and all other land uses. Buildings are still constructed without any notion of what they will do to parking, walking, or traffic patterns. Even simple planning could yield better results than we now get.

Because universities influence land use over large areas, it is helpful to get others—such as real estate developers, city planners, and state and federal officials—into the land use planning process. Far too many beautiful university campuses are now surrounded by the worst kinds of junk because their administrators did not involve the surrounding community in land use planning. There are many irresponsible land speculators, but there are also many serious and capable officials and entrepreneurs who would cooperate with the university.

Land aquisition and short-term land use can be political and social dynamite, as Columbia University discovered. Expanding universities are always playing land markets, and often they hold land for years before using it. But the university as slumlord, or as owner of those dreary shack stores at the edge of campus, provides an inappropriate and unpleasant image. Land use, like parking, is a potentially explosive issue that can swamp any university administration. Maybe you are lucky, but this is not an area to test your luck.

Land speculation can be very profitable, particularly if university insiders know far enough in advance what is going to happen in a few years. No university ever has enough money, and so real estate speculation is tempting. Property tax exemptions may make it even more tempting. But speculation can be dynamite, politically and socially. It may also prove embarrassing to administrators, particularly if insiders use information for private purchases and gains.

As with buildings and equipment, it is very easy to forget that land is a means, not the end. One often gets the impression that some universities are more interested in land speculation than in education. Strongly held ideas about what surrounding land use should be contribute to this situation. There may be a temptation to try to influence, by fair means or foul, what the neighborhood should be.

Conclusion

Minor input mishandling can put an administration in deep trouble. Many small but controversial input questions do not receive much attention from top level administrators until the demonstrations start or embarrassing revelations appear in the press. How should such questions be handled? It gets back to goals. We must have a clear idea of what outputs are wanted and in what order, and then we can figure out what inputs are useful, remembering that the quality of almost any input can be improved, but that resources are not infinite. We must also keep in mind that an apparently trivial decision (such as purchase by a university of a run-down apartment near campus) can be disastrous.

Any discussion of inputs therefore must focus on goals and targets and on systematic evaluations of how to meet them. Subordinates handle many input questions, but the results they are supposed to achieve are often not clear. Administrators can improve performance if they suggest relevant targets, taking into consideration the potentially dangerous value judgments of observers and critics.

It is easy to confuse ends and means and become bogged down in process. Anyone who has worked with a property purchase, plans for a large building, or personnel standards for typists is aware of how quickly one can become totally absorbed in short-term problems. A basic aim of this chapter has been to present some guidelines and techniques for getting above process in handling input allocation and selection.

Chapter VI

Power

Eric Hoffer once commented that some people believe that power comes in cans, and all one has to do to get more is to somehow acquire more cans. Clark Kerr (1970) has pointed out that there are more claimants for power with regard to colleges and universities than ever before. Government spending takes power from boards of governors and institutional presidents, and students have been gaining in power, in Kerr's view. He also has stated that since there is no more power to be divided, a zero-sum game is involved.

The truth of the matter may often be quite different, as we shall see. There is frequently an expansible supply of cans, so the common view of power as a fixed pool is perhaps erroneous, at least in many instances. If you get more, I get less, may not necessarily be a correct operating assumption. It is quite possible that people in the system can pick up more power—without others ᴸᴼ⸗ᴸ_ any in the net sense—if they know where to look. Gross and Grambsch (1974; chapter 4) present some quantitative evidence in their study of university power and goals in support of this contention.

The expansibility of power results largely from the ambiguous nature of power in academic institutions, which relates, in turn, to their ambiguous goal systems and to the fact that the systems tend to be imperfectly understood or utilized. Thus, if someone comes along who understands and knows how to maneuver in the system, he becomes to the power centers in the system, valuable and hence more powerful.

It tends to be true that, as more people exert power and influence in the system, decision-making often becomes slower and more complex, conflicts are likely to increase, and more compromises are likely to result. However, even though more people become involved in the decision-making process, the compromises and power trade-offs involving various kinds of decisions can result in a net increase in power and influence extended to all of the people involved. Even more important, there are frequently many power vacuums in the system. Therefore, many people can fill such power vacuums and initiate actions and decisions in ways that lead to more power and influence for them, but not necessarily less for anyone else.

This chapter focuses on both power and influence with regard to academic institutions. We treat power and influence together here as a single process, because both are central to decision-making, policy formulation, and the institution's goal system and priorities. We explore who tends to have and exert power and influence, why, and in what areas, and also who can get power and influence, why, and how.

Although we treat power and influence as part of the same process, there are some technical differences between these two concepts. An individual can exert power if he has or is perceived to have the means or ability to employ coercion, penalties, rewards, or incentives to get something done. If he is a manager or administrator, much of this power stems from the formal authority that goes with his position, and this involves formal or official power.

However, he may also have personal influence that exceeds his formal powers, and this influence stems from personal qualities (including, for example, expertise, knowledge, and some personality traits) and from various situational factors. Such influence is manifested in the ability to produce an effect or get something done without the exertion of coercion or the direct exercise of command. It involves getting the voluntary cooperation of others, though it may also mean convincing or swaying them in a desired direction. Effective leadership is often based more on influence than on formal authority or power, especially in academic institutions.

People who are not managers or administrators can also exert power, as well as influence, because power is not just a hierarchical concept related to formal authority or one's official position. For example, a professor can exert considerable informal power with regard to some decisions—hiring or promoting other faculty members, granting tenure, developing curricula and courses—because he or she has or is perceived to have the ability either to use or to determine that others use coercion, penalties, rewards, and the like. And the faculty as a group may even have the power to get an administrator removed from office. It is common for nonmanagers however to exert considerably more influence than power, and often the dividing line between power and influence is unclear. Here, too, influence stems from personal qualities and situational factors. Although formal authority and official power are needed to ratify and implement decisions, those behind decisions may have considerable influence and possibly also much informal power but not any formal authority or power.

Because leadership stems from personal and situational factors, and not only or necessarily from formal authority, informal leaders of various types emerge in all kinds of organizations. This is especially true within the faculties of academic institutions where expertise of many types is pervasive. And interested faculty members frequently find that there are many power vacuums that can be filled and various kinds of actions and decisions that they can initiate.

Universities and colleges are becoming both more important

and more costly. As a result more persons seem interested in obtaining power and influence within or over such institutions, especially as conflicts increase, often because of budgetary constraints and scarcer resources (Perkins, 1973; *Governance of Higher Education,* 1973; Hodgkinson and Meeth, 1971). One key to this struggle for power is the struggle between various value systems as to what is important—and this relates directly to institutional goals and priorities. If an individual controls the university, or even just the budget, he can more easily obtain his own goal preferences.

Rather quickly any discussion of university power becomes an ethical debate about what should be done and why. And as noted in Chapter Four although power has been shifting significantly in many academic institutions—often externally—the goal preferences of the different constituencies do not seem to be shifting nearly as much. This is the basic reason for so many of the conflicts.

In the balance of this chapter, we discuss some important studies involving power and academic institutions and then we present our conception and analysis of institutional power. We attempt to analyze and taxonomize power comprehensively, in managerial rather than legalistic terms. In the process, a geography of power is created, a road map if you will, of the places and situations where power actually is (or at least seems to be) in a modern academic institution.

Not too surprisingly, perhaps, power and method are closely related, because management implies power of some sort. Our analysis is admittedly incomplete, rather crude, and perhaps presumptuous in its claim—but we know of no better or more comprehensive analysis. It is also fiendishly complicated, because power is complicated, as is the real world of academic institutions.

You can read a state law and see where the power technically lies within a state university. Similarly, you can read the charter, statutes and bylaws of a private college. Typically, this legalistic answer is grossly inadequate, because the real questions do not deal with who is legally responsible, but rather with how a complex organization really functions, what kind of goal system it really has and pursues, and how well it achieves its goals.

If any large state university acted in strict observance of the statutes, it is quite possible that there would be little or no meaningful output at all. Trustees and other governing bodies recognize this, and so the actual distribution of power is quite different than the statutes would infer. The same is frequently true of the formal organizational structure as depicted by boxes and straight lines on organizational charts and in official policy manuals. However, many groups and individuals misunderstand where power is, and a basic purpose of this chapter is to clarify some of the key power issues in academic institutions.

There is a large residue of power, influence, and management that can never be reduced to neat, tight analysis. Charismatic leaders—both formal and informal—often achieve power in peculiar ways, never foreseen by others, and some have power accidentally thrust upon them. We can only recognize this and proceed. It is still possible to analyze somewhat systematically where power is and why it accumulates where it does. Later in the chapter consideration is also given to what management—or other interested parties— might, can, and should do with regard to institutional power.

Gross and Grambsch Studies

In their 1964 survey, published in 1968, Gross and Grambsch found that administrators typically made the big decisions, although faculty power was by no means negligible. At almost all the sixty-eight universities in their sample, the president was perceived as having the most power. And the trustees or regents were perceived as having only slightly less power than the chief executives. The faculty ranked seventh and students fourteenth.

Table 6 presents the 1964 rank-order findings on the perceived power structure of the sixty-eight institutions. The mean scores suggest that power is considerably more diffuse in state universities than in private institutions. Quite a few constituencies, especially external groups, have significantly more power in the public sector. Moreover, the total of the mean scores in the public sector is substantially higher than that in the private sector, suggesting an expansible supply of power, and that power is not a zero-sum game.

In their 1971 survey, published in 1974, Gross and Grambsch

Table 6.

PERCEIVED POWER STRUCTURE FOR SIXTY-EIGHT UNIVERSITIES

Power Holder	Rank	Total Sample Mean Scores	Rank	State Universities Mean Scores	Rank	Private Universities Mean Scores
President	1	(4.65)	1	(4.62)	1	(4.70)
Trustees	2	(4.37)	2	(4.41)	2	(4.24)
Vice-Presidents	3	(4.12)	3	(4.07)	3	(4.10)
Professional School Deans	4	(3.62)	4	(3.53)	4	(3.64)
Graduate Deans	5	(3.59)	5	(3.53)	6	(3.54)
Liberal Arts Deans	6	(3.56)	7	(3.43)	5	(3.57)
Faculty	7	(3.31)	8	(3.27)	7	(3.29)
Department Chairmen	8	(3.19)	9	(3.13)	8	(3.16)
Legislators	9	(2.94)	6	(3.45)	15	(1.63)
Federal Government	10	(2.79)	11	(2.79)	11	(2.53)
State Government	11	(2.72)	10	(2.91)	13	(1.86)
Large Private Donors	12	(2.69)	13	(2.49)	9	(2.84)
Alumni	13	(2.61)	12	(2.57)	10	(2.53)
Students	14	(2.37)	14	(2.34)	12	(2.25)
Citizens of the State	15	(2.08)	15	(2.28)	16	(1.63)
Parents of Students	16	(1.91)	16	(1.90)	14	(1.70)

Source: Gross and Grambsch, 1968, pp. 76 and 79.

found little significant change in rank orders compared with 1964. Students increased from fourteenth to twelfth place. Graduate school deans and legislators moved up one place, while liberal arts deans, department chairmen, private donors, and alumni dropped one. The

other groups remained the same. The higher level administrators
and regents continued to dominate the power structure.

Both Gross and Grambsch surveys revealed little difference
in rank orders by type of university, except for the type of control
—state versus private—involved. Legislators and the state government ranked higher in public universities, and private donors ranked
higher for private schools. In the 1971 survey compared with 1964
students rose to tenth place from twelfth in private universities, and
to twelfth from fourteenth for state universities. In the private sector,
legislators, the federal government, and the faculty moved up one
place, while deans of the graduate school, alumni, and parents
dropped one place. For the state universities, legislators moved up
two ranks; liberal arts deans and the state government moved up
one place; the graduate school deans dropped two ranks; and professional school deans, department chairmen, private donors, and
alumni all dropped one rank.

In the 1971 survey there was a high overall correlation in the
perceptions of higher and lower level administrators and the faculty
with regard to the overall power structure. The most significant
differences involved a higher rank for faculty and students by higher
level administrators than by lower level administrators and the
faculty, and a higher rank for legislators by faculty, especially in
public universities, than by both groups of administrators.

In their 1971 study, Gross and Grambsch (1974), pp. 129–
135) also asked the respondents to indicate the degree to which the
power and influence of each of the groups had changed since 1964.
The derived scores revealed a ranking quite different from the above
power-position rank orders. The responses to changes in power indicated a general tendency to believe that the most groups either had
held on to their ability to influence and control others or had increased it. This finding suggests that a more important role in
decision-making has become available to a wider spectrum of participants who are now able to influence each other to a greater
extent than previously. It supports the contention that power is not
a zero-sum game and that it is quite possible for many people in the
system to pick up more power without others losing any in the net
sense. Those whose power was believed to have increased most
significantly were regents, legislators, state and federal government,

as well as faculty and students. Those whose power was believed to have declined were department chairmen, alumni, and parents. The power of administrators (other than chairmen), citizens, and private donors was believed to have remained about the same, with most of these groups showing slight increases.

Gross and Grambsch conclude from their 1971 study that the power structure of universities had not changed if structure means the pattern of relative distribution of power. Presidents continued to sit at the top, with trustees and other key administrators not far behind, and students fairly far down. But Gross and Grambsch felt the modest gain made by students to be impressive, especially because no comparable gain was shown by the administrators. Similarly for other perceived power gainers, even a tiny incremental increase was felt to be a major achievement.

In our view, as noted in Chapter Three, it is likely that power conflicts between faculty members and administrators have increased—and will continue to do so—at many universities and colleges since 1971, given the serious financial problems confronting them. Similarly, power conflicts between external constituencies and insiders (especially the faculty and probably some key administrators) has probably become—and will continue to become—intensified. Moreover, the power structure at many institutions has probably been shifting substantially to outsiders and perhaps also to a lesser extent to potential students as compared with the faculty and administrators.

Baldridge's Political Model

J. Victor Baldridge's political model (1971a and 1971b) was outlined in Chapter One. At this point we shall focus and elaborate on some of the power aspects of this model.

Baldridge's model has been developed in conjunction with empirical studies dealing with academic institutions and various constituencies during periods of turmoil and dramatic change. He has found that especially under such conditions formal authority has been seriously limited by the political pressure and bargaining. Decisions often involve negotiated compromises among competing groups. Therefore, leadership and personal influence tend to be even more important than formal authority and official power. However, this is not an argument for not giving the institution's chief executive or central administration clearer or even greater formal authority. And if the central administration has and maintains budgetary control, its formal power tends to be greater than that of any other on-campus group. It can use the budget to set both time and resource constraints in connection with institutional goals and priorities.

From Baldridge's study of New York University during the 1960s, it is clear that greater central authority and power had evolved as the chief executive and his key deputies took the lead to restructure the university to meet the threat of increasing competition from state universities. They also took the lead in having interested participants and constituencies present their views and in making a series of changes to cope with critical problems that were threatening the viability of the institution. These steps were taken under acute internal and external pressure.

Intense conflicts emerged when old philosophies were being destroyed. However, under the leadership and direction of the central administration, compromises were forged, new policies were implemented, priorities were reordered, and severe adjustments were made in the strongly opposing schools. A sizable number of academic and nonacademic personnel were retrenched in the process. The central administration was supported most strongly in its quest for desired changes by the trustees, the graduate faculties, and the graduate business School. The strongest opponents included the education and undergraduate commerce faculties, the heights campus, alumni favoring a school-of-opportunity concept, and various faculty members fearing—or at least claiming to fear—dilution of quality from undergraduate consolidation.

Some of the major changes in the university's goal systems and priorities have included the following:

1. Upgrading of undergraduate admission policies across the board in an effort to move the university out of direct competition with the public institutions for the bulk of the medium-ability students. This meant discarding the school-of-opportunity philosophy in favor of a more selective approach. This has had drastic effects on several schools and faculties.

2. Most of the key decision-makers thought that the multi-school system of undergraduate education would have to be abandoned so that duplication of efforts could be avoided. At that time there were five major undergraduate units. A plan for partial consolidation gradually evolved amid strong opposition for many quarters. A new coordinated liberal studies program was the eventual outcome.

3. A new urban university theme was adopted. This new image or goal was carefully articulated around service to the New York community, research in urban problems, and preparation of urban specialists in science, education, public administration, and social science. The university was soon focusing more than ever on the problems of urban society and concentrating its limited resources in one area rather than trying to be all things to all men.

4. The upgrading of quality involved an attempt to get more full-time students instead of the large part-time group that NYU had long attracted. Moreover, this implied a massive effort by the university to provide student residences, something never done on a substantial scale.

5. An increasing proportion of the university's energies have been concentrated on graduate and advanced professional training.

6. Faculty recruitment has placed much greater emphasis on obtaining more full-time people with advanced degrees.

Whether NYU can achieve its goals and priorities effectively and efficiently in the long run is still open to question, because finances continue to be a critical issue. However, the possibilities for revitalization have been recognized and acted upon to a considerable extent.

The conflicts and power struggles at NYU were not due primarily to misunderstanding or communication breakdowns. They were chiefly strategic in nature and related largely to the allocation of scarce resources and very real external competitive forces. This is also true at numerous other academic institutions, although blind proponents favoring some kind of utopian collegial, democratic, or permissive model of academic governance fail to recognize this.

Power and influence are more eagerly and actively sought after when the resource crunch comes. And control of the budget becomes even more critical when this happens. As long as the chief executive maintains control of the budget, he may continue to be a truly powerful individual. However, if he is to survive in his job, and also carry it out effectively, he—or he and his top management team—must also be effective as leader, mediator, negotiator, statesman, entrepreneur, and overall professional manager. In this regard, his personal influence and abilities become significantly more important than his formal authority and power, but the latter are still clearly important as well.

It is interesting to note that NYU faculty senate surveys showed that the degree of faculty confidence in the central administration was significantly higher in 1968 than in 1959 (Baldridge, 1971a, p. 48).

The 1968 NYU survey also examined the degree of faculty participation in the governance of departments and colleges and at the all-university level. Baldridge found that many people were active in departmental decision-making, but only a small minority participated in college or all-university decision councils. This lends considerable support to his contention that small groups of political elites—especially key administrators—dominate major decisions, but different elite groups control different decisions. And the trend seems to be toward more democratic academic governance. All of this proably tends to be the case—though in varying degrees—at many if not most universities and colleges.

The 1968 NYU survey also dealt with who has influence and how much in ten major decision areas (Baldridge, 1971a, Figure 9–3). The findings clearly indicate that the central administration has been by far the most powerful group at NYU. The same is no doubt true—though again in varying degrees—at many, if not most, academic institutions. However, the trustees have probably become more powerful than the central administration at quite a few institutions, especially those that are in serious trouble and have ineffective or weak chief executives.

It is significant to note that even though individual professors have had very little power at NYU, departmental and college faculties have had only modest power overall, while the central administration has had a great deal of power, followed by the deans and the trustees. The degree of faculty confidence in the central administration was considerably higher in 1968 as compared to 1959.

Baldridge's studies suggest that power and influence do not necessarily come in fixed cans, and that by filling power vacuums and initiating actions and decisions, one can often gain power and influence without others losing any of theirs, in the net sense at least. For even in conflict and power struggle situations there are usually many common interests and leeway for negotiation and compromise among the participants. Moreover, many of the interfaces or interactions among the interested participants often involve shared objectives and cooperation even as they battle over conflicts and power. This, too, can often provide a basis for compromise, new initiatives, and the creation and filling of power vacuums.

Cohen and March Study

As noted earlier, this study (1974) is based in large part on interviews with forty-one university presidents, as well as interviews involving thirty-six chief academic officers, thirty-six chief financial officers, twenty-eight other officials close to the president, and student leaders and editors at thirty-one campuses. Cohen and March found that power—including presidential power—tends to be quite ambiguous at academic institutions. This, in turn, relates largely to the ambiguous nature of institutional goal systems.

Our position is that this may well be an accurate description of reality at many, and perhaps most, universities and colleges. However, there seems to be no inherent reason why the formal authority, official power, and roles of the president, other administrators, and, in fact, all major constituencies cannot be adequately articulated and clearly defined. Areas like personal influence and informal leadership can never be absolutely defined, but greater role clarification in conjunction with a contingency approach should reduce the ambiguity of power. Moreover, the personal satisfaction and morale of most of the participants are likely to be greater, as long as their most potent personal needs are not sacrificed too seriously in the process. And if such clarification leads to greater institutional viability and success, the satisfaction of participant needs and achievement of personal goals are likely to be enhanced.

Although Cohen and March point out that the president usually has only modest control of events, they do acknowledge that he does typically play a dominant role in decision-making, especially with regard to the budget, academic policy matters, tenure appointments, planning, and academic development.

Cohen and March have found that power in universities and colleges is diffused, that participation is fluid, and that the amount of effort and time that participants devote to the organization varies. Individual participants vary from one time to another, and this is a basic feature of *organized anarchy*. However, an effective president can still exert the most power over the major decisions, especially through control of the budget. And participation can become more productive and effective through clearer role and process definition and articulation.

Cohen and March found that the president is often resented because he is perceived to be more powerful than he should be. He believes he should have more power, others believe he has too much. If he underestimates his power, inaction is the result; and if he overestimates it, conflict and antagonism often result. Here, too, clear definition of the president's formal authority and official power could do much to minimize confusion and problems. And much more can be done in this regard, especially if the institution's goal system becomes more operational.

Cohen and March recognize that the president typically has more potential for moving the organization than have other participants, but this potential is often less than others believe he has. His power to accomplish things depends on what he wants to accomplish and ultimately on whether the goal system is highly ambiguous or adequately operational. Cohen and March feel that the ambiguous nature of power leads to ambiguity in responsibility and blame. This, they claim, serves the president well, because he can take credit when things go well but avoid blame when they do not. We feel that there are many exceptions. Many presidents resign or are fired when the institution runs into serious trouble, because they are ultimately held responsible by the trustees, the faculty, the government officials, major private donors, citizens, and other influential groups.

Cohen and March point out that most people—especially faculty—most of the time tend to be less concerned with the content of decisions than with eliciting an acknowledgment of their importance. In other words, who has the right to decide, claim power, and participate is more important than the choice or outcome. As a result, much of the argument is really over the symbols of governance and ritualized legitimacy. Status and self-esteem needs can often be fulfilled, and conflicts reduced, by providing various kinds of parallel and overlapping committees and channels for participation in decision-making. In turn, this can enable the key administrators greater leeway in making those decisions that they feel are the most important.

Cohen and March conclude that "the president is like a driver of a skidding automobile. The marginal adjustments he makes, his skill and his luck may possibly make some difference to the survival prospects of his riders. As a result, his responsibilities are heavy. But whether he is convicted of manslaughter or receives a hero medal is largely outside his control."

This is no doubt a pretty accurate description of the president and the presidency at quite a few universities and colleges. However, this does not mean that the chief executive has to be or should be this much of a dependent variable, captive, or passive force, in terms of the system or even of the external environment. Cohen and March's descriptive-explanatory study provides a much better understanding of why so many academic institutions, as well as their key administrators, are in so much trouble. It also can be of considerable value to academic administrators who must clearly understand both their institution and their own position in it, if they are to exert greater power effectively and become more effective managers and leaders.

Cohen and March present eight valuable tactical rules (Cohen and March, 1974, pp. 205–217) for those who seek to influence decisions and exert power, and some of these rules are discussed later in this chapter. But apart from this, they do not have many suggestions for correcting academic mismanagement. We disagree with their contention that little can really be done empirically, and in terms of observed and verifiable behavior, with regard to studying power in connection with academic institutions. This is clearly a particularly messy type of research, but a great deal more can and should be done than has been to date. Although we have not done very much systematized research in this particular sphere, we shall shortly present a conceptual and analytical framework and related methodologies that may prove quite useful.

Demerath, Stephens, and Taylor Study

This study (1967) was conducted at forty-five major American universities and colleges (twenty-three public and twenty-two private) during the 1950s and early 1960s. Although not very recent, the study does contain some findings and implications that are relevant now and for the foreseeable future for many academic institutions. Our major interest is in the data about the University of North Carolina under two different presidents. Demerath, Stephens, and Taylor (1967, Chaps. 6–8) conducted empirical research and personal interviews on that campus and made use of two faculty questionnaire surveys. The two key reference points are 1956, the year in which Chancellor Robert House resigned from office after serving as chancellor since 1945, and 1960, about four years after William Aycock became chancellor. When Aycock took over so did three new deans—of the faculty, the graduate school, and the college of arts and science—as well as a new chief business officer. Faculty surveys—sponsored by the faculty council—of all full-time (voting) faculty members were conducted in 1956 and 1960. The response rate in both cases was 63 percent, and all of the returned questionnaires were usable.

The administrative style of the university under Chancellor House was traditional and patrimonial, and also had many bureaucratic qualities because the university is state supported and subject to much legal and rational or formal authority. There was relatively little in the way of faculty participation or representation. This was a basic cause of faculty dissatisfaction, as were low salaries, unfilled vacancies, poor communications, and professionalism in athletics. The faculty protest movement began in 1947 and became increasingly strong in the 1950s. By the mid-fifties the institution was clearly ready for and in need of a change.

In 1957 Chancellor Aycock took over, and other major administrative changes (some of them noted above) were made. Orderliness in the administrative system was emphasized; rules and procedures were clarified and systematically followed. Actions were organized by structural definitions and more effective communication, not by punishment. Procedures by which budgets were made, academic policy issues were explored, and operation problems were analyzed and decided were now spelled out for all to know. Lines of authority and responsibility, advice and consent, decision and action were simplified, clarified, and reinforced by the very behavior of the chancellor and his top staff in daily relations with the faculty and other personnel. This was not the traditional Weberian kind of routinized bureaucracy, however. It did not involve a proliferation of offices and bureaus, but it did lead to greater participation, collegiality, and democratic governance.

In his social interaction, Chancellor Aycock was an able competitor who wanted to succeed in human relations and generally did. He had extensive faculty contacts and carefully consulted the faculty except in rare instances. He used clearly spelled out executive authority to define and accomplish tasks, in conjunction with a collegial approach and collegial authority—chiefly at the departmental level and with regard to academic policy matters—in reaching decisions. He worked from a collegial base that lent support to his innovations, chiefly in managerial methods and only indirectly in educational affairs. (His innovations were improved organization and a new administrative style, but not new educational programs.)

Faculty satisfaction and identification with the university increased significantly with the evolution of the above changes. However, salary increases, bigger budgets, new faculty additions including quite a few good appointments, and the strengthening of the departments were also major factors.

This study has a number of general implications with regard to power and influence. It demonstrates that power in academic institutions need not be nearly as ambiguous as is commonly assumed. It is true that there is a higher degree of democratic governance at many universities and colleges today than there has been at North Carolina, but this does not mean that other universities cannot also do much more to define and clarify formal authority, power, and participatory roles and relationships. The study indicates that it is possible to combine hierarchical authority with adequate faculty participation and collegial governance processes. This involves a contingency approach rather than a single model of governance to be used under all conditions.

It is also true that little attention was given to educational innovation at North Carolina, and that if there had been significantly more of this, power and influence might have become more ambiguous. However, a dual system of formal authority and decision-making and participative management within budgetary constraints can still be utilized. In fact, educational innovation—and especially its implementation—is likely to be more effective when formal authority and participatory roles and channels are reasonably clear and adequately defined.

A key reason why there was not more educational innovation at North Carolina seems to have been that the top management was not very interested in it. This suggests that top management must often take the lead in bringing about substantial educational innovation. Effective leadership, personal influence, and participative management all tend to be critical in this regard; however, formal authority and budgetary control are also important.

The faculty at North Carolina felt that its influence was considerably more adequate under Aycock's chancellorship, even though formal authority relationships were emphasized—and more clearly defined—than under the previous chancellor. Excess ambiguity in the organization structure frequently leads to member frustration and dissatisfaction.

The new chancellor got higher salaries for the faculty, filled vacancies, got bigger university budgets, and good faculty and administrative appointments were made. No doubt these factors had a great deal to do with the improvement of morale and satisfaction on the campus. It is quite possible that virtually any kind of administrative or managerial style and power-influence mix would have led to greater faculty morale and satisfaction, at least for a while, because some of the most important personal needs and goals of the faculty members were fulfilled to a higher degree.

Higher salaries, more resources, more hiring, more opportunities for advancement, less concern about losing one's job—these are things that most faculty members attach very high priority too, whether they say so or not. And whether the chief executive is an autocrat, a benevolent dictator, permissive, paternalistic, or democratic may not really matter very much at many academic institutions, especially in the relatively short run, compared to whether he can deliver these things. The same is likely to be true with regard to the actual power-influence mix. The faculty at many universities and colleges facing serious financial problems may well be willing to accept various alternative kinds of university governance or power models, as long as this results in job security, adequate pay, and sufficient (in their view) perquisites and personal freedom to do their own thing.

However, in the longer run, effective professional management and leadership are crucial to institutional viability and success. The faculty—as well as other major constituencies—will always have some gripes and express some kind of dissatisfaction with the institution and its management, as indicated in the Demerath, Stephens and Taylor study. But if enough of their own high priority personal goals are fulfilled to a sufficient degree (in their view) the faculty related problems and conflicts are not likely to become serious.

A fundamental task of effective management and leadership, including the use of managerial authority, power, and influence, involves facilitating the attainment of the potent personal needs and related goals of a sufficient number of the institution's interested participants. In turn, this involves balancing the institution's inducements paid out (money, job satisfaction, status, esteem, trust, confidence, or whatever) with the contributions it receives from the participants. Both power and influence must be used wisely if this is to be done relatively effectively and efficiently.

In many cases it may be feasible for academic managers to use their power, influence, and budgetary control to achieve trade-offs with the faculty by assuring more job security or less faculty retrenchment, adequate salaries, and the like, in return for faculty cooperation in restructuring various institutional goals and priorities and in bringing about program changes and educational innovations. By doing this, management is also likely to enhance its ability to obtain more external resource support and to attract more students to the institution.

Sources of Power

Before presenting our methodology, analytical framework, and analyses of power, a short discussion about common sources of power and influence in organizations—especially with regard to

organizational decision making—is in order. This discussion is based
not only on our own research, observations, and experiences, but also
on many other studies. Some of the most important of these are
Filley and House (1969, pp. 60–66); Berelson and Steiner (1964,
Chaps. 8 and 9); Gibson, Ivancevich, and Donnelly (1973, pp.
287–293); French and Raven (1960, pp. 607–623); Pichler
(1974, pp. 400–434); Petit (1974, pp. 434–438); and Laing
(1974, pp. 439–444). Most of these works have comprehensive
bibliographies.

Some of the sources of power listed below are essentially
organizational in nature, some relate to group characteristics, and
some are essentially personal or individualistic. Many of them are
interrelated in various ways, and many depend on situational factors.
Items 12 through 16 are based largely on Cohen and March's study
(1974, pp. 205–216).

1. Formal authority to decide and act. This involves authority to make various kinds of decisions.

2. Authority to enforce various policies, procedures, rules,
methods, and so on.

3. Responsibility and function. For example, "he is responsible for that activity, or he makes that kind of decision," even if
formal authority is not spelled out in this regard. This often involves
custom, habit, or being left alone to decide, and it can relate to
groups or constituencies as well as to individuals.

4. Expertise, skill, and knowledge relating to specific kinds of
decisions.

5. Information. When an individual is thought to be a
significant information source with regard to certain kinds of decisions, this perception can be a source of power and certainly of influence.

6. When an individual is perceived to be in a position (either
formal or informal) to facilitate or hinder the satisfaction of the
personal needs and related goals of others in the system.

7. Manipulative ability and political effectiveness in getting
things done.

8. Referent power or influence by association. When an
individual is perceived to have a close association with people more
powerful than himself, this perception can be a source of power. The

same may be true of associations with high-status people. The president's secretary is often a good example.

9. When an individual is judged by others to be fair, open-minded, and trustworthy, especially in negotiating compromises and resolving conflicts.

10. Permanency of the participants in conjunction with the size of the groups or constituency. A sizable group of tenured faculty members are likely to exert more power generally than a larger number—and especially than a smaller number—of nontenured faculty.

11. Default and avoidance by others in conjunction with personal initiative. This relates to creating and filling power vacuums while others fail to do so or to act.

12. Willingness to spend time. When someone in an academic institution is willing to devote considerable time in meetings, on committees, developing contacts, and the like, with the aim of influencing various decisions, he is likely to have an effect on the outcomes. He provides scarce energy resources, he may become a major information source if he does his homework, and he is more likely to be present when something important is considered and done.

13. Persistence. This can also relate to time. If an individual persists, he is likely to influence decision outcomes and implementation of those decisions.

14. Exchange status in the short run for substance in the longer run. Most issues in academic institutions tend to have pretty low salience for most participants. Self-esteem and social recognition are often more important to them than the content of the decision.

15. Where possible, overload the system. If an individual presents many projects for organizational action, this makes large claims on human resources and energies for the analyses of problems, discussion of issues, negotiations, meetings, and so on. It is likely that at least some of the desired projects will get through. Persistence and time are also critical in getting higher-priority projects acted on and implemented. It may also be possible to act on various projects by default.

16. Provide "Garbage Can." Providing many projects and issues—which take up much time and energy in philosophical and

unoperational discussions—can often draw much of the "garbage" away from interfering with really high priority projects and concrete day-to-day decisions. It may be wise not to place the critical items or high priority decisions near the top of the agenda, since they could very well attract too much garbage. If they are placed lower on the agenda, many participants may be worn out by the time the critic items are reached, and it may be easier to get them through.

17. Personality factors (charisma) or personal qualities.

18. Institutional dependency or the relative importance of a given part of the overall system—how much the institution generally is or perceives itself to be dependent on a given group, unit, constituency, or individual. It relates to the unit's relative importance. This may vary, even quite dramatically, over time.

19. Get involved in critical interfaces of the system. An interface is the point at which interrelated parts within and external to the organization intersect and act upon or communicate with each other. The more relevant and significant interfaces are those where power is a real issue, and those that commonly involve problems, if not outright conflicts. They also require managerial attention and involve the more important kinds of organizational decisions that are made. If one has a good understanding of the overall system, he is likely to be in a better position to get involved in those interfaces from which greater power and influence can be derived.

In general, involvement in more of the critical interfaces can be a very important source of power, since it relates to quite a few of the other power and influence sources noted above. For example, one can become an important information center in this way, and also develop knowledge about the system, as well as expertise and skill relating to the acquisition of power. It can lead to increased power through association, as well as greater manipulative ability and political effectiveness (if one does not mind the somewhat Machiavellian connotations that might be implied). If an individual engages in more critical interfaces, he is likely to be in a much better position to be present and give inputs when important decisions are made, to create and fill power vacuums, and to generally take more initiative with regard to decision-making. Time, persistence, exchanging status for substance, overloading the system, and providing "garbage cans" also all relate to gaining more power through interface activities. And increased visibility in the system may by itself be a source of significant influence, if not outright power.

Road Map of Power

We have developed a rough framework of analysis for power and the related broader issues of academic management. Inputs enter the system, are utilized or transformed, and emerge as outputs. Various environmental constraints control key interactions and developments within the system. If this framework is correctly built, then it should be possible to use it to analyze important and interesting problems. The problems focused on here are those of power within the system.

The weights assigned to each of the items in the four classifications presented in Chapter Three are placed across the top of Table 3 for each of these items. Table 3 deals with external interface relationships—that is, the critical interfaces each subsystem has with inputs, outputs, and environmental constraints, but not with the other subsystems. Although it is usually not possible to assign a meaningful weight to any one specific interface, it does seem possible to assess in the importance of interface patterns involving a given subsystem item and other parts of the system over time. To do this, we use the weights assigned earlier to each of these external items. If a given subsystem interfaces with many parts of the overall system, it is more likely to derive greater power and influence for itself than if it interfaces with fewer parts. More important, it is likely to gain even more power and influence if it interfaces with the more important other parts of the system. The assigned weights are a reflection of the relative importance of each part.

Whenever a critical interface is indicated (by an X) in Table 3 for a given subsystem, the weights of the other items involved are added, and shown at the end of the table as a total external interface score. This score reflects the relative importance of each of the subsystem categories in relation to their external interfaces—that is, inputs, outputs or goals, and environmental constraints.

We noted earlier that interfaces with other parts of the system—including outside interest groups and participants—can be a very important source of power, because interfaces also frequently relate to many other potential sources of power and influence. These include information, knowledge, referent power or power by association, the need satisfaction of others, opportunities for creating and filling power vacuums and taking initiative, and providing significant decision inputs. Those groups and individuals who interface and deal with the more powerful and important persons, groups, and parts of the system will typically be the ones who play significant roles in making the interesting and important organizational decisions.

Table 4 in Chapter Three lists the internal subsystems on both the vertical and horizontal scales. On the horizontal scale, the external interface scores for each item from Table 3 are included, but they have been reduced by a factor of 10 and rounded to whole numbers. The external interface scores are used in Table 4 as a reflection of the amount of power and influence gained by a given subsystem in its interfaces with other subsystems. If the subsystem interfaces with other subsystems that have high external interface scores, it is likely to derive more power and influence than if it interfaces with only those having low scores. A higher subsystem external interface score suggests that the subsystem has more power and influence—apart from its own inherent or relatively independent power—than one having a low score.

The subsystem interface scores for each subsystem in Table 4 have been added up, and the totals for each one shown in Column A. Column B lists the assigned weights for each subsystem item from the system taxonomy. These weights indicate the relative amount of importance and power each has, apart from the power and influence it gains through critical interfaces. The total subsystem interface score for each item is multiplied by its assigned weight, and the result is the total power score for each item shown in Column C. Multiplication rather than addition of Columns A and B is in order, interactive or multiplicative effects are involved.

The total power score reflects the overall importance of each subsystem category in terms of power and influence in the university, relative to the other subsystem categories. In other words, the total power and influence exerted by each item in the system is a function of both its own internal power and importance and the power and influence it derives from its interfaces with other parts of the system.

Table 7 gives the rank ordering of the various subsystems in terms of their total power scores. The same methodology can be used in deriving power scores for the external groups considered in the classification of environmental constraints in Chapter Three. We shall deal with these groups further in the chapter on environmental constraints.

The power rankings contained in Table 7 are basically quite consistent with the rankings emerging from the Gross and Grambsch and Baldridge studies discussed earlier, to the extent that the same categories have been used. However, their rankings have been based on surveys rather than on an analytical framework and related methodologies that provide a means for much more in the way of description, explanation, prediction and prescription. Of course, vastly more systematized empirical research needs to be done with our approach, but even without this, it will hopefully provide many readers with a useful do-it-yourself kit.

One can intuitively confirm our kind of analysis by reflecting that everyone knows the university president's name; that most persons within the system are aware of endless types of public relations materials, and that relatively few people know who is the head of any given student organization outside of student government, or the name of the leader of a nonacademic trade union on campus.

If the various tables are studied closely, it is possible to map out where power is in the institution now, and also to suggest how one might get more. Consider a student government interested in becoming more important. It is not very powerful now in most universities and colleges, and it ranks 14 out of 21 items in Table 7. This group might be able to increase its weight by getting more formal authority in some areas, especially those areas—like budgets —that are among the most important in terms of power. Even if the group cannot achieve this, it could increase its power and influence by being more involved in activities and interfaces where power is. If the student government could provide and obtain inputs and some decision-making power on budgets and on the hiring and firing of professionals, could influence employers of the institution's graduates, and could get a student lobby recognized by the state government, it would gain considerable power and influence. When

Table 7.

SUBSYSTEM POWER RANKINGS

Rank		Total Power Score (*From Table 4*)
1.	Central Administration Political-Authority System	2430
2.	Trustees	2370
3.	Schools	2265
4.	Central Administration Functional System	1980
5.	Deans	1572
6.	Public Relations and Information	1278
7.	Data Processing	1232
8.	Library System	1135
9.	Interdisciplinary Studies	1044
10.	Faculty Council	875
11.	Department Chairmen	854
12.	Other University Publications	808
13.	AAUP	770
14.	Student Government	576
15.	Social Subsystems	560
16.	Other Student Organizations	540
17.	Placement	510
18.	University TV and Radio	455
19.	Registrar	365
20.	Nonacademic Unions	228
21.	University Press	220

considered this way, it is not surprising that many astute student body presidents ask for (or demand) access to such key issues. They know full well that this is the road to power. The same is true for astute faculty members who really understand the power system and try to get directly involved in the budgeting process.

If the university under study decides to give significantly higher priority to career preparation and jobs for students as a goal, the student placement subsystem would gain in power and influence. If the placement group also got a significant voice in the budgetary process and interacted in significant ways with trustees, department chairmen, professional groups, faculty leaders, and more informational subsystems, it could move up at least several ranks in Table 7.

Examination of Tables 3 and 4 in Chapter Three also reveals why some groups lack power. They do not interrelate with the critical issues or parts of the system that bestow power. You can read accross these tables for any part of the university and see which types of involvement a group has. Where it does not get involved, it loses potential power.

The tables also suggest why coalitions form. Usually no individual has enough power to carry the day on a key issue, so he or she must find partners. When another group or part of the system has similar feelings about a problem or decision, coalition is possible. Even the central administration, using its double-counted and therefore exaggerated power scores (exaggerated because central administration is considered both in terms of functions and as the political-authority subsystem) usually cannot act without some support—at least passive support—from other groups since the others can, for practical purposes, veto many acts. The same is true of the trustees.

Suppose that the trustees decide to cut salaries. They can do this, and it is a tempting thought if resources are cut badly by financial supporters. There is normally no legal reason why this cannot be done. But if it were done, a possible coalition of deans, schools, faculty council or senate, interdisciplinary studies, student government, and possibly others could be formed to protest. If the coalition battled cleverly enough and hard enough, they have the power to overwhelm the nominal power of the trustees. Because such coalition-building is so important for any one group seeking more power, it is common to find a hotbed of potential or actual coalitions being formed all the time by various parties, including the central administration and even the trustees.

Internal coalitions also are common, as study of the tables suggests. Again, no one group has enough total power to dictate to all the others, so coalitions have to be formed to fight the issue.

Interestingly enough, administrators at all levels normally are not tenured—at least in their administrative jobs—and serve at the pleasure of their bosses. In a critical fight, deans, central administrators, the university press head, heads of various publications, the TV-radio staff, and the registrar could possibly be removed or asked by the trustees to resign. However, if all of these people formed a strong and unified coalition, such mass resignations or firings would probably not take place. But if they were not unified and were out to save only their own jobs—which may be quite understandable— it would be more likely that they would all lose their jobs. In general, the balance of power is often held by individuals whose ability to serve rests with the pleasure of the trustees or other governing body. The remaining internal groups are frequently not powerful enough, even in a coalition, to force really major changes.

Moreover, conflicts are quite common within each group in Table 7, and these can reduce considerably the power of the group in various situations. For example, different schools or faculties, deans, department chairmen, central administrators, and student groups often have different aims and interests, so the power scores for each of these groups may be far too high with regard to various kinds of specific decisions. Similarly, university publications as a group are fairly important in terms of power and influence at the university under study here, but no one operating a single journal or paper is very important, because he does not control all of them. Collectively, editors of the business journal, the history journal, the publisher of the newsletter sent to parents, and all the rest, may be truly significant, but no one of these people is in a truly critical position. This problem suggests the critical nature of the unpacking of taxonomies. Because the categories used here are quite broad, such actual power as may accrue to a person further down in the system is not readily apparent. A manager or administrator who wants to get something done might follow a policy of "divide and conquer," or to at least take advantage of this common dispersion of group power to accomplish something that he feels is important and in the institution's interest.

This discussion suggests why student government leaders or faculty representatives typically never seem to get control of really important things like budgets. They are few in number and do not usually have strong or unified backing from all or even most of their constituencies. Usually, when student or faculty representatives or activists try to get control of really important things like budgets, the management quietly gangs up, forms a coalition, and makes sure that real control and power is not given away. If an administrator or manager was inclined to share control with students and so informed board of trustees, he might be asked to resign. Because the top officials can control their key manpower, they can exercise effective control on key issues, leaving the unimportant things to other groups. Many faculty members and students do not understand what—or even where—power really is, and spend a lot of time arguing about things that do not really matter.

This power map might prove useful in another way. The scores given various components of the system, environment, outputs, and inputs, are suggestive and for a given period of time, not definitive. Suppose that one or more scores changed, because of a change in policy at the very top. Thus, the education of undergraduates might become of greater importance. It would be possible to raise this score (say, from its present 5 to 10), and then go back through the matrix and recompute power scores to see who would be more or less important. Such basic changes in goals (or in inputs, or environmental constraints) would mean that some subsystems would become more significant and others would lose in relative importance. This, of course, is happening all the time in a viable organization, as various subsystems struggle, for better or worse, to become more significant. And from time to time such efforts succeed, and the whole matrix and its power scores change.

The weights and scores suggested here and in Chapter Three are for one university only. They may be most applicable to large, complex state universities, although the weights and scores of other institutions of this type would vary, in many cases dramatically. If other types of universities and colleges are considered, their scores and weights would probably vary even more because some inputs, outputs, environmental constraints, and subsystems are not part of their overall systems. Thus a small liberal arts college with no graduate schools would not have many of the goals suggested in the output taxonomy. The University of Chicago would not have many problems with athletics (O-4), and the relationships of a church-

related college with government (C-3, C-4, and C-5 in the classification of environmental constraints) would be different from those
of a state-supported college. This, of course, would significantly
change many power relationships within the system.

Finally, the tables presented and the related discussion suggest why so many faculty, students, administrators, and others in the
system are confused about power. If you really think that power
comes in cans, then you fight to get more cans. You may succeed,
and then you are able to enter the inner sanctum of the university
where the decisions are really made. You are on the budget committee, or perhaps the committee on tenure, or the committee that
is going to decide where to build the new laboratory. And instead
of finding power, all you discover is a dreary series of committee
meetings, where seemingly innocuous people just like you wallow
around in confusion for long periods before even tentative recommendations are made. Somehow, power always seems to be someplace else, no matter where you are. Even university presidents argue
that they cannot control the place—the power is somewhere else.
No one has enough to do with what he feels needs to be done. This
can be a traumatic discovery for a novice in the power game.

However, the effective manager or administrator can achieve
considerable control in making or seeing that important decisions are
made and significant changes are implemented that are beneficial
and warranted in terms of his institution's viability and success.
The analytical framework, methodologies, and taxonomies presented
here will hopefully be of considerable use in this regard to many
managers, administrators, and others seeking greater power and
influence. We can only hope that they use their power wisely and
judiciously.

Problems

Many kinds of power problems are implied in the above
analysis. Some of them are extremely intractable, in that no one
really knows what to do about them, even if they are recognized in
advance. Here are a few of the sticky ones we now face in American
higher education.

Universities and colleges historically have been havens for

gentlemen and ladies who knew the rules and were usually willing to play by them. The occasional lapse into vulgarity, bad manners, or refusal to play the game could be handled quietly without much fuss. But in today's world of varied values, we find that there are few gentlemen in the old sense of the word. The game is played by strange rules, or no rules at all. How is this problem handled? It usually is not. And so we are in deep trouble, because we have no mechanism to cover such problems. Ultrarightists and ultraleftists these days are so far out that none of the ordinary, informal, or formal mechanisms of power can deal with them. If ordinary sanctions are imposed, the nonplayer simply ignores them. Then we turn to law, only to find that we really do not have any law covering such problems. This leads to regulations, rules, due process, and final resort to sterile legalisms—at which point the university may be close to death without our really knowing it. The nonplayers may be unable to take over power, but they may well be able to deal the organization a death blow simply because it cannot, from any of its numerous power centers, deal with this particular kind of cancer. Some persons may argue that the institution is so corrupt that it really does not matter whether it lives or dies or who gets hurt in the process. Perhaps—but some of those interested in viable institutions may have to solve this problem before they can deal with any of the others. We have no particular wisdom to present here. However, the turmoil on many campuses several years ago need not be repeated if institutions have effective management and leadership, including sound contingency plans to use if such problems begin to emerge again.

Committees are one solution to the critical interface problem. If an administrator has a problem affecting several groups, he forms a committee to plaster up the differences, develop coordination mechanisms, or otherwise do what is necessary to keep this interface from becoming critical. Committees handle problems with relations between subsystems. For example, a committee may be set up to study the reporting system for grades (here, informational-functional subsystems). Political subsystems rarely get handled in committees, and social subsystems almost never get handled there either (except in odd cases of professional misconduct or deviant behavior). Other committees may handle environmental constraints—for example, budget constraints. Others—such as admissions committees—worry about inputs. Still others worry about outputs (for example, the quality of certain students). In short, wherever a key interface appears in Tables 3 and 4, one is likely to find a committee at work, trying to coordinate and inform a wide clientele. Note that this is a means of defusing complaints and keeping the interface below the critical point, and also a way of sharing power. This is one important way of decentralizing the kinds of power decisions that are not too critical. Paradoxically, formation of such committees may enhance an administrator's power, which is why so many people are willing to form new committees. If people agree in advance to abide by a committee's decision, potentially dangerous problems are defused and the administrator has time to spend on other, more significant issues.

In any complex system many astute persons intuitively understand that information is power, and they may carefully hoard the information they generate or control. Or they may present it in unusable forms. If only they know what is going on, they have power. If they can structure information, they can influence results.

Such information distortion becomes particularly important in forecasting that has major input implications. Consider the problem of how many students will be at a university in 1977. If it has 28,000, the problem faced will be very different than if it has 30,000. But those in a position to forecast accurately can distort information or present it in ways that make it difficult to interpret. (They also can make simple mistakes in forecasting, which compounds the problem.) Note here the inherent power in information—the trustees or the president cannot do all of the field work that leads to the forecast—they have neither the time nor the expertise. In a very real sense, they are prisoners of their own technocracy and information systems. This problem is also critical in the presentation of data. If an administrator wants to know what it costs to run the power plant, but the accounts are kept in a way that makes it impossible to determine such information, he lacks the power to do much—until the proper data is gathered. Any large university is faced with such problems all the time, in part because of external constraints about how accounts and costs are to be structured and maintained. Without data, the presumed power center is powerless to act. Relatively little systematic work has been done to improve the amounts and usefulness of available information, although much work is now beginning. Until we can state with confidence that all relevant data is readily available and usable, this will continue to be a very real problem for all administrators and participants.

Control of personnel is crucial in any power system. Some management writers have gone so far as to suggest that a manager who cannot control the people he works with cannot manage. He only administers a system powerlessly while those who are free of control do their thing. Although this probably is an overstatement, it is true that the manager or administrator who cannot hire and fire his people has much less power than one who can. The administrator of a university, with tenure and long-term contracts, is in a peculiar power position. Outsiders, accustomed to the harsher world of industrial discipline, find it difficult to understand why the president does not just fire those who give him trouble. The lack of ability to dismiss leads quickly to diffusion of some kinds of power. This has led some to suggest that the university is unmanageable. Certainly it has a diffused power system as a result, as Table 7 suggests. University administrators are denied the weapon against personnel that most organizations have. An organization full of high-talent manpower rarely uses this weapon—but it is a very handy thing to have in reserve.

One of the changes that could shift power in the university would be removal of tenure. New York state is already discussing elimination of tenure for primary and secondary teachers. Predictably, the teachers are fighting violently for this right, because they also clearly see the implications of change. Any effort in any university or college to remove tenure would focus attention on this subject for perhaps five years, and that alone could destroy an institution. It hardly seems worth the effort.

So, how does the manager or administrator operate? Generally, his options are restricted to long-term resource allocation. If he is lucky, he has inherited a reasonably good pool of manpower and talent with goal systems reasonably close to his and those of his external clienteles (the state, major private donors, parents, alumni). From there he can move slowly toward creating new positions, reducing the importance of (but not necessarily eliminating) old ones, and generally moving toward whatever goals he has in mind. If he is unlucky, he inherits much deadwood, disruptive personnel, and general confusion. We all know colleges and universities that, because of past personnel policies, are for all practical purposes dead. Power is not concentrated enough to use, and the situation is not likely to change very much.

Students are the basic clientele of academic institutions and a key issue is that of student admissions. The quality of student inputs largely determines the reputation of the school. A mediocre faculty, blessed with top flight students, will look good; a great faculty with poor students will not look good. Rather curiously, faculty do not usually press for the power to control admissions, although they may have veto powers. On occasion, some little old lady clerk in the registrar's office may hold more power on this issue than the president or faculty.

One reason for relative lack of interest is rapid turnover. If we goofed this year, we can wait a few years and rebuild the quality —we think. But reputations change quickly, and once this key point begins to slip, external power sources may drain off an institution's ability to attract top students. Professors who have given advice on the desirability of various colleges to high school students, seniors for graduate school, and parents can perhaps appreciate this point. Some schools we just do not recommend, in spite of their alleged reputation, because we know that those schools have not been attracting the best students. Here we are external power centers to other systems, in a modest way, taking advantage of the situation to influence their results and problems.

If there is anything really different between universities and other organizations, it lies in the battalions of high-talent, creative personnel universities have. Aside from a few research laboratories and think tanks, almost no other large organizations have this characteristic to this degree. But you cannot order creativity as you would pencils or punctuality. The creative person either does it or does not do it, depending on how he feels. A terrifying view of a great university is one in which all professors do exactly what they are told—no more, no less. The place would collapse in chaos within weeks. Here again is a gentlemen's agreement, in that most professionals will go to great lengths to work creatively in areas in which they have interest or competence. If they withdrew this creative part of their work, they indeed have power—which is why Table 7 looks the way it does.

Hence, power does not come in cans, nor are the cans finite in supply. It is quite possible that any person in the system can pick up power without anyone losing any—if he knows where to look. The expansibility of power lies in the fact that many of the key interfaces in Tables 3 and 4 in Chapter Three are imperfectly understood or utilized. Thus, anyone who comes along and works with any or all of them tends to become more valuable and hence more powerful in relation to other power centers in the system. Curiously, other power centers may actually gain power as a result, because they now know more about the system, and hence know more about how to make it work.

The section on sources of power suggests ways of attaining power and influence. A few other guidelines or tactics that relate to the above discussion are worth noting here. (1) Observe situations where key interfaces are imperfectly meshed, not understood, or close to crisis. Even casual system observers can find plenty of these around any university. (2) Do some research. It helps to find out what is really going on. (3) Get listened to. One point often overlooked by power-seekers is that it pays to have a strong base from which to operate. A competent teacher or researcher will be listened to more closely than an incompetent one; a good accountant with a reputation for precision and good work will likewise be listened to with interest; and so on. (4) Do some planning for the key interface. This gets to the notion that if something is wrong, a plan should be suggested to make it right. Planning also requires the proper structuring of the information relevant to the problem. (5) Resource reality helps. Good plans that make wildly unrealistic demands for resources available are neither useful nor exciting. In short, pay attention to potential budgetary limitations. Also pay attention to payoffs, especially in proportion to costs. (6) Publicize the idea. There are all sorts of information channels that can be used. Lots of people will see it, and some may borrow from it, but this is a sign that something useful is happening.

After a few exercises of this sort, a power-seeker is spotted as a comer by those above, who always find such talent in short supply.

The half life of most key administrators is only several years, so plenty of vacanies will shortly occur.

We have participated in lots of situations where a new president, chancellor, or dean was initiating his regime. Out there in the audience were dozens of potential professional marshalls, their batons tucked in their knapsacks, ready for the call that never came. One could read in their studious faces the eternal question—"What's his magic? Why him, not me?" The above six points, as well as many others covered in this chapter may explain why.

Concluding Remarks

Universities and colleges are extremely complicated organizations. They are very difficult to manage efficiently, because the goal systems are so ill defined. One cannot get there from here very efficiently or effectively, if "there" is undefined.

This exercise in systems analysis, taxonomic creation, and interface relationships is an attempt to define the problems of university management by focusing on power and influence in organizational decision-making. We would all like to see easier solutions, and much easier formulations of the problem. But the formulations are difficult, and many are more misleading than helpful because they do not get at all the key problems. We would argue that it is necessary to spell out all significant problems in considerable detail before it is feasible to dissect them into relevant components.

This type of analysis can be helpful in working through the many interrelationships within universities. Far too often, simplistic solutions are suggested for currently pressing problems, but proponents of the changes do not consider the effects of such change on many other components of the university. It is not enough to argue that A should be tried, because changing A slightly may also change B, C, W, and Z in ways not originally intended.

The exercise in power determination suggested what might be done with such analysis. Moreover, this sort of exercise is verifiable, in that any shift in any of the system components should lead to power changes that could be observed in the real world. If a goal changes significantly, then some system elements will become more important and others will lose significance. Using this methodology, such a change could be calculated in advance, and then checked to determine if it in fact occurred as predicted. If not, back to the to the drawing board!

No exercise of this sort can ever include all relevant components in a complex system. It cannot handle the charismatic personality, the addled fool in a key position, or the sudden, dramatic shift in key environmental constraints. There are too many behavioral variables in this system, and too many places where such variables can become very important even in the short run, to ever handle such changes. But as always, what else do we have? Prehaps it is true that academic management will always be more art than science, but the basic argument is that some systematic sorting out of key variables will allow any interested person to operate the system better than if everything is done by intuition.

The following two chapters explore internal interrelationships and environmental constraints in greater detail.

Chapter VII

Internal Interrelationships

Administrators have to worry about outsiders but they also have to mind the shop. Big universities—with thousands of professors, tens of thousands of students, and dozens of special centers, projects, and research operations—are extremely complex organizations. They are made even more complex by their diffuse goal structures. Even if an administrator is capable of developing a smooth, well-running system, it is never clear exactly what this system should be. Even small colleges are complex organizations. The university or college has to be organized and operated. Basic functions are performed, such as teaching and research; the rest rooms are cleaned; the professors paid on time, and programs are carried out.

Suboptimization Concepts

One basic concept in our analysis is suboptimization. Most individuals have a worm's eye view of the organization for which they work; most are interested in what is happening to them, or to their small unit. Most people try to suboptimize in organizations—they try to make their groups perfect, no matter what happens to the total organization. If every group is trying to do this, with more or less success, the result is extensive suboptimization, with the overall organization functioning much less smoothly and efficiently than it might.

A few examples might suggest how this works out in a large university. Consider a school that allows its English department to do what English professors feel is correct and proper. Such behavior might include extensive work with advanced graduate students, much time allotted for research, and allocation of funds for esoteric journals of great interest to English scholars but not to laymen. The department would have a high payroll, because the most qualified and famous English scholars are not cheap and the school would have to pay market rates to attract such people. This department might be world famous among the knowledgable as a great department, and its doctoral students would be in demand at other schools. Its scholars would dominate meetings of various professional associations with presentations of the best learned papers, and other aspiring scholars in the field would yearn to visit the department to take part in its exciting activities.

While this optimization of performance was occurring, other parts of the university might be in trouble. Over at the business school, many students badly need remedial work in freshman or sophomore English. Few students seem to be able to read rapidly, spell correctly, or write lucidly. So the business school dean (head of this subsystem) approaches the English department chairman to ask for more intensive and better work in basic English than has been available. The business dean is likely to be disappointed. First-rate English scholars are not interested in drilling business sophomores. Even if they are forced to do it, they will probably not be effective. They will dump the task on their graduate students, who are not very interested either. After all, the graduate students came to the university to study under masters, not to drill freshmen in basic English. So there never is enough system capacity to handle the dirty work of drill and rote teaching. And even when it is done, it is done badly. One could turn this around and ponder a situation where the business school dominated proceedings. The English department would be operated as a service area to business, providing good, routine instruction but accomplishing little scholarly work.

Wherever there are two subsystems with potentially competing goals, we encounter the potential for suboptimization. It works outside of academic departments as well. The maintenance crew may be able to dispossess a class because the school is more interested in maintenance than in teaching. Or, conversely, the building may fall apart because academics are always in the way when vital maintenance functions should be performed. Perfect optimization of any subsystem normally means that the system as a whole is performing badly. This point is lost on subsystem leaders. Most individuals feel that if they are optimizing, then the whole system must be optimizing. But the optimal system is one in which no subsystem is optimal. Everybody operates with less than perfect efficiency (as they see it), in order to get overall optimum system performance. Top administrators are always in trouble on this point, because few of their subordinates understand this problem very well. The problem is more complex in university environments than in most large organizations because of the diffuse goal systems of academic institutions. You can only optimize if you know what total optimization might be, and, again, this is not always clear.

Top administrators often spend more time on this internal problem than on anything else. A further complication is that a university, by its very nature, is an extremely diverse organization. The many schools, departments, scholars, administrators, and students really have little in common, and they have much to fight about. Jurisdictional disputes can be a burden, as can direct philosophical (goal system) conflicts. When disputants lack anyone else to talk to, they appeal to top administrators—who have to figure out where to cut, where to change, and where to pressure. Because academics are by nature articulate, eloquent, and persuasive, such controversies can become extremely involved.

Somehow these problems must be resolved. Unfortunately the university administrator, unlike his counterpart in business, cannot attack problems with more simple-minded goal systems (for example, how does this decision contribute to profits?). He must decide what the goal system is and how it best might be achieved by which overall system integration and optimization. And then he must spend months arguing with irate deans and chairmen about why he did what he did.

Hierarchical Problems

We live in a world of hierarchies for one very simple reason —they work relatively well, or at least adequately, in complex situations. Young revolutionaries may dislike cumbersome bureaucracies, and many others may not like complex, pyramidal organizations, but to date no one has figured out any other form of organization that, by itself, would work half as well. In intriguing experiments, many other kinds of organizational structures have not performed well. So we all have bosses and subordinates. Like other large organizations, universities have a formal authority hierarchy composed of chiefs, subchiefs, and the rank and file. One typical pattern is shown in Figure 2. The board of trustees, regents, or governors is typically a part-time policy-making body at the top. In state universities, the board normally holds all of the formal power to operate the university, including the power to hire, fire, spend, and set priorities. In descending order down the pyramid are the president, vice-presidents, deans, departmental chairmen, and finally the faculty.

Universities have many nonacademic functions, and these normally are handled by experts. Thus, one vice-president may handle finance. He is responsible for the accounting division, maintenance functions, and leaders of nonacademic personnel. Other nonacademic vice-presidents handle planning, building construction, purchasing, and other services that have to be performed well if the university is to operate efficiently. These operations form a matrix organization in which each group services the others. The accountants keep records for all academic groups, yet may report directly to the vice-president for finance. The maintenance section does work in classroom buildings; the purchasing agent buys equipment for everyone; and so on. Organizational difficulties arise here, because it is not always clear who should do what for what purpose. One basic organizational rule is that no one should have two bosses, but most universities violate this on occasion.

An enormous amount of work has been done in management

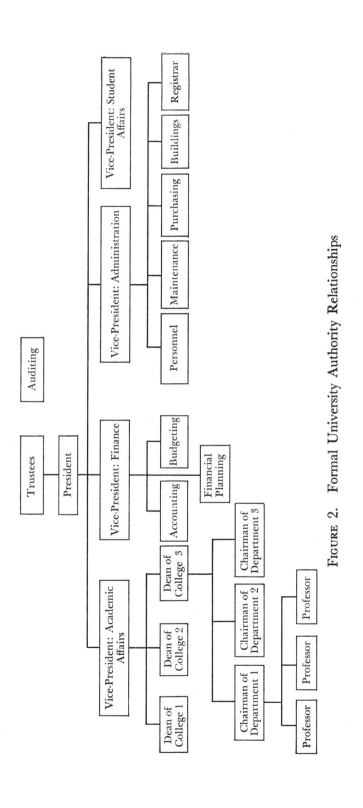

FIGURE 2. Formal University Authority Relationships

and administration on organization theory, some of it useful for many kinds of university administration. Yet few administrators consult with their own expert departments on such matters. Certainly the peculiarities of many university structures suggest that these two groups operate without any communication. One very useful (and cheap) thing to do is to talk to the organization and management experts who are found at any university. The administrator may be surprised to find a pool of technical expertise right under his nose, and payoffs can be large.

The functional subsystem of the university normally is the only one which appears on the formal organization chart. Outsiders observing the structure and organization may conclude that the university is tidy and well organized. Insiders are aware that there is confusion, that many people are working at cross purposes, and that a university is full of people who formally hold little power but who seem to have a lot.

Two factors are responsible for this situation. First, you cannot order a man to be creative, and the university is full of creative people. Thus, if the chairman orders one of his professors to do something, it may or may not get done, depending on how the subordinate feels. These creative people may spend a lot of time figuring out how to frustrate some order they do not like. It is rather frightening to think of brilliant people trying their best to frustrate some order of a dean or chairman. Most perceptive deans, vice-presidents, and chairmen recognize this possibility, and they are careful to avoid confrontation—and a lot of trouble.

Second, the functional organization is only about one-fourth of the total organization problem. Figure 1 in Chapter Three shows the functional, informational, political, and social subsystems, all of which are interlocked in a variety of subtle ways. Few organizational charts show more than the functional subsystem, and fewer show all of them. The result is that the formal organization may be almost irrelevant to what is really going on. The other forms of organization may be much more interesting and relevant.

Academics tend to generate much more complex informational, political, and social subsystems than workers in a factory. Much management and organization theory evolved out of industrial experience of fifty years ago, when the worker-supervisor relationship was simple and goals were also simple. Under such conditions, the functional subsystem was the critical one. Moreover, the spatial layout of facilities was such that the other three subsystems followed the functional. Needed information tended to be closely related to function; socializing tended to be closely related to persons in the same functional subsystem; and political activities also were restricted to persons in a small work area.

But the modern university, with its highly educated people, fuzzy goal structure, and undefined work tasks, tends to develop very complex subsystems that are not related to the functional subsystem. This is why so much confusion is generated in the internal university system, and it also is why so much of university administration is misunderstood by outsiders. Most outsiders are familiar with traditional hierarchies, where people respond properly to orders received from above and other subsystem relationships are either not as important or very closely linked to the functional subsystem. Outsiders often cannot understand why no one seems to pay much attention when the university boss says "Jump!"

Because this point is so critical to proper university organization, function, and process, we consider the information, political, and social subsystems below. Many of the difficulties of internal university administration stem from failure to perceive that these subsystems can be quite unrelated to the functional subsystem.

Information Subsystems. The business of any university is information, yet rarely is the information subsystem organized in a coherent manner. Typically, this subsystem has evolved through time, in bits and pieces, as required. We are interested here in the information that is used for internal administration and control purposes. Enormous amounts of other information also is generated, including research results and teaching materials, but none of it is directly relevant here. These other types, however, are what interest the faculty and students the most. Much usable information is necessary if the university is to function well. But information has often been structured in a very suboptimal way. Here are some of the major informational channels—common to most universities— none of which are necessarily related to any others: Some information flows in accordance with the functional subsystem. This is the traditional method of passing around useful information. Such things as course assignments, budgets, and pay changes follow the hierarchy on the organization charts. Some information relates to the students—grades, specific assignments, and degree requirements. The registrar may keep these records, and a professor or dean may not even know what his various students are doing. This is particularly true for students crossing organizational lines—for example, when a student in liberal arts takes a course in the business school. Some information pertains to an academic discipline. Information of relevance to students, administrators, and professors may be tracked along discipline lines—for example, what a medical student needs to know about licensing requirements or an accounting student wants to know about CPA examinations. Some information involves professors—what the professor is doing in research or public service, for example. A man may be on an air pollution commission outside the university (yet doing work very relevant to his career), and few within the university may know much about it. Some information involves various staff functions—the blueprints of building electrical wiring systems may be in some maintenance office. Technical information is often categorized in this way. Some information relates to the social subsystem. Participants may pass on information to people they know socially. This information flow cuts across all subsystems, but whatever is transferred tends to be informal and casual. Some information involves the public relations function—press releases to newspapers on internal developments, for example. Often a professor or student learns about a staff change when he reads it in the newspapers.

Some information involves critical interface relations. The interface is where two subsystems meet. For example, a committee might report on some item of interest to two different schools within the university. Some information pertains to interdisciplinary groupings. A student may discover that the Latin American Studies Center has scholarship funds available for students in economics, political science, or history, although none of these academic departments may know about the awards. Some information relates to nonprofessional staff—rules and regulations about work and trade union activities, for example. Some information involves programs. A candidate for the PhD degree might discover that some critical information is available in the doctoral program office.

All of these information flows mesh at various points, although relatively little work has been done to make sure that all of it flows to the right places at the right times. Consideration of these flows suggests why the system evolved casually. From time to time some development made it imperative that interested persons know something, so an administrator, professor, or student developed an information flow. Often these flows become institutionalized without much thought as to who should really know what is going on. As a result, university information flows tend to be very inconsistent, sporadic, and confusing. It is often difficult to find out who knows what is relevant. And often the information available is organized in the wrong manner for the purpose at hand.

This confusion about the information subsystem is closely related to goal system confusion. An individual needs information to check a deviation, to get feedback on some process, or so that he can plan better for future activities. But if no one is really sure what the norm is, or what should be done, there is not much interest in information. Who cares if the power bill is high, if it does not matter? Who cares if a professor never shows up, if there is no penalty? Who cares what the costs per student are in various disciplines, if it is generally agreed that such information should not be used for planning future programs?

Goals can be seen as norms, if they can be measured, and to measure them one needs all the relevant information. Some university goals are carefully considered, and the information system around them is highly developed. Thus, grades and records necessary for graduation are highly developed, as are employee payroll records. If professors really did not care much about money, we could expect that this part of the information system would be messy, like so many other parts. One can infer much about what is really important around a university by observing just how well the record system is able to report results.

It may also be true that if good information were available to show what is really going on, some things might change quickly. Thus, it is common to find faculties avoiding good information about teaching performance, and there is not much reliable information about how professors really spend their time. On the other hand, it is normally easy to discover who published what or how much he is paid. Absence of information, or lack of properly organized information, means that the administrator cannot operate properly or efficiently. If you do not know what is wrong, or to what extent, you cannot correct anything. A few examples of this problem may suggest how difficult it is to operate without appropriate information.

A school wished to reduce maintenance costs, which were believed to be too high. It turned out that no one had any records of existing costs, except very gross figures such as total payrolls. This school had the usual mix of old, very old, and relatively new buildings, each with many special maintenance problems. But no one could say for sure which problems required the most attention and cost. Moreover, there were no performance norms for various craftsmen. No one knew how much a plumber, electrician, or carpenter should do in a day. Before it could even begin to tackle the problem of reducing maintenance costs, this school had to begin to develop—at considerable cost—a complete maintenance records system. This is a large school, and maintenance costs were already more than $1.5 millions per year. Yet it was impossible even to determine if these costs were high or low until new data could be gathered.

Another university wanted to give more attention to teaching excellence, particularly through promotions and pay increases. It quickly discovered that there was no information in most professors' files about how well they taught. Indeed, even evaluation systems were not well developed. The evaluation procedure had to be done on a very casual, ad hoc basis for years, until better information about teaching performance was developed.

A state university had experienced many student riots and disorders, and the legislature demanded a crackdown—or else. In the next demonstration, the university officials carefully took many pictures of persons involved, only to find out that there was no effective way of identifying anybody. They had forty-five pictures of individuals, and these had to be checked against twenty-seven thousand pictures in students files. Some files lacked pictures, some of the women had dyed their hair, and some of the men had grown beards or shaved them off. It took six weeks and several thousand man-hours to do the sifting.

A young, quiet professor was up for tenure consideration in a major state university. His records did not suggest adequate competence, and so he was dismissed. The university then faced student protest, because the professor was highly regarded by his students. Moreover, the administration later learned that he had consulted with the state Department of Education the previous year in regard to retarded children, and one of his suggestions, when adopted, had saved the state some $14 millions per year. This public service was not in his records. This matter was played up in the newspapers, and the administration was made to look like a bunch of incompetents who did not know what their own faculty were doing, which they didn't.

A major state university, in response to many student and faculty requests, made very complete changes in the rules and regulations governing campus police operations. The employees were upset, and the administration discovered that many of the changes were in direct conflict with the union contract. The administration eventually had to retract many changes, with some embarrassment.

There is presently a great deal of interest in systems analysis for universities and colleges. Many private firms have moved into this area, offering special training, seminars, and analysis. Typically, the information and functional subsystems are being integrated. Here are the steps in this process. (1) Decide what is going to be done—what information is needed. This relates to goals again, but many subgoals are fairly easy to decide on. Records are needed of grades, of maintenance costs, of relevant information about students and faculty, and about building utilization, for example. (2) Once these goals have been set, figure out what information in what form is necessary to measure the desired results. Since most subgoals are measurable, this is possible. (3) Decide on norms of performance. If you are going to do better, you have to know what is considered good. (4) Design an information flow through all relevant subsystems so that the administrator responsible for performance will get all the information he needs to control the system. Often this phase requires computers, redesigned records systems, and similar changes. But if the design is developed step by step, it is relatively easy to do. As many as six to eight subsystems may be required to generate information in the functional system. This process is unfamiliar to university administrators, who normally are not trained in such analysis. But a whole discipline exists to serve their system, so the necessary talent is around. However, such expertise is relatively scarce, and so it is not cheap. What emerges is an integrated system that provides a flow of relevant functional information to decision-makers. This system also decides what to measure, what the norms are, and how to determine when norms are not being met. So far, few universities have made substantial progress in this direction, although current information problems will require the development of such systems as rapidly as possible.

Political-Authority Subsystems. In most complex organizations, the political subsystem follows the functional subsystem, because those in formal positions of power have the ability to push others around—and they sometimes do. There are exceptions when some power behind the throne maneuvers for advantage, but the functional organization chart usually depicts the power structure. One intriguing exception is the person who has the ear of the leader. This situation personifies the informational subsystem in action— and illustrates a source of political power.

Power and political subsystems are intimately related. Although Chapter Six focused on power, further elaboration regarding political subsystems is warranted here because of their pervasive importance, along with power and goal systems. Moreover, political subsystems are closely related to other subsystems, and an elaboration of those relationships—in particular the relationship between the political and informational subsystems—is needed.

The interrelationships between subsystems contribute to the diffusion of power in the university organization. The information subsystem is rarely well organized, and the individual who controls critical information may be much more powerful than his position on the organizational chart would suggest. In universities and colleges, there are many such people around.

Chapter Six discussed this power question, and, in Table 6 and 7 of that chapter, the power matrix of one university was suggested. These charts indicate why the political subsystem in a university will be much more complex than in many other large organizations for information control. In a large organization with unstructured goals, it is not too clear who should do what. And so there are ample opportunities for individuals to seize control of some apparently irrelevant function. Because no one is really clear what should be done, or what is important, the person reaching out is not always immediately cut off. Later on, when he has funds, personnel, and a strong suboptimizing goal system, it may be difficult to control him.

Other factors contribute to the diffusion and complexity of the political subsystem. Academic personnel look two ways in their jobs—inward toward the university in which they work, and outward, toward their disciplines. The faculty can be categorized in these terms. The insiders tend to be men of lesser stature in their disciplines, and to follow the functional subsystem for their search for power. They want to be in on the game as chairmen, deans, and so on up the hierarchical ladder. Outsiders tend to be publishing scholars, known in their fields. The rules and regulations of the place they happen to be working seem trivial and burdensome, and they feel that power and political gain come from national or international professional recognition. Presidency of a major professional organization or election to a prestigious scientific fellowship is more important to them than participation in local activities. This outward orientation, if done successfully, can lead to power accumulation that administrators find difficult to handle. University presidents just do not tell Nobel prizewinners what to do. If a distinguished faculty member wants to do nothing but research, he does it. If he wants to teach the freshman basic course in his discipline, he does that. Moreover, he can obtain large grants for research at any time, so cutting his budget does not work as a constraint. Rather, the university administrator will plead with such a faculty member to get his grant request in to the National Science Foundation on time. In this situation power follows the discipline, not the internal functional system. These prestigious members of a faculty are the focus of the outside recognition of any university. Few economists could name the presidents of the ten schools they consider best, but they could easily list the prestigious and brilliant economists on each faculty. If an administrator wants to run anything but a dreary cow college, he must learn to put up with these brilliant outsiders even though their prestige tends to erode the internal political system.

On occasion one encounters a faculty leader who, by reason of his personality, professional competence or local prestige, is seen by many as a spokesman for a large constituency. This image is often related to his professional status, because such a man is usually known as an extremely competent scholar in his own field. This combination of qualities makes such an individual more influential than his position as mere professor would suggest.

The organization of a university contains a number of *blockage slots,* positions where key decisions—who gets grant money, who gets in, who gets the coal contract for the power plant—are made. Often these decisions are not considered important to either faculty or administrators, unless some specific nasty problem comes up. Thus, a position with blockage, or veto power can be critical. One example is the admissions office. If you can't get by the director, you can't get into the system at all. And that is power. Consequently, a lot of politicking usually surrounds the kinds of decisions made in blockage slots.

Political maneuvering in a university environment is facilitated by several interconnected factors. (1) You cannot order creativity. (2) Tenure rules and long-term contracts curtail the use of the usual penalties for misbehavior. (3) The professional is supported from outside by his discipline, particularly if he is well known in his field. (4) The fragmentation of the information system means that various persons in the system have key bits of information that give them power, or at least influence, regardless of their positions in the hierarchy. (5) Blockage possibilities can be combined with all of the above to create power. (6) An individual may represent some formal coalition, such as the AAUP. The individual professor who is able to take advantage of all of these factors can become a formidable political opponent of any administration. One result is that an administrator may have an informal (though sometimes formalized) advisory committee. Such a group provides information that enables the administrator to avoid making proposals that are in direct conflict with potent persons or groups.

An administrator interested in regaining lost power must develop a strategy that will give him control of a tightly organized information system from which he will receive relevant feedback on the critical dimensions of his problems. He also needs a system for informing all interested persons about critical items and a rapid retrieval system to provide information that is not normally compiled regularly. University systems analysis programs perform exactly these functions, so it is no surprise that there is presently great interest in them. Such programs tie the information system closely to the functional system. The political system then also meshes consistently with the functional and information systems.

Any group of highly educated, articulate individuals involved in a complex organization is sure to include some very political animals whose behavior will be reinforced in a system that provides much free time. Some will work hard at conventional tasks, such as teaching or research, but others will consider such latitude an open invitation to active political maneuvering. Given the constraints imposed on administrators, this is inevitable. A lot of the political activity is noise, and one must be able to sort out the noise from the significant political activities. It is not always easy to do this, although good administrators must quickly learn how.

Social Subsystems. A university is conducive to mobility. The nature of job tasks and typical special arrangements means that talented people float all over the place. These factors lead to complex social interactions. The many committees, work groups, and interdisciplinary activities also lead people to meet others in many complex ways. Hence, it is very difficult to analyze in any systematic fashion the patterns and purposes of socialization. University location can be a major factor in socialization. The professors at an urban campus often live miles apart, and the resulting social arrangements and interactions are quite different from those on a campus located in a small town or city where many professors are neighbors.

The importance of this social interaction depends more on one's philosphy than on any hard data. Some would argue that the social system is the key system, that the old school tie and the buddy system works in university administration as in all other complex systems. An individual can be perfectly qualified for promotion or power, but never make it because of some fatal defect in his social relations or background. Others would suggest that, although key persons in the hierarchy must be reasonably compatible socially, it is difficult if not impossible to run something as complicated as a university on the buddy system. Social relations are significant, but they are not everything. An examination of key figures in both formal and informal university power structures reinforces this view—they come in all sizes, shapes, religions, sexes, races, and philosophies. Competence is critical in the modern academic institution, but compatibility counts, too. The casual (and correct) comment made at a cocktail party can be crucial. Much more work is needed in this area before anyone can state with confidence what the social subsystem counts for.

Interface Problems

Examination of Table 4 in Chapter Three, plus consideration of this chapter, suggests that there will always be major problems at the key interfaces between subsystems. This is where various parties fight to suboptimize, often at the expense of some other subsystem; this is where compromises have to be worked out to accommodate everyone. This also is the point where blowups can happen, and where top administrators can be faced with distressed subordinates who are convinced that someone in the system is out to get them. Some of these interfaces are quite precise and well drawn, as in relationships between the liberal arts college and various professional schools. Often they pop up unexpectedly as critical points of contact between the informal subsystems (mainly political and social). All cases must be handled correctly, or the whole system may get out of control.

Committees are the classic means of plastering over the interface cracks. All factions with an interest in the problem can meet to figure out what the problem is, whose interests are at stake, and what should be done. This gives most factions the feeling of having been in on the decision and may calm some of them if the decision goes against them. Committees also are invaluable in developing and disseminating information. In situations where the information subsystems is disorganized and diffuse, this is a key function.

These two considerations may explain why committees proliferate at universities. It is often a lot easier for an administrator to appoint a committee to study some problem than for him to make the decision and then find that many subsystems and individuals are furious. If it appears that two or more subsystems are going to be involved in something, it is far better to get them in at the outset than spend long hours fighting them afterwards. Moreover, many problems really are not important for the total organization, although they may be of critical importance for some subsystems. No matter what is decided, the university can survive. Hence, a committee can make the decision and keep everyone informed and reasonably happy, and top administrators can do something else with their scarce time.

A second method of controlling key interfaces is to develop and analyze the critical information needed to resolve problems. This is often difficult, but the administration does have potential informational resources not available to all subsystems. Judicious development of such information can produce a fair and just evaluation of a subsystem interface conflict. This evaluation, presented to all parties, can produce the right decision, and everyone concerned will know what happened.

Another means of resolving subsystems conflicts is to be authoritarian. The decision is made at the top, and heads are banged together below to make sure that what is decided is done. This is the traditional way of getting things done in hierarchies. It is seen by outsiders as the best way for a university to operate, because most outsiders are still used to this type of administration and management. There are two major reasons why this technique frequently does not work well in universities, although one can find many places (all seen by academies as really dreary, fourth-rate schools) where it occurs. The particular qualities of the university environment and of its participants militate against this solution. It is not a moral issue—it just may not work very well. Possibilities for sabotage, information distortion, and goldbricking are so real that unpopular decisions can easily lead to the demise of administrators rather than to efficiency.

The second major reason why autocratic direction often cannot be efficiently employed is that the information needed for good decisions is so great as to swamp top administrators. Either decisions are made without good information, or a very elaborate staff is built up to furnish the information. When the latter situation prevails, we find that decisions are no longer highly centralized. Some group is presenting highly condensed (and therefore manipuable) information to a few top people. This changes the nature of the decentralized system, but it does not centralize.

This autocratic system, if comprehensive and consistent, also is expensive. It is possible to obtain free or cheap labor on committees, because interested persons are eager to take part so that they can be in on the final decision. But if they do their homework, attend regularly, and participate actively, you have to hire staff men to do the job while professors glare at them from the sidelines. Expensive talent is thus used to do something that could have been done free. Many man-hours are required to do this job properly, because autocratic systems are characterized by widespread efforts to distort or hide key information.

Given all of these difficulties, most top managers go back to committees and information-dispensing. But they typically are under pressure from the outside to crack a few heads and show who is boss. A good administrator who can avoid such pressures normally can live relatively comfortably with his employees.

Conclusion

It is impossible in any short book even to list all of the possible interactions within a complex university system. Tables 3 and 4 in Chapter Three suggest some of the important critical interfaces, and this chapter has attempted to spell out some of the important aspects and defects in the critical subsystems.

Once again, we come to the same point. If we lack precise goal systems, it really does not matter what is going on in the subsystems. As long as universities and colleges have ill-defined goals, administrators do not see the need to accumulate systematically information about those goals. And so they cannot manage very effectively or efficiently. Outsiders, accustomed to precise goals and structured hierarchies, observe in bafflement the struggle within the university. This chapter tries to explain these struggles.

If we stop here, we admit that universities and colleges really are unmanageable. The only way they can be controlled is to set quantifiable goals, measure results, and correct deviations from stated goals. This means that shortly we will see imposed, internally or externally, goal systems that financial backers and students can observe and measure, whether or not the academic community approves. In the 1950s and 1960s, academics in effect said, "Give us money, and we will give you great results." The money was given, but the results have not pleased very many people. And so things will change. This chapter has provided some indicators of the kinds of changes that can be expected.

Chapter VIII

Environmental
Constraints

A university is a part of its total external environment and is constrained by it. It depends on its environment for critical resources because few universities generate surplus funds. And the external environment determines what the institution will be to a considerable extent. This chapter considers the problems that university administration or management has with its environment and how various conflicts and problems can be resolved. The conflict situation results largely from different goal preferences between the university and interested outsiders. When an outsider wants something that a university does not want to provide, or something that has low priority inside the university, how is this conflict resolved?

The analysis follows the taxonomy of the environmental constraints in Chapter Three. Major segments of the environment will be considered in turn, and the critical interfaces of each with the university will be studied. We are interested in devising the best strategy for handling the university's operations and goals when faced with outside pressure.

Nature of Environment

The university's environment provides inputs, takes outputs, and constrains action. Let us examine each of these.

Inputs. From the environment come students, faculty, other employees, money, and equipment. The quality and quantity of these inputs determines how well the university functions. If we want bright, highly-motivated students with good academic records, the number of such young people available determine whether we will get our share. If we need many professors of physics, the number of well-qualified men in this field will give us our probability of getting the right men; and so on.

Outputs. Others outside the university hire graduating students. They also use research—what is generally available (as when a professor publishes a paper) or what is contracted for and purchased by the outsider. And most public service activities are used by outsiders—a professor helps his state government reorganize its highway department, or an educator helps his local school district work with disturbed children.

Constraints. Universities may want to do various things, but someone in the environment will not let them, or will try to influence what is done. In short, the environment tries to establish goal systems. This is accomplished in three ways. The first is through laws. The relevant legal jurisdiction has laws about who does what, who has the power to act in various ways, and so on. The second environmental constraint is manifested in academic rules. Various state, national, and international associations provide some measure of quality control. For example, certification groups decide if the university or any of its subsystems are properly qualified to do their job. Little of this quality control has the force of formal law, but virtually all schools pay close attention to such certification requirements. The third environmental constraint takes the form of informal pressures. All sorts of nonuniversity elements try to influence the university. The governor or a large private donor calls the president and suggests something; newspapers editorialize; alumni write letters to key officials, advocating some course; or a national fraternity tries to exert influence through visits, letters, or phone calls. All of these informal pressures always are potentially or actually present, and although they do not have formal force, administrators pay attention to them. Administrators and managers should be careful not to antagonize too many of these outside clienteles at once. Persons or organizations who care enough about what is going on to protest or give advice normally are—or should be—listened to.

Critical Interfaces

We are interested only in relevant external factors, not in all of them. As suggested above, most external forces are *potentially* relevant, but at any particular time only a few are critical. What follows is a discussion of those external factors that seem to be most important most of the time.

State Government. This is mainly critical to public institutions, although private ones may have more minor relationships and problems relating to laws, nonprofit status, and similar matters. Public institutions get most of their financial support from state governments, they are regulated by state law, and selection of the trustees or regents of state universities and colleges is regulated by state laws. Many states currently are concerned about how their universities are operating. This is in part a financial concern— modern universities and colleges are very expensive, and often 20 to 30 percent of state expenditures are for higher education of some sort. A second concern relates to the shift from elite education as recently as twenty or thirty years ago to mass or even universal education now. Thirty years ago, perhaps 10 to 20 percent of eighteen-year olds went on to college in most states; now 40 to 60 percent do. And, because college is usually the only route to upper-middle class status, a lot more voters are concerned about what goes on than before.

The state university or college provides something that the state wants—a type of education that has a high payout to residents and states. The university often provides valuable research (for example, in agriculture). But the problems and conflicts that arise between universities and their main sponsors originate in concerns about how much these outputs cost and how well the right kinds of things are being done. In short, there is goal divergence between the parties. This is what most of the discussion about universities and their financial needs is about most of the time. When a university shows signs of diverging too much, the state tends to try to pull it back to correct attitudes.

Table 8 suggests common major goal system discrepancies between state multiversity administrators and professors—assuming they are in basic agreement—and their external clienteles. Nine of the ten goals presented earlier in the taxonomy of environmental constraints are used for illustrative purposes. The things university personnel consider critical are often of less concern to outsiders, and the result is constant antagonism. If the multiversity is like the old elitist Ivy League schools with very large endowments and such deviations get too big, trouble is usually certain.

Because goal divergencies are important, top administrators spend a lot of time plastering over and buffering this key interface. One can usually forecast quite accurately what the president will be saying to outsiders the week after some particularly nasty incident involving goal divergence. He will point to the kinds of research that have created twenty thousand jobs in the state; he will note how well farmers or various industries are doing as a result of the university's efforts; and he will point to some all-American fullback who just happens to be a Rhodes Scholar as well. And of course he will note how badly the university needs more funds to continue the vast, important works in process.

If goal divergence continues and is perceived to be a major danger, the state can retaliate in a variety of ways. The following list of pressure-response patterns suggests ways that university administrations can counter such problems.

External Pressure	*University Response*
(1) Cut cash	Try to find new sponsors; raise fees

(2) Pass new laws	Lobby against; if passed, passive resistance, short-term; sabotage efforts wherever possible
(3) Do not send students	Change curriculum; beef up internal professional staff; push for more cash to do this; coalition with similar unfortunate schools
(4) Discredit	Do (3), with even more intensity
(5) Do not hire graduates	Beef up placement; shift curricula to match needs
(6) Harrass university personnel	Back-room agreement; legal response (through AAUP); change rules
(7) Use public relations pressure	Counter public relations pressure
(8) Do not buy research	Beef up internal professional staff and facilities; actively seek new clients

The state normally resorts only to items (1) and (2) in this list; items (3) through (8) are done by other outsiders. Academic goals will probably never correspond very precisely to state goals. Yet the university is far too important to destroy—it provides the state with needed services. The state can only pressure academics and hope that something useful will happen. The top manager or administrator thus is faced with a perpetual problem—what his organization wants to do and feels is important is often seen as wrong by his major sponsors. But his strategy, as suggested by the above list, is relatively clear-cut.

First, some money and talent must be put into high priority state goals. Study of Table 8 suggests that many state goals can be achieved rather cheaply. Thus, business and various other vocationally oriented or applied schools do not require as much cash as many other programs, particularly at the undergraduate level; good coaches and recruiters can win football games and, with luck, break even financially; and medical research is one of the easiest areas to find support for. Small incremental expenditures in key areas, when properly supported by good public relations work, can pay big dividends.

Table 8.
GOAL DIVERGENCE: SUGGESTED RANK ORDERINGS

Rank	State Multiversity	Professional Accrediting Agencies	Parents, Alumni	Federal Government	State Government	Manpower Users
1	Protect professors and faculty benefits	Graduate education	Jobs for graduates	Research, especially applied	Jobs for graduates	Applied undergraduate education
2	Research	Protect professors and faculty benefits of the professional school	Cultural assimilation	Graduate education	Cultural assimilation	Applied graduate education
3	Graduate education	Undergraduate education	Undergraduate education	Jobs and status for graduates	Undergraduate education	Public service
4	Undergraduate education	Research	Athletics	Undergraduate education	Graduate education	Research
5	Truth	Truth	Graduate education	Public service	Athletics	Cultural assimilation
6	Cultural assimilation		Public service	Cultural assimilation	Research	
7	Public service			Protect professors and faculty benefits	Public service	
8	Jobs for graduates				Protect professors and faculty benefits	
9	Athletics				Truth	

Second, talk a lot outside the university about goals that coincide with those of outsiders. It is possible to stress things that seem to matter on the outside. Any multiversity, or even a good state college, can show all sorts of good things going on, given a bit of imagination.

Third, use the university information system to buffer these goal discrepancies. In earlier chapters we have already suggested the potential power of information systems, and they can be very useful here. There are any number of good channels to use in presenting useful information about what the university is doing. Everyone has to be selective in information receptivity, so the trick here is to maximize the desirable information people receive. Good news is more effective when presented on the six or eleven o'clock TV news than in an obscure academic journal. An imaginative public relations staff can sometimes pull such things off—which suggests how valuable it can be to a university administration.

The really prestigious private universities and colleges may have fewer goal divergence problems, which is a major reason why many of the best universities are private. Note that *best* here is an academic evaluation; that is, it corresponds to the goal system for academics noted in Table 8. Because private schools have different fund sources and a different policy-making framework than public schools, they often can do things that public schools find difficult to achieve. Hence, high-level doctoral programs and esoteric theoretical research, for example, often come from private rather than public schools. The clients of such schools, along with sponsors, tend to expect something quite different than do the sponsors of state institutions. Indeed, most of the prestigious state multiversities achieved greatness in spite of, rather than because of, their legal status.

Federal Government. Universities and colleges are high-skill labor-intensive, which these days means that they are very costly to operate. As institutions of higher education have moved from the periphery of society to the center, and the numbers and percentages of young persons in college have grown, fund sources have been falling steadily behind. Traditional fund sources were gifts and states; since World War II, the federal government has been increasingly supporting both public and private schools. Federal support seems very appealing at the outset, because our tax structure generates lots of funds at the federal level while states have difficulties increasing their tax share. If some of these federal funds could be passed on to universities, lots of problems would be resolved. Federal officials might be more willing to provide funds with fewer strings attached. The ideal source of funds, from a university administration's point of view, would be cash from a donor who has no say in how it is to be spent. Such funds are rare, and the federal government is one of the more likely sources of such support.

Moreover, even if federal funds do have some strings, federal donors are more likely than private or state donors to take a global view of what is important. A suspicious state legislature may not be too keen to support a Latin American studies program, or study of esoteric languages rarely spoken or used in his state, but from the national point of view such programs might seem very useful. Science students who tend to leave their own states to work in California, Illinois, or New York may not really be supported locally, but supported by federal authorities.

Because most large universities see themselves as a part of the world and the nation, not the state, and because their prestige depends largely on programs not too relevant to the particular states they are in, the possibility of donors with a global view is indeed attractive. Given these possibilities, it is not surprising that virtually all large schools have looked very closely at the possibilities for obtaining federal funds.

Consideration of the federal goal column in Table 7 may suggest why most schools like federal funds. The federal goal system, in regard to higher education, tends to be more meshed with the goal systems of university administrators and faculty than do the goal systems of states. As a result, tied federal funds are more palatable than tied state funds. A major gain here is that the federal government, in all its many and complex branches, tends to buy research of all sorts, and professionals like research. The desired research may not be exactly what a professor would do on his own, but at least it is better than teaching all of those dreary freshmen.

One major drawback of much federal funding is that much of it must be distributed along political rather than merit lines. This is not true when the federal government wants something important, such as new rocket or atomic research. For this, only the best schools need apply. The *best* are the schools that historically have had the best natural science, engineering, and atomic research capacities.

Local Government. Local government normally is not too directly involved in university problems. There still are many municipal colleges and universities, and much of what was said about state government problems applies to local governments. However, local governments have had severe tax and revenue problems, and in recent years many excellent municipal schools have become state-supported institutions. The trend here is toward obtaining support from the governmental unit that has the best taxing power.

Professional Constraints. This environmental set refers to all the external constraints that affect the educational functions of university or college. The most important of these are the various certification processes, although other universities and colleges also have some direct effect on any school. Certification is done by many organizations for many purposes. Some accreditation is for the university generally, to achieve quality control. That is, if a university is certified, its degrees and courses are accepted by other members of the accrediting group. Students transferring or going on to graduate work can transfer work. Some certifications are for specific programs, such as business, medicine, or law, and the certifying group is an association in the relevant field.

The usual certification routine looks occasionally at the types of programs offered, the caliber and quality of faculty, types of relevant facilities, and so on. Decertification can be a powerful tool —so powerful that it is rarely used. If students cannot transfer their work, a school is in deep trouble. Typically even the veiled threat of a major decertification is enough to make administrators move quickly to remove alleged deficiencies.

In addition to providing quality control, certification has several other important effects on universities and colleges. One major one is to raise costs. If more professors need advanced degrees, or if natural science programs need more laboratory facilities, costs go up. Administrators can use these requirements as a weapon in dealing with major financial sponsors.

Certification requirements also provide minimum standards

for administrators to follow. Often specific minima are set for given items—for example, the percentage of the faculty with terminal degrees. This provides a target to exceed or equal and is used to reinforce the judgments of university decision-makers.

Table 8 shows the typical goal system of a certifying group. Not surprisingly, this goal system corresponds rather closely to the university's, because most certifiers are academically oriented. Rarely is there overt conflict between the certifiers and the schools, although much discussion may take place when a university falls below some stated minimal standards in one area. Administrators argue that such a failure to meet standards really does not matter much, and besides, they are about to correct the situation. The threat of failure to be accredited can be a very useful weapon to use for getting funds from the state legislature. But because the certifiers and the schools tend to want the same things, agreement here is easy. The hard part is getting enough resources to meet the minimal standards.

Certifying groups perform a valuable national function. Without such groups, it would be very difficult to rate universities, and it would be very easy to cut corners in areas that specific administrators see as not too important. But steady national or regional pressure toward minimal standards can only benefit faculty and students alike.

Most certification necessarily focuses on minimal, not optimal, performance. It may protect marginal schools, but it cannot make them good schools. To achieve greatness (as defined by academics), certification is not enough.

Parents and Alumni. Table 8 shows the general goal system of this group relative to the university's internal goals system. There are some potential areas of direct conflict here. And there are plenty of examples of difficulties, but they often seem much more important at the time than they prove to be in retrospect. However, this group tends to support the university more than some others because parents and alumni are getting quite a bit out of it. The university is where one now goes to get plugged into our class and status system. Parents may be alarmed about some of the wild things going on, but there may be no better way to get a higher education at present. About the only thing one can do is send kids someplace else. Public schools rarely get so far away from this support group that they lose more than a limited number of students. The problem for many expensive private schools is often more severe.

Administrators will spend quite a lot of time with influential, wealthy alumni (always a tiny minority), who may have very firm ideas about reform. They also have money to give, and that makes them worth listening to. But any clever administrator can usually handle such problems—the easiest way is to get the alumnus down to see for himself. Most students are quite nice and stable, and so this technique often works well—it can even lead to a new library wing or business school building with a nice bronze plaque on the door. Very active alumni often do spend much time around the campus, and they often have a much better idea of what is really going on than do outsiders who only read the newspapers and watch TV. Unless the school is really hopeless, administrators often find some firm support from this quarter.

Manpower Users. This set includes all of the organizations that use college-trained people. It is a diverse group, including all the professions and organizations that feel that college training is useful to future employees—and are willing to pay for this belief. To date, there has been relatively little pressure from this group, although this does not mean that there are no serious problems. There always is some group that wants to avoid training costs by using university funds and powers, and administrators soon get adept at avoiding such horrors as welding classes and baking management.

But many users—particularly those interested in professional schools—have interests relatively compatible with those of the university. Thus, medical doctors are very interestetd in high quality, as presumably the university also is. Young persons trained in the natural sciences have pretty clear ideas about what kinds of training will qualify them, and both universities and users want such training to be as good as possible. Most professional schools work closely with users in figuring out what is needed for new entrants to the profession.

Here is where colleges are getting into major difficulty with all their sponsors, however. Over the past twenty-five years, our major multiversities and other schools have shifted from elite to mass and new universal education. Instead of dealing with a small group of upper middle-class students who would have gotten ahead in any case, they now deal with the upper half of all young persons. And because they do, the pseudocorrelation of success and college attendance is breaking down. No longer does merely going to college guarantee a good, safe, and interesting job. Young graduates find, to their dismay, that they cannot even get jobs, let alone good ones. This is most true among the not quite good enough students from not quite good enough schools, but the problem is spreading. Demographic factors in the 1970s are creating further pressure here—the percentage of young people in the total population is greater than it was in the 1950s, or will be in the 1980s. The child boom of the 1950s and 1960s is at or approaching university age.

Because this was not an important problem in the past, no one worried much about what graduates (or dropouts) did. Now, schools will have to worry, because few outsiders will support an expensive educational process that does not lead to what is commonly considered productivity. Universities and colleges will have to produce economic payout. Most academics were educated in a more elitist atmosphere, and most would disagree, but it does not matter. They will change, or else.

Professional schools at all levels are much better equipped to handle this problem than are more general programs. The mark of a good professional school has always been its ability to place students within the profession in the best possible jobs. It is interesting to check job placement records within any big university. The schools of business, law, medicine, and education will frequently know where their recent graduates are and what they are doing. The philosophy, history, and English departments typically do not know and do not care. If external clienteles demand results, one can confidently predict that history, philosophy, and English will change their ways, or many of these departments will disappear. It is as simple as that.

Uniqueness of Goal Deviation

Academic institutions, almost alone among major institutions, are characterized by having significant goal deviations from their major supporters. This is particularly true of state schools.

Other kinds of organizations tend to be stuck with the goal system their major supporters want. We rarely find, as one example, employees or managers of a business corporation saying publicly that the board of directors or the stockholders are wrong; such a person would not last long. But influential faculty members make such comments almost daily. However, professors have tenure, and goal systems as seen by university insiders can be very different from goal systems seen by major supporters. The whole academic tradition leads to goals that others find obscure, ridiculous, or just plain wrong. Yet outsiders are somewhat reluctant to push a university down a chosen path. That somehow is dangerous.

So the tension continues, and the university administrator is caught in the middle. His position is doubly precarious, because he typically is an academic. If he tries to shove his staff in an unpopular direction, the situation can get very rough. He can easily become an outsider to his own faculty, which in practice means being cut off from information, formal and informal, to the point where he may be unable to operate. But if he fails to act on at least some of the pressures from outside, he may be asked to resign. It's a tough life, and it may get worse. There is ample evidence that outside supporters of universities are beginning to demand changes in internal goal structures. If the university refuses to move in directions financial supporters consider proper, funds will be cut. They already have been in many states. Moreover, the kinds of schools (such as junior colleges) that do mesh with both perceived and preferred external goal systems will get the money to expand, while funds for more traditional universities will be cut. This also has happened, and will continue to happen, in many states.

It is not fun to be known as the administrator who was in charge when the system came unstuck. And it is not fun to be caught in the middle of a fight about what is to be done when faculty, students, the state legislature, and others have strong and quite divergent views. But this is the basic plight of the senior university manager or administrator in the 1970s. There is no way to escape, because the financial resources required to play the game in the old way are so large as to make a "do it the old way" strategy impossible. Academic goal systems will have to be restructured, and this means changing professors. This group of intelligent, articulate people are about the hardest group to change in all society.

Academic institutions are now mass institutions, and they are very important to lots of outsiders. But internal goal systems have not changed much yet. Professors and other professionals still want their universities to reflect their values and judgments; they face, through historic accident, financial supporters who have quite different ideas about what an academic institution should be. Conflict is certain, and the top administrators and managers are stuck with the problem of plastering up these key interfaces as best they can.

There is no possibility that this particular conflict will be resolved easily or quickly. Schools that give in and follow overall goal systems preferred by state governments or others are soon seen as second- or third-rate by those in the profession. Since you have to get professionals to cooperate with you to make the place go, it is not likely that good schools will move in this direction readily.

This problem is also complicated by the Baumol crunch, which involves very rapidly increasing university costs. When universities were relatively cheap, it did not matter much what they did or how their goals diverged. But now they are costly, and goal divergence has become very significant. Unless universities fall in line with their financial backers, many will be in deep trouble soon.

There is no easy way out for any manager or administrator here. Some academic institutions may become unmanageable, because the goal systems of insiders and supporters are so divergent that no compromise is possible. In such situations the outsiders can win—but the cost will be the destruction of the university as we have known it. We may see much of this in the next decade, and if we do, many administrators will be in very difficult personal positions. However, there are many ways that effective management and leadership can avert such disaster or extreme consequences. Some have already been suggested, and many more will be discussed in the following chapters.

Chapter IX

View from the Top

This chapter focuses on managerial issues involving university boards, the presidency, and senior management. We use the terms *trustees, regents,* and *governors* with regard to boards synonymously unless otherwise noted. We also use the term *president* synonymously with *chief executive officer, chancellor,* and *principal.* He or she is the top administrative official of a given university or college. Some multicampus state universities have presidents at one level and chancellors and vice-chancellors at another. Governing boards—in theory at least—have the ultimate authority and legal responsibility for the financial and administrative affairs of the university. In reality, the degree of involvement of such boards in actual decision-making and in the affairs of the university varies widely among institutions.

Boards

Trustees are more conservative than their faculties and students. They are typically establishment types—affluent, elderly, and leaders of business and industry. In recent years an increasing number of women, students, members of minority groups, community citizens, and other nonestablishment people have been appointed or elected to the boards of colleges and universities. In general, such boards and their memberships are often probably better than the educational institutions deserve, given the selection process and the other activities and full-time jobs that their board members are involved in (Hartnett, 1969, 1970; Rauh, 1969; Perkins, 1973; Hartnett, 1971; McGrath, 1971). Most—but far from all—board members tend to do their homework, or at least enough to keep the place going.

Desire for status, prestige, publicity, and power, as well as business and social contacts—and possibly political aspirations—are important factors motivating people to become university or college trustees. However, dedication to the institution and a desire to do a genuine and effective public service are also motivating forces. If the board members actually understand, accept, and basically support the goals and key priorities of the institution, they are even more inclined to do a truly dedicated and effective job.

Types. Some boards are totally or primarily self-perpetuating. The board members select their own successors within various rules and procedures set forth in the institution's charter or constitution. These are usually private universities, but in some cases this is the pattern in state or public institutions, or at least in those that obtain much of their financing from the government. The membership of this kind of board is often rather homogeneous in their values. Where the institution has limited and clear-cut goals that remain relatively stable over time—for example, private religious schools, military colleges, or at colleges strongly espousing a certain idealogical viewpoint—this type of board can prove effective and can function with relatively little internal conflict. If the institution is well endowed, or otherwise has a good deal of money for what it wants to do, this makes the board's—as well as the administration's—job that much easier. As long as the institution can maintain its comfortable place in higher education, things go smoothly.

Some self-perpetuating boards try to have fairly diverse representation among their members. This can be healthy if the institution is striving to achieve a set of diverse goals or if it is attempting to redefine its goals and priorities and redirect efforts to achieve them. However, if a university is confronted with serious financial problems, there can be significant conflicts within the board. Conflicts are also likely if the board selects, as a compromise candidate, a rather ineffective board chairman. This is also often true with the choice of a president.

Another type of board is one where a majority, if not all, of its members are government appointees. This can lead to much conflict and to institutional instability over time, especially if each election brings in some new political leaders and key government officials whose views about higher education differ from those of their predecessors—or even if those who remain in power change some of their own basic views because of political pressures and realities. This kind of board is more likely to become politicized and polarized.

It is quite common to have a majority of board positions filled by ex-officio appointments. Here various government officials, the heads of certain organizations (like the Mechanics Institute in California), the head of the university's alumni association, certain university officials, and individuals holding other specific jobs are automatically appointed to the board. If the members of such a board have diverse views about higher education and this particular institution's goals, and the institution is confronted by serious financial constraints, there can be considerable conflict. It may be possible to reach a workable compromise on key goals and priorities at a given point in time, but if and when some influential members are replaced by other strong-minded people with different views, the conflicts may well resume again.

If the institution is big enough to sustain a wide range of diverse goals—to perform at least some part of all the functions its board members and major constituencies want it to perform—even when it is confronted with significant financial problems, the conflict and instability are not likely to be as acute. And if a board is responsible for the entire system of higher education in a state rather than for only one college or university campus it is also more likely to perform a range of functions and thus reduce the possibility of conflict. If it is responsible for a number of campuses of a multi-campus university—but not the whole system—it is somewhere in between. However, if a board is responsible for the whole system or a greater part of it, and a homogenous group dominates the board, this kind of concentration of power might be damaging to all higher education in the state over time.

Another kind of board is characterized by having many of its members elected by various constituencies such as alumni, students, the faculty or academic senate, and even the public at large. This is quite common among both public and private universities. It is usually found in combination with ex officio appointments, some self-perpetuating membership, and—in the case of state universities—some government or political appointments. This is the most democratic kind of board because it represents diverse constituences. However, the members of such a board will have diverse views regarding the goals and priorities of the institution.

Here, too, less serious conflict is likely. The board's job is easier if the institution is large and can generate enough resources over time to pursue a range of diverse goals in a sufficiently efficient and effective manner. This means a large enough endowment or sufficient revenues generated from contributions, fund-raising, fees, government allocations, and research grants. If resources are not abundant, limited goals and priorities will have to be pursued and a coalition of the most influential and powerful board members will determine what they should be. If the board chairman is strong and respected, he will—and should—have a big voice. Similarly, if the president is a powerful and respected individual, he could play the most critical role in this process, and this would be the healthiest situation under such conditions. The wise academic manager will take into account which of the above conditions are relevant to his institution, and will then develop appropriate plans and strategies. This calls for a contingency approach.

Institutional Goals. It is impossible to overstate how important it is for board members to both know and accept the goals and priorities of the university, especially in times of crisis. At least the most influential and active board members, including the chairman, should understand and clearly support the institution's goals. If the goals and priorities are not clearly defined and adequately understood, the result is likely to be that much unproductive time will be spent talking around the major issues, and the board will have serious problems selecting a proper president and other key administrators.

If the institution is confronted with very serious financial and other problems, the board can play a key role in redefining goals and priorities and redirecting efforts in ways that will make the university more viable and effective. It can help the university achieve a better fit with its major constituencies, its external environment, and the broader society. The board can assist in determining what niche the university can best fill and what kinds of related markets the university can best serve, given its strengths, limitations, and potential. Once the board, or at least its key members, understand and are committed to the institution's goals and priorities, it can attract and maintain members who would, and could, effectively sell the university externally and support it internally. This includes assistance in getting financial resources for the institution.

Any university or college can usually pursue some new programs that would increase its viability and prestige, result in increased board support, and enable it to attract and keep effective board members. These may include such programs as external degrees; extension and other part-time adult degrees and non-degrees; specially tailored and accelerated courses for practitioners, professionals, and semiprofessionals; correspondence courses; classes conducted for organizations; part-time classes during the day and at night for mothers and senior citizens; work-study classes; year-round operations; student internships; classes in fields where critical manpower shortages exist and are likely to continue; applied and vocational training; and research directly related to major problems in society.

Few universities can successfully emulate Harvard or the University of California, and therefore they must be selective in their goals and priorities. They can serve selected markets effectively and in this way create viable niches in higher education, serve society, and achieve prestige for themselves and their board members. This course of action calls for a contingency approach and goal systems; choices should be based on institutional strengths, existing and potential competitive advantages, and a realistic assessment of resource availability.

Chairman. The board chairman is more often than not the key individual who sets the tone of the board. If he is clearly dedicated to the university and committed to its goals, he can create greater dedication and commitment among other members. If he is also an effective and respected leader and manager, conflicts will tend to be less acute, and workable compromises will be achieved where this is the only feasible alternative.

The chairman cannot expect all board members to be interested in and to keep up with all board activities and concerns. He should make sure that individual members are given assignments—individually—through subcommittee appointments or on special task forces that are in line with their particular interests, knowledge, and expertise. For example, some may be most interested in finances, other in physical facilities, some in particular kinds of educational programs, and others in personnel matters.

It is of utmost importance that the board chairman and the president or chief executive officer trust and respect each other. Even though they will have disagreements, they should have an open relationship, communicate regularly, effectively and honestly, and have the same basic understanding of the university's goals and priorities. In a state university, it is valuable if the chairman gets along well with the key politicians and government officials who deal with the university; but it is even more important that he have a good relationship with the chief executive. The chairman should keep the president directly informed about any relevant information he gets from board members—or other parties—about the president, and the president should keep the chairman informed about all matters of direct interest to the board.

The Board and the President. At many universities there is a tendency for the board to become captives of the information system of the central administration. Time lags and poorly designed and inadequately functioning information systems contribute to this situation. It is therefore critical to find a president who is both capable and honest in his communications. The board should be prepared to support the president—at least publicly—during crises and to defend his budget requests when they are well documented, legitimate, and tie in realistically with the institution's goals and priorities. When the chairman or a majority of the board members feel they can no longer support the president on a growing number of major issues, this is usually a clear signal for them to replace the president or resign from the board.

Evaluating how good a job the president is doing is frequently not an easy task. Some quantitative or hard data are needed for this, as well as much qualitative data and judgment. An analysis should be made to see whether the institution is doing a good job in meeting the key goals and priorities that are defined and accepted by both the board and the administration. It is usually best to make such an evaluation annually but within the framework of a longer-range plan. Are the new programs on target and reaping the desired results? Is student recruiting and placement going according to plan? Are costs being kept in line? Is the university losing a significant number of good people? How is it doing with regard to research grants, quality, and output?

It is also very useful, where possible, to evaluate the institution in a relative way by comparing its performance to those of other institutions—or parts of them—that are adequately comparable. If this is a multicampus or multicollege entity, useful comparisons might be made within the system. Such things as expenditures in relation to revenues, student-faculty ratios, course and departmental loadings, student contact hours, cost per student, quality of students and faculty, salaries, the jobs graduates get and their career advancement, and costs of similar kinds of programs can be used for evaluating performance. However, problems of measurement and true comparability often limit the meaningfulness of such comparisons, and many qualitative factors and considerable judgment judgment often must be used in conjunction with quantitative or hard data.

The board should be aware of symptoms that indicate that the president and his staff may not be doing an effective job and that the institution may be heading for real trouble. These are really process items rather than a direct analysis of goal performance, but in time they are likely to have an adverse impact on goals and priorities. If administrators under the president, or students, staff, and faculty members frequently bypass the president and go directly to the chairman or various other board members with what they perceive as significant problems, this can indicate that the president is not functioning very effectively. On the other hand, the chairman or other board members should not normally bypass the president in seeking out information or investigating problems from people at the lower levels, unless the president is aware that this is happening. If board members do this, or if someone volunteers sensitive information, the president should be kept informed of anything critical that evolves. Similarly, other board members should keep the chairman informed about critical information that they might get through informal channels.

If the board receives deficient, inaccurate, or incomplete information on important matters from the administration more than rarely, this is often another trouble symptom. Fairly widespread student, staff, or faculty dissent and opposition to the central administration, in any of various forms, can be important indicators that the president is not doing his job properly. A significant number of complaints from people outside of the university about the university, as well as unfavorable media publicity, can also be critical symptoms, especially if much of this negative feedback turns out to be justified. Frequent and serious crises within the university or college are sure signs that something is wrong in the administration. Often a leadership or managerial crisis is considerably more damaging to the university than a financial crisis. The former can make the latter much more acute than it need be.

Activities. The board should play a major role in defining and, if necessary, redefining, the major goals and priorities of the university. However, it cannot impose these on the institution unless the president and a clear majority of other key administrators also accept and support them. It is up to the president and his administration to get adequate acceptance of the goals and priorities from the faculties, students, and other internal constituences. A determination of the goals and priorities should be accomplished through a democratic process that takes into account the interests, needs, capabilities, and limitations of these constituencies. Total consensus and unanimous agreement is indeed rare at universities, and it is the responsibility of the president—not of the board—to achieve a workable internal concensus on goals and priorities through effective management and leadership.

The board approves the overall university budget. If it has confidence in the central administration, the board will usually only be concerned about the global figures and broad budget categories, and will not examine the budget in detail. It may also approve major shifts in sources and uses of funds, major new programs, new schools and faculties, and important decisions involving facilities and the location of activities. The board should also approve targets for external financial support and should help to achieve them in whatever legitimate ways it can. If the institution is state supported and the government's funding formula and allocations have serious flaws that lead to unstable university operations, the board should work to get a more feasible formula. If the board is working with salable institutional goals and priorities, it will be in a better position to help deliver the desired funds and resources. The board can do much, both informally and formally, in the sphere of public and external relations through the numerous contacts of its members.

The board approves the appointment and, if necessary, the dismissal of the president. It should be given the opportunity to voice its opinion on other senior administrative appointments and to raise questions about them. But the president should really make these staffing decisions. The same should be true of faculty tenure and promotions. The board may have an inherent veto in such personnel matters if enough of them raise serious objections; but normally this is just rubber-stamp approval if the president has the board's confidence. On the other hand, the president can use the board to get him off the hook when he wants to make a negative personnel decision that would lead to an outcry from various quarters internally.

The president should be able to use the board as a whole (or any of its members) as a sounding board and in an advisory capacity on any subject. He should not, however, get them involved in or concerned with detail and trivia, or his own image may deteriorate. Board members should be encouraged to put forth their suggestions and initiate new ideas, and the president should make sure that these ideas are responded to appropriately.

Pressures on board members come more from sources external than internal to the university. Board members are asked to assure adequate financial resources, and they must cope with political problems, public antipathy, and nitty gritty items like letters from concerned parents and nuts. Even if the university is being run by an effective president and competent administration, there will always be some kinds of external pressures and problems involving the board.

The administration should always be kept informed about sticky public relations problems that come to the attention of board members first. The president and his staff should normally make official public statements on behalf of the institution. Whenever possible, board members should avoid making statements that are not in line with what the president or his deputies have been saying. If such a statement cannot be avoided, the president should be informed about it before it hits the public. Generally, it is best to thrash out such disagreements privately.

Choosing a President or Chief Executive

It seems that the position of president or chief executive is up for grabs at 10 percent or more of all North American universities. Recent estimates reveal that there have been about three hundred colleges and universities in the United States—out of a total of around two thousand six hundred—looking for a chief executive. Quite a few schools have been operating with acting presidents. In the past key administrators in higher education tended to be quite immobile, staying in their jobs forever, and faculty members used to change jobs frequently. Now the reverse seems to be true. The end of the big boom in higher education, overcapacity, limited resources for growth, less research money, greater competition, more emphasis on costs, growing problems involving relevancy, major conflicts and confusion over goals and priorities, and the shortage of well-trained, first-rate academic administrators and managers are among the chief reasons for this dramatic change.

There are few if any universal policies or guidelines applicable to the choice of a university or college president. A contingency approach is needed; and this relates to a number of conditions, several of which are considered below. A basic issue involving the selection of a chief executive—or any important manager—is whether the individual should be selected on his ability to fill a predetermined job or the job should be designed to fit and suit the individual. Often a balance or blend is best, especially in high-level and other key jobs. Below, we outline some basic guidelines for choosing a university president, recognizing fully that no gods are available. However, many boards, search committees, and faculty members still do not seem to be convinced of this (Bennis, 1973; Cohen and March, 1974).

If goals and priorities are reasonably clear, things are going smoothly and are expected to continue doing so, a competent administration is in place, weight should be given to finding the most suitable person for a largely predetermined job. In other words, the chief executive should have specified qualifications if things are not expected to change dramatically in the foreseeable future. The candidate may be external or internal; but internal selection may prove more feasible because the person chosen would probably already be familiar with the institution's goals and priorities, operations, personalities, and problems. And there would be less chance of ending up with a poor fit. If an adequate consensus cannot be reached about the choice of an internal candidate, it may be best to look elsewhere. In any event, it may be wise to have the incoming president work with the outgoing one as an apprentice for a period of time.

At the other extreme, some universities and colleges are confronted with very serious financial problems, major deficiencies in the existing administration, and unclear or ineffective goals and priorities. Here it may be best to try and find a president who has good and creative—but realistic—ideas about what the university's goals and priorities should be and how it should be managed and led, and what seems to have the capability, know-how, and talent to deliver. This would mean building much of the job around the man. If there is a solid enough consensus among board members and the other major constituencies that a certain individual fills this kind of bill, he should be selected and given considerable leeway in designing and carrying out his job. This may even mean letting him make a number of new administrative appointments and personnel changes. It is important, however, for the board to set up some strategic standards for evaluation of the new chief executive's performance. Under this set of circumstances, this kind of individual is likely to be chosen from the outside, and he is likely to be much more of an entrepreneur than the first type.

Probably the most common set of conditions falls somewhere between the above two extremes. Some goals and priorities should be taken as given by the new president, while he defines some new directions, priorities, and programs. He may make a limited number of administrative and personnel changes, but much of the system will remain intact. This kind of individual may be either an internal or external candidate. However, going outside is more costly, because of the extensive search and travel expenses and also because an outsider who is selected is likely to be in a stronger bargaining position.

If the choice of a particular internal candidate as president is likely to result in much internal conflict, it is usually wise to find a suitable and more widely acceptable external candidate instead. And it is usually better to go outside than to appoint a compromise internal candidate who does not really have the qualifications for the job. It is also better to appoint an acting chief executive than to move too hastily and fill the job with a permanent compromise candidate who is clearly not adequately qualified. Usually an acting chief executive will be selected from inside the university. In some cases this kind of person turns out much better than expected in his acting capacity and may become the regular president. It is usually less feasible with an outside candidate to use the acting route as a test for permanency. If a candidate is really good, he will probably be reluctant to come in on an acting basis.

If a university is undergoing a severe crisis—especially in its leadership—the board may have no choice but to appoint an acting president quickly, and under some circumstances he may have to be an outsider. If a major hatchet job and much cost cutting must be done quickly for survival, an outsider may be the only feasible alternative. Or the board may choose to set up some kind of interim top management committee or trusteeship to run the institution.

Because there are so many unfilled university and college presidencies, a given institution may have to appoint someone with an unproven record in high-level university management. Depending on the key goals and priorities of the institution, a top scholar with at least some administrative experience may prove to be a good choice, especially if he has a competent supporting administrative staff. A proven leader from government, from a profession like law or medicine, or from the private sector may be a wise choice, providing that his attitudes, values, interests, and expertise fit reasonably well with the goals, priorities, and basic operations of the university. Such a president should have much contact with the academic side of the institution, to get tuned in to significant differences with his previous experience.

An individual who has not been very successful as a high-level or top-level manager at his own academic institution might prove to be effective at another university or college. His previous lack of success may have been primarily due to conflicts between his own values, attitudes, and desired goals and priorities for the university and those of various other powerful constituencies—including perhaps the board—rather than because of inadequecy in managerial skill or basic leadership ability. If there seems to be a much better fit at your institution, he may well be a good man for the job.

The successful university or college president usually has, as a minimum, the following basic qualifications: He or she is cool-headed and a good negotiator; communicates effectively both orally and in writing; consults quite widely with different constituencies and uses two-way communication; has the critical information at hand when needed; is an effective organizer and chooses competent deputies; has a democratic rather than an authoritarian leadership style, but can be tough and make sensitive or critical decisions when necessary; backs up decisions with well thought out explanations and meaningful documentation when necessary; is a good planner and follows through with effective controls; and has tremendous energy.

The board has the final approval over the selection of the

chief executive. As a minimum, the board should consult widely and sincerely with representatives of all the major constituencies that are related to the university on the choice of a president. Both formal and informal channels can be used for this purpose. Long lists of names can be compiled, and once the choice is narrowed down to a small number, appropriate constituency representatives should have the opportunity to meet with all of the candidates brought in for interviews and negotiations. They should then be given a chance to state and explain their preferences.

It may be wise for the board to set up a special search committee for selecting a new president. Some of its members could be elected representatives of their constituencies (for example, faculty or senate and student representatives), while others might serve in either an ex officio capacity or be appointed by the board. Such a committee would be advisory to the board, with the board making the final decision; but the committees view should be seriously considered by the board.

It is very unlikely that everyone connected with the institution will be happy with the board's choice. However, if the board has consulted effectively and has sound reasons for its choice, there is much less chance of severe repercussions. Where serious conflicts do arise between the board and major constituencies (or among various board members) some resignations may be inevitable.

In order for a university to get a truly outstanding—or even a first-rate—new chief executive these days, it may be necessary for the board to meet some rather tough conditions beyond the individual's salary and other requirements. The appointment may involve a clear mandate to make major changes, and even a guarantee from the board that it is willing to go along with a sizable deficit for some time or with a decision to clear up the existing deficit and bring in a sizable amount of new funds. More academic institutions are now appointing chief executives on the basis of fixed term contracts. This tends to be a wise policy, especially in a rapidly changing environment.

President and Central Administration

In times of crisis in particular, the chief executive's job at a university is often a very lonely and frustrating one (Cohen and March, 1974; Ritchie, 1970). He typically has no direct major constituency, except his personal staff, to give him positive feedback, comfort, and support. An effective dean or department chairman is likely to have at least most of his own faculty supporting him. But the chief executive is likely to spend much, probably most, of his time ironing out conflicts and seeking workable compromises among various constituencies that are fighting for scarce resources and their own particular interests. With this kind of job, positive feedback is often a rarity.

An integral part of the president's job should involve defining, redefining, supporting, and implementing the goals, priorities, and changing programs of the institution. This requires much consultation, a two-way communication, follow-up, and leadership. Moreover, reward and information systems of various types must be designed and utilized in support of the goals and priorities if they are to be achieved. Scarce resources should be allocated and utilized efficiently and effectively, and this gets at the heart of the budgeting process, which is very time consuming.

It is wise for the president not to make private deals behind closed doors with deans and other constituencies regarding the budget and resource allocations, especially in times of financial stringency. Major budget allocations should be determined in an open meeting of the major constituency leaders or of managers in some kind of president's council or committee. This enables the appropriate representatives to give all of the reasons and evidence bearing on their requests, and the president can explain openly the reasons for his decisions.

This kind of forum can also be used to get the weaker—in terms of their revenue generation and the market test—parts of the university to realize that their viability, interests, and goal attainment are directly dependent on allowing the stronger parts to get adequate resources and grow even stronger, where this is possible and in line with the more critical goals and priorities of the university. In other words, the stronger faculties can, in effect, subsidize the weaker parts and make it possible for them to survive. For example, by allowing the management school or the new environmental studies program to flourish and grow because the demand and opportunity is there, it may be possible for the Albanian classics or medieval history department to survive.

The president should usually be willing to make use of a

variety of committees and task forces involving faculty and possibly even student representation for such things as the budget, tenure and promotions, new programs, educational innovation, interdisciplinary purposes, and the like. Some of these groups might be given decision-making powers, but usually they should be advisory to the president or his line executives or used primarily for informational or co-ordination purposes. If the line executives abdicate their powers and responsibilities for making the final decisions on important admin-istrative and financial matters, the institution is likely to be heading for trouble, especially in periods of financial stringency and cutbacks. On the other hand, the president and his key executives run a serious risk if they more often than not ignore the recommendations given to them by the appropriate advisory or other committees. On occasion the president may set up a committee primarily to buy some time on a problem. This may be wise, but if overdone could create antagonism.

Purely academic matters, such as approval of new courses and relatively minor curriculum changes, can and normally should be within the jurisdiction of the academic senate or faculty council and it, or its various committees, can make the final decisions. These are typically decisions that do not require significant additional costs or resources. Similarly, the faculty through its various bodies and committees can play a central role in determining procedures, criteria, and regulations involving tenure appointments, promotions, and dismissals. However, the central administration should deter-mine the total amount of funds available for faculty advancement and compensation. It is critical for the president to maintain a good relationship and to communicate honestly, effectively, and regularly with the university's academic senate (or faculty council) and its leaders. This should involve two-way communication and informal as well as formal discussions.

A key executive under the president, especially in times of financial stringency, is the senior financial officer, often called the vice-president for finance. Business experience can be very helpful in such a job, but the individual should also be sensitive to signi-ficant differences in goals, values, attitudes, and requirements be-tween the business and academic worlds. Someone with government experience may be a good candidate for this job, because he has had experience working for a nonprofit organization. However, if he is used to spending large sums without really being accountable in a cost-benefit analysis sense, he may not be the man for an institution that is trying to tighten its belt.

Most universities have a senior executive, often called the vice-president for administration, in charge of such things as physical plant, nonacademic central staff, logistics, union relations, various information systems, central services, procedures and regulations, and a host of other administrative functions. In smaller universities and colleges, this responsibility may fall within the jurisdiction of the senior financial officer. Unfortunately this position is often filled by someone who is underqualified, because the job is not considered important.

However, large amounts of money are spent on such things as physical plant, central services and staff, and logistics, although such areas frequently function far below potential. Moreover, there is often much antagonism about the quality of such services within universities. It may be wise and economical over time to place a first-rate executive in charge of administration and pay him accordingly. And this executive should be given leeway to bring in more first-rate people under him and to reward them accordingly—not only with more pay, but also with more challenging and creative work. This policy can reduce the total number of personnel and the related payroll, and the quality of performance can be improved Universities tend to overcentralize services, staff functions, and other activities. Many of these functions and activities can fruitfully be pushed down into the schools, departments, divisions, and other units which make use of them. More is said about this in the next chapter.

Many universities and colleges have a senior executive in charge of academic affairs who reports to the president. He may be concerned with such things as new and various existing academic programs, coordination among programs, faculty advancement and development, various other academic personnel matters, and possibly research programs. He has jurisdiction over important activities and decisions that are academic rather than financial or administrative. This individual should usually be a respected scholar known for his intellectual ability and integrity. This can be a very sensitive and powerful job, especially if it involves decisions on faculty tenure and promotions. Ideally, he should already have had some significant experience in academic administration. If the university is reasonably clear about and satisfied with its goals, priorities, and academic functioning, an internal person may be best for this job. However, if it wants to bring about some major changes, someone from the outside with fresh ideas and relevant related experience may be the best choice. Here, too, a contingency approach is in order, depending on the situation and problems involved.

It is common for the deans in large universities to report to the vice-president or vice-chancellor for academic affairs instead of or in addition to the president. However, the president should still be readily accessible to the deans and should have adequate personal contact with them. The decision-making roles of the vice-president for academic affairs and the president vis-à-vis the deans should be clearly understood by all involved. If the institution is going through a serious crisis or redefining its goals and priorities, it is even more important for the president to communicate and meet personally with the deans. The same is true when a new president first takes over. It may be feasible for some very large and diverse universities to consider having two top academic affairs administrators—one for professional faculties and schools and one for nonprofessional faculties. There may be great enough similarities among professional schools, and big enough differences between them and nonprofessional faculties such as arts and humanities, to warrant such an organizational setup.

Publicity—public relations or public information—has recently become an important function for many universities. This activity involves public image-building of various kinds for the institution. The president should have close contact with the head of this unit, especially during times of crisis or if the university is trying to create a new image. There should also be adequate liaison and communication between this unit and the board.

The president should not fall into the trap of isolating himself from his major constituencies by building up a large or arrogant personal staff. He should delegate as much authority as possible down the line, rather than giving or letting his personal staff usurp excessive power and influence. And he should make sure that his staff is responsive to his line deputies and honest with him. If he does not have adequate confidence in executives under him, he should replace them rather than adding to his personal staff and giving it more powers.

He will, however, probably need some personal staff—such as a secretary, an administrative assistant, possibly a driver, someone to handle appointments and logistics, and to take minutes. He may also really need an executive assistant and a few special assistants for budgeting, special projects, and the like. However, they should act as staff and not as line executives. We do not believe that any university president needs a personal staff of more than about seven or eight people.

The secretary of the university usually reports to the president. He is often a key information center, especially if he is the liaison between the central administration and the academic senate or the board, or both. He typically is responsible for a range of important correspondence, keeping and disseminating minutes of meetings and various other kinds of communications.

Depending on their formal authority, autonomy, and the way they actually operate, the deans of schools and faculties may be either senior or middle management. Where they have wide-ranging powers and much independence in running their entities, they are senior executives and function much like a president of a small or medium-sized college or university. In recent times the trend has been toward more centralization of authority at North American universities—usually because of scarce financial resources. And so, increasingly, deanships are turning into middle-management jobs— even clerkships in quite a few cases. The most notable exceptions are typically found among prestigious professional schools that are recognized by the board and the chief executive to be important to the achievement of key institutional goals and priorities. They are also typically the schools and faculties that best meet the market test, that get external funds on their own, and whose graduates typically have no problem in getting good jobs. Top medical and dental schools, followed closely by the more prestigious business, management, and law schools, are among those whose deans most commonly function as truly senior managers. However, because most deanships are probably now essentially middle management jobs, we shall postpone any further discussion of deans until the next chapter.

Chapter X

Middle Management

The term *middle management* applies primarily to what people do in their jobs rather than to their titles, which can be deceiving. Someone with a grandiose executive title may in reality be little more than a clerk, while an individual who has a humble title may wield much influence and power.

In trying to define middle management, we come directly to the question of centralization versus decentralization of authority, which is not an absolute but a relative concept. In general, middle management is responsible for the implementation of higher-level decisions. Implementation may require decision-making, planning, determining strategy and tactics. But most if not all of middle-management activity takes as given, or as its premises and constraints,

244

decisions made and approved by top-level or senior management. Whether an individual is a senior or middle manager depends on the importance of the decisions he makes, the amount of authority, power, and influence he exerts, and the degree of autonomy with which he functions. Making major decisions about budgets and personnel and raising and spending funds from external sources independently are typically top and not middle management functions in academic institutions. Lower management implements decisions and directs and controls people and operations. The decisions made by lower-level administrators or supervisors are typically routine and derive from higher-level policies, procedures, and regulations.

Centralization versus Decentralization

At universities and colleges generally there has been and still is a trend toward greater centralization of authority and decision-making, primarily because of growing financial constraints—as well as other reasons discussed in earlier chapters. Most deans in charge of individual faculties and schools are now middle managers, and quite a few seem to really function as lower-level managers and junior executives. There are notable exceptions of course, found mostly at leading professional schools.

Where the dean functions as a senior executive and is willing to delegate substantial authority to his deputies—associate and assistant deans, department chairmen, division heads, executive officers, and administrative assistants—the latter can legitimately be considered part of middle management. Where the dean has very limited authority and autonomy, his deputies typically operate as lower-level administrators or clerks. The personality and ability of a given dean or other administrator can have a significant bearing on how he actually operates and what level of management he is really in. For example, even within a university where authority is highly centralized, a particular dean—because of his drive, initiative, influence, personality, and competence—may be, in effect, functioning as a senior executive. However, even this is becoming less common as central controls become more pervasive and stringent.

As a minimum, deans, department heads, and other middle

managers should be consulted with regularly and should have easy access to their superiors. They should be kept informed about what is going on and should serve as key communications centers in the system. If this is not done, their leadership and managerial status is likely to be seriously undermined and many serious problems can result.

The question of centralization versus decentralization of authority also relates to support services such as student recruitment, registration, placement, purchasing, course and classroom scheduling, maintenance of faculties, computer facilities, typing pools, printing and production, public and external relations, budgeting staffs, and accounting. There are two areas of concern here. One involves who makes the decisions and how authority is delegated; the other involves where the services are located—a geographical question. Because there are no universal answers, a contingency approach is called for. The best arrangement depends in large part on factors to be discussed shortly. Various services may be geographically decentralized—for example, located within a certain faculty—but subject to a high degree of functional authority and control exerted by the central administration. However, the general pattern and trend seems to be greater centralization—of both location and authority—of support services. Here too, financial constraints are influential. In reality, the benefits derived, in costs and economies that can be readily quantified, are probably often more than offset by diminished service, information, and communication, and by problems, alienation, frustration, errors, waste, and unproductive time and effort expended in achieving the organization's goals and priorities.

A few people near the top, who are in charge of major support services, may function as senior executives, providing that top management delegates substantial authority to them. Most administrators of support services can be considered to be middle- and lower-level managers. Those within the central administration who exert a fair amount of authority and control over their respective units, and also exert considerable functional authority and control within their counterpart services lower down and within individual faculties, schools, and departments, are essentially middle managers. It is much more common for those involved with the administration of services within the faculties and schools to function as relatively low-level administrators or supervisors, because of the proliferation of central directives and controls. Only where the dean has considerable autonomy in various areas, and is willing to delegate significant authority and independence can various administrators at this level function as middle managers.

Effective Decentralization

In our opinion, the trend toward increased centralization if often excessive, unwarranted, unwise, and dysfunctional to the goals, priorities, and viability of the institution. Excessive centralization leads not only to the loss of power and autonomy for middle management, but also far too frequently to slower and poorer decisions, faulty communications, and much information-clogging and distortion. This stems from not utilizing a contingency approach based on an adequate assessment of salient conditions and of the results desired. There is a clear tendency for top management to centralize, standardize, and tighten up across the board and in a uniform fashion when the financial crunch comes—and this then often continues to be the situation indefinitely into the future. It would often be wiser to allow different degrees of autonomy to different faculties, schools, and departments, depending on the goals and priorities and specific circumstances of each. Instead of centralizing, it would be more effective to build and capitalize on strengths while containing and, if necessary, cutting back most acutely the relatively weak parts of the system. This enables the stronger parts to subsidize the weaker and keep more of them viable, thus enables the university to pursue more of its varied and diverse goals. However, top management and the central administration should not abdicate too much of their authority to a powerful dean, or serious suboptimization is likely to result. A particular faculty should not usually be allowed to hire as many new people as it would like to while others are faced with the need to cut back considerably.

Those faculties and departments that are actually or potentially the strongest, and thus the ones to which greater decentralization of authority and autonomy should typically be granted, tend to have at least several of the following characteristics.

1. They best meet the market test and satisfy the priorities, needs, and interests of those who provide the funds, of the community, and of broader society.

2. They have the strongest external supporters, and quite possibly also the strongest supporters among key board members.

3. They are in the best positions to contribute to achievement of the university's goals and priorities, as well as to achieve their own.

4. They are in a position to obtain, on their own, sizable amounts of financial support, including contributions from private organizations and individuals, research grants, and revenues from special programs.

5. Enough jobs are available for their graduates, and most graduates get relatively good jobs and move ahead rapidly in their careers. (This characteristic influences future alumni support.)

6. The external visibility and reputation of the faculty is relatively high. This reputation can be the result of superior teaching, research, publications, consulting, speaking engagements, public service, and so forth. And it may also be the result of involvement in various educational and training programs for adults and practitioners, part-time degree and nondegree programs, extension or correspondence programs, and programs conducted for external organizations.

7. They can readily redeploy faculty resources to meet changing needs and demands for new programs, courses, research projects, and the like.

8. Management by objectives and performance evaluation can be applied more easily than in other faculties. Here, the goals and priorities of the faculty, as well as its contributions to the institution as a whole, can be assessed and determined—albeit not usually in a very precise way. This assessment covers such things as: enrollment trends; revenues generated; costs in relation to revenues and results; amount of outside funding obtained independently, what happens to graduates; relevancy of research and publishing output to financial supporters and the broader society; effectiveness of programs in relation to goals, results, and costs; quality of the reputations and productivity of faculty; public service; and pertinent external contacts. Many of these things

must be analyzed and measured in a relative way, if not in absolute terms. This may be done by comparing the unit with other faculties, schools, or departments. Where management by objectives can more readily be applied, this can facilitate effective decentralization of authority and strategic rather than detailed control by higher authorities.

9. They are or could be relatively self-sufficient with regard to various academic programs and support services. Where some academic programs must should be done jointly with other parts of the university, some higher-level coordination and control may be feasible. However, where this can be accomplished directly through the joint cooperation and decisions of the faculties or departments involved, it may be best to keep higher-level control to a minimum. Of course, if it is a major new program that can have a truly significant impact on the university generally, then even top management may legitimately want to be directly involved, at least until operation of the program is stabilized. As for support services, the faculty can be more legitimately self-sufficient if it is large enough to support a substantial amount of such services and has enough volume so that services operate at a reasonably high degree of capacity. However, there usually are trade-offs between direct quantifiable costs and hidden costs, including the quality of service, problems and conflicts between those promoting the services and their clients, and so forth. Often it is better to decentralize services that function smoothly, but at only 70 percent of capacity, than to centralize them and have people who seem to be working most of the time but are not really being very effective or efficient much of the time. Moreover, part-time personnel can often be used to keep the costs down. It is also usually easier to decentralize services effectively where the goals and priorities of the faculty are reasonably clear, and an assessment can be made of how the various services contribute to attainment of the goals and priorities. Where the uses, kinds, or importance of support services are unique, it may also be better to decentralize them. For example, where a given faculty does considerably more research and publishing and has much greater legitimate use for computer time than other faculties, related services should be provided within this faculty to the greatest extent possible. It may also warrant its own library.

Where the markets for recruiting and placement of students are relatively clear-cut, as compared to other faculties, this may call for independent recruiting and placement operations.

10. Where the faculty is growing—and is expected to continue to grow—and is also effectively innovative and has good management and leadership, greater decentralization of authority may well be warranted. Although there are notable exceptions, professional schools typically meet these conditions to a significantly greater degree and extent than most other faculties, and are likely to continue to in the foreseeable future. They also most commonly have their own buildings—usually the newer and better ones—and more of their own facilities and support services. Moreover, they often have higher pay scales for their faculty members, because they tend to have more job options open to them elsewhere—and not only at other universities. In spite of this, inadequate decentralization is becoming significantly more common even with regard to professional schools, as well as various other relatively strong parts of many universities and colleges. This tends to be both unwise and dangerous in terms of the university's overall health and viability. It also tends to make it much more difficult for universities to attract and keep first-rate deans and middle managers, while many who perform what are essentially lower-level managerial or clerical jobs are overpaid for what they actually do. If the latter are relatively high achievers and really competent, they are not likely to be happpy—or to last very long—in their jobs. Although the growth of various professional schools may well diminish or even stagnate in the future—for example, if there is a prolonged and serious economic recession—they are likely to continue to be relatively strong and viable compared to most other faculties. Many law schools seem to be running the risk of seriously overanticipating future demand for their graduates—especially graduates who want to practice law as a profession. Many law schools have been expanding enrollments sharply, in large part by taking in increased numbers of women and minority group members—which we feel in itself is admirable. Many engineering schools, and possibly to a lesser extent business schools, could run into serious problems during a recession. However, business, management, and often engineering graduates tend to be in significantly

greater demand, even in a recession, than many other kinds of graduates. Medical and dental schools seem to be in the best shape generally for the foreseeable future.

Selecting a Dean

Many of the criteria, conditions, and procedures discussed in Chapter Nine in connection with the selection of a president or chief executive also apply to selection of a dean. In both cases a contingency approach is called for where the goals and priorities of the particular faculty or school are reasonably clear and viable and things generally are going quite smoothly—and this is expected to continue, the new dean should usually be selected largely on the basis of the qualifications of the job that can be spelled out clearly. If a good internal person is available and has adequate faculty consensus, there may well be less risk in selecting him than an external candidate.

At the other extreme, if the faculty is confronted with serious financial and internal problems and has unclear goals and priorities, it may be best to try to find a first-rate individual whose basic philosophy meshes well with that of the faculty at large, and then to let him pretty much create his own job. An external choice is likely to be more common here. If fund-raising is seen as one of his key tasks, then a basically nonacademic type—especially for professional schools—may be desirable.

If the new dean is not viewed by his faculty as a scholar or academic, then—regardless of how big or prestigious his previous job was—he could run into serious problems on academic matters. If he tries to impose new goals and priorities on the faculty or tries to make major changes involving academic matters—such as programs, curriculum, courses, and academic personnel evaluation—without adequate consultation and effective salesmanship and leadership, there may well be a huge outcry from the faculty. In such circumstances, it may be wisest for the dean to appoint a key deputy (for example, a respected academic as associate dean) to directly handle most of the sensitive academic matters while he deals chiefly with administrative and financial affairs and external relations. He still could exert adequate overall control through his budgetary, financial, and administrative responsibilities. If a scholar who has had little or no major managerial experience takes over as dean, he should make sure that at least one of his key deputies is competent and well informed with regard to administrative, financial, and budgetary matters.

The most common situation calls for a balance in matching the new dean to the job and the job to him. Some goals and priorities may be taken as given, while others are undetermined or flexible. The faculty is confronted with a number of significant problems, but not a real crisis. Here the choice can be either external or internal, a scholar or an administrator, depending on many conditions.

Imposing a really unpopular choice on a faculty is likely to lead to disaster. It is much better to appoint an acting dean until a suitable and acceptable permanent choice can be made. It is also very important to consult genuinely and broadly with the faculty before a choice is made. A faculty search committee, or adequate faculty representation on a university search committee which is advisory to the president or chief executive, can be valuable.

It is critical that all serious prospective candidates for dean be given as accurate a picture as possible about where the university is heading and what the new dean's job will entail, not only in the immediate future but over the minimum period he would expect to remain in the job. Thus, the candidate needs to ask the right questions of the right people, not only in his own prospective faculty and in the central administration but also of board members (especially the chairman), other deans, and various people that he is likely to have significant involvement with. And honest and accurate information must be provided to him.

It is critical that there be a reasonably good fit between the prospective dean's basic philosophy, aims, aspirations, interests, and priorities with regard to the job and those of both his own prospective faculty and the university's top management. It may not be easy to determine if this is really the case, but much effort should be made to do so.

If the prospective dean is not from the academic world—for example, a business executive or government official—it is possible that some key people in administrative jobs at the university may have either covert or overt negative biases toward him just because of this. The vice-president for academic affairs and various other deans may fall into this category, although this negative bias is the exception rather than the rule. (Incidentally, it is quite common for prominent outside practitioners and professionals who became deans to get significantly bigger salaries than other deans and even vice-presidents.) It is important for the new dean to become aware of such biases, even if they are not in the open. If the president does not share this bias and is expected to be around for some time, there may be no major problems. Similarly, if those who have such a bias are not going to exert much influence or authority over the new dean, their attitudes are less likely to pose serious problems for him.

When a new dean takes over he should try to get a good fit between his interests and capabilities and those of the key deputies he appoints. If he is an outsider, he should definitely appoint someone who can provide him with accurate and unbiased information about the faculty and its problems and personalities. He should not hastily dismantle or change things dramatically, unless or until there are potentially better and feasible alternatives and options that can and will be implemented. We have known deans who did this and never fully recovered from the mess of problems that resulted. On the other hand, the new dean can often effectively make the most major changes, and relatively quickly, during his honeymoon period, especially if he has been a highly popular choice as dean. Incidentally, this also applies to a new president or chief executive.

Dean's Job

Apart from external relations and fund-raising, the most important matters for which a dean is responsible relate to budgets, personnel decisions, general administration, and academic programs. If he spends much time outside of his own faculty, he should delegate many of these internal matters to competent deputies (Hodgkinson and Meeth, 1971), pp. 45–53; Gould, 1964).

If a dean is not regarded as a scholar or academic by his faculty—but rather as only an administrator or manager—it may be wise for him not to get too directly involved in academic personnel matters, curriculum, and other purely academic problems. It may be best to handle them primarily through his deputies and faculty committees (mostly advisory in nature). However, he still can keep control of available resources, goals, and priorities through his budgetary and other administrative powers. He can veto faculty promotion decisions, new programs, and the like. He should, where possible, give proper guidelines and provide enough information and, if necessary, quotas, so that those deputies and committees charged with making recommendations or certain types of decisions know in advance what the resource constraints are likely to be.

When vetoing promotion, tenure, dismissal, and salary recommendations, a dean who is not viewed as a scholar tends to run greater risks—if he does this more than very occasionally—than would a dean who is regarded as a first-rate academic. Regardless of the dean's background and whether he is viewed as a scholar or as only a manager, he is wise to set up some faculty committees to deal with academic personnel, academic programs, and curriculum matters. It may be a good idea for the faculty to elect all or most of the members of academic personnel evaluation and selection committees, perhaps with some provision for representation of different professorial ranks and areas.

When a faculty or school is required to dismiss a number of faculty members for budgetary reasons, the effective dean typically relies on his department chairmen (or their equivalent) and the appropriate committee to recommend exactly who should be laid off and to support their recommendations with as much documentation as possible. The dean should give operative guidelines on the magnitude of the cutbacks required and the related deadlines, and the faculty is then charged with implementing them and fighting things out. This procedure enhances the likelihood that in the end the faculty's recommendations will be sounder and create fewer problems than if the dean had acted on his own in a vacuum. If the dean feels that he must veto a particular recommendation, he should have enough documentation and evidence available to clearly explain why he is doing so. He could attribute the blame for dismissal of a faculty member to the budgetary decisions made by the central administration or to uncontrollable external conditions. But if the cutbacks in his own faculty are relatively greater than in others, this may not go over too well.

The truly effective dean will anticipate such cutbacks through some meaningful contingency planning, if there is a significant chance that they will arise in the foreseeable future. He will let the faculty know adequately in advance that there may have to be cuts, and then he will establish priorities for cutbacks, should they be needed, in a calm atmosphere rather than in a crisis setting. He may also make more appointments of a contractually limited nature and for shorter periods, so that cutbacks become more automatic and routine. And he can tighten academic standards for retention, tenure, and promotion, and avoiding excessive overstaffing.

The amount of autonomy and authority a dean has over his faculty budget is determined primarily by the degree of centralization in the university—although his own personality, initiative, and behavior might lead to greater autonomy than is prescribed in the formal rules. As a minimum, even if the dean functions as a true senior executive, higher approval will be needed for at least a number of broad categories, and for the total budget figure. These categories include such things as payroll for academic personnel and support staff, total revenue, the amount to be turned over to the central administration, capital expenditures, and other major expense categories. Higher-level approval will also usually be required for tenure appointments and perhaps for some special salary situations.

When the dean functions as a low-level manager or clerk, a myriad of categories and details require higher approval. These include separate categories in both dollars and bodies for various kinds of personnel, a very detailed breakdown of revenues, specific categories for telephone, postage, Xeroxing expenses, and so forth. Moreover, he has little or no authority to shift funds among the detailed accounts should the need arise. (Ways can be found to do some of this fund shuffling, which may more often than not be in the best interests of the university.) And detailed audits may even be conducted on a monthly basis by higher authorities.

Excessive standardization goes hand in hand with excessive centralization and is very common at universities and colleges nowadays. Some standardization is clearly warranted. However, applying the same standards, criteria, procedures, policies, and regulations across the board, to such diverse faculties as medicine and arts or business administration and science, tends to be both unwise and dysfunctional. As noted above, a contingency approach makes the most sense, since this takes into account the results desired and the most appropriate means for achieving them, given particular conditions. One faculty may legitimately have to use the telephone much more because of its interfaces with the outside world. Another faculty may do the kind of research and publishing that entails much greater short-term output, reproduction, and paperwork. A particular faculty may have a legitimate need for various kinds of expensive equipment and technology. Student-faculty ratios and class sizes differ considerably among faculties.

It makes much more sense to compare the budgets and performance of a particular faculty or school with those of other reasonably comparable faculties—even if they are not in the same university—and not to highly dissimilar faculties. In large and diverse faculties, the same is true for various departments. To some extent, various—but not all—faculties and departments within the same university can be grouped together for some kinds of meaningful comparisons. For example, law and business and perhaps medicine and dentistry can be meaningfully compared on various items. The same may be true for engineering, applied sciences, and perhaps architecture. Similarly, some useful comparisons can be made between arts, the humanities, and possibly education.

If committees make major budgetary decisions, it is difficult to place the blame, responsibility, or accountability for overspending and errors. This is a primary reason why an individual administrator should make the final decisions or give his formal approval. Higher authorities at universities could very often spend their time much more fruitfully if they designed effective control systems and focused attention on strategic controls of critical items, rather than relying on excessively detailed and standardized controls that typically lead to serious informational deficiencies, behavioral problems, and other dysfunctional consequences. Then if a particular faculty overspends significantly, the dean can rightfully be held accountable and if necessary reprimanded or punished. If the situation is serious enough, he might have to make up the difference in his future budgets.

If the chief executive has confidence in his deans, he should give them increased leeway to shuffle funds among broad accounts. If the goals and priorities of their faculties are reasonably clear, operational, and accepted, and if there is adequate information available to make a reasonbly meaningful judgment and evaluation as to whether goals and priorities are being achieved to a sufficient degree, top management should be primarily concerned only with this achievement. It should not be or become preoccupied with endless detailed controls that are, after all, not the primary purpose of the institution. In fact, various controls are frequently deficient as a means of achieving the desired goals and priorities.

Chapter XI

Professors

In the end, the quality and reputation of any university or college depend primarily on the faculty. All the other inputs and outputs are secondary to how well the faculty does its job. The reputation of top managers and administrators, both within and outside of the academic community, will in large part depend on how well they manage to keep their diverse professors productive. If the administrator wishes to stay on the job, or if he wishes any reputation at all, he must pay very special attention to the care and feeding of his faculty.

Professors (typically) are very complex people, both individually and in groups. They live in a world apart from most people, complete with special interests, training, and hang-ups. We have noted earlier that most people are accustomed to hierarchial structures, and that the university is presumably organized as a hierarchy. But as we also suggested, it is almost impossible to operate a university with a vigil, authoritarian hierarchy, because the one order that cannot be given is "Be creative!" Yet faculty creativity is exactly that quality which is critical. How, then, does a university manager handle his personnel? Faculty can be guided, led, or forced to do things, but they must frequently be handled in quite special ways. Managers who learn how to do this will go down as great men. Those who fail to grasp the minimal essentials of the problem resign early.

Goal System

Like everyone else, professors try to maximize something. One thing they try to maximize is money income, although money certainly is not everything. Other things, such as individual and professional prestige, job satisfaction, geographical location, and satisfactory interpersonal relationships are items to be considered when making career decisions. Our estimate, based on practical grant receiving and giving, is that all factors other than money typically count for about 20 or 30 percent, with money making up the remaining 70 or 80 percent of the maximization package. One does encounter exceptions from time to time, but not too often. These exceptions as usually true scholars (very rare) whose major interests are totally unworldly, and very successful academics who already are making enough money so that they are well up in the top one or two percent of all income earners in the United States (that is, they make more than $30,000 per year). At that level, other things become much more important to many. But less than 1 percent of American academics make over $30,000 per year in total income, so these persons also are rare.

The way to maximize one's interests, whatever they may be, is to try to do one's job so that these things are maximized. Each individual must decide what to stress and what to minimize, so that the probability of success is maximized. The following are strategies professors can use, and comments about how these approaches might assist a faculty member toward his goals. These strategies also have significant implications for academic managers and administrators.

Teaching. Most laymen think this is what professors do. Actually, in the modern university, this is often one of the lesser items on a professor's list of activities. With faculty-student ratios at prominent schools running from about ten-to-one to twenty-five-to-one, and with each professor teaching from six to nine semester hours, most professors actually see only a handful (say twenty to one hundred) students per quarter or semester some six to nine hours per week. Even when you add preparation time, conferences, office hours, advanced graduate students on special work, and all the rest, you find that most professors probably do not work with students for more than twenty hours per week.

Teaching comes out badly in a typical professor's maximization criteria. Teaching minimizes, rather than maximizes, a professor's income. Few people, beyond the professor's students, typically know or care how good a teacher he is, but everyone knows who writes in the discipline. The scholar is the one who gets outside offers at fat salary increases and makes his reputation giving papers at key conferences. The teacher can enjoy only the satisfactions of working with his students.

It can also be quite traumatic to be a teacher, because the most relevant feedback loops about success or failure are so long. An individual may feel that he is doing a good job, but he can never be sure until his students are far along in their careers. It is relatively easy to be popular, but it is not as easy to learn how to teach well. Most professors, even those who are not so interested in students or teaching, spend a lot of time agonizing about this without becoming better teachers. Much work has been done on measuring teaching performance, but little has been learned. However, most schools still probably do not even make widespread systematic efforts to evaluate teaching, instructors, and courses, and this would be useful.

A professor who does nothing but teach may contact from two to ten thousand students in his thirty to fifty years of professional life. If this is all he does, then these are the only people who know how good he is. For some, this is more than enough. But a single, truly significant article, or book in many disciplines may educate more persons than a lifetime of personal teaching.

Research. This is where the high payoff for academics is now at numerous institutions. Those who can do research well can look forward to higher incomes, more professional prestige, and better students, particularly at the graduate level. Perceptive students try to learn under the best men, and the way we evaluate best in academe is by the quality and quantity of a man's writings. Students half way around the world can read and study a man's papers, and with luck have a chance to take his seminar some day. And it does seem to be true that the most able researchers are frequently among the better teachers.

Published research also leads to professional reputation and prestige. Any scholar worthy of the name will be able to indicate quickly just who the ten or fifteen best men in his field are, and they will all be published writers. Deans and chairmen, when looking for the strong man to fill a prestigious chair, will look to publications for guidance. The well-published professor will have significantly more offers at other schools, which will help his chairman or dean at the next departmental salary discussion.

Truly outstanding scholars are still often able to obtain research grants. Often these grants are large and contain a significant margin for overhead expenses. A million dollar grant—of which half goes directly to the institution for overhead—benefits the institution as well as the faculty members. These overheads are rewards to the administration for their astuteness in getting the man to join the faculty.

Lots of people try to win this way, given the very large pay-offs, but relatively few succeed. One study suggested that only about 10 percent of all economists with PhD degrees ever write anything beyond their theses, though many try. Good research, written up well enough to get published in the right scholarly journals—or as books or monographs—is tough to do and few can consistantly carry it off.

Observers, noting the endless streams of materials emanating from campuses, may feel that everyone is pouring out publications, but that there are relatively few prolific scholarly writers. This proposition can be tested by sampling any faculty, including those with impeccable scholarly reputations, and discovering how few professors actually do very much writing. There are many more professors around now than a few decades ago, so there is a larger absolute amount of materials being produced, but the proportion of writers to the total may well be about the same.

Another side effect of this general inability to write well is a constant petty jealousy in almost every field. Those who do write may be sticking their necks way out. A piece of work, once published, is there forevermore for the critics to clobber. If a professor never writes, he never has to worry about critics and visibility. But then, he does not get very far professionally. Administrators quickly get used to biting commentary directed at some of the best men on their faculty.

A subbranch of research is the writing of textbooks and other educational materials. This tends to have high professional payoff in two dimensions. One is that most good text writers become widely known in their fields. This means invitations to give papers at the right conferences, and job offers. The second dimension is financial. Writers get royalties, and 10 or 15 percent of current text retail price can mount up. Many academic institutions have a handful of textbook millionaires around (they are not really millionaires, but a few do earn well over fifty thousand dollars per year in royalties).

There is considerable status confusion about texts. Many academics feel that this is a low-grade activity, not worthy of serious consideration professionally. Others feel that this is an important part of teaching. A text author may reach with one small edition more students than he will ever teach personally. And observation suggests that text-writing professors fare very well indeed in terms of promotion and status—often better than research writers.

Public Service. This is a catch-all category, embracing all sorts of services not normally included in the first two categories. One professor may spend much time and effort as a member of his local school board; another may consult with the United Nations on some key issue in his realm of competence; another may advise the governor about some problem; still another may work extensively with his church. As long as the activity is seen as socially desirable, schools will encourage it, even when it requires time during the working day.

Probably most professors do some of this; some even take leaves of absence for special situations such as appointment to a government post. The level of activity tends to be quite closely correlated with research and scholarly work. Those most widely known and respected are asked to perform high-level tasks. Those known only locally perform important but less significant local services.

The payoff ranges from the purely personal satisfaction felt by a man who runs his church's fund drive, to national or even international fame achieved by a professor who operates a major AID mission for the government or becomes a cabinet member or key presidential advisor. A man who has advised presidents will not usually lack offers of prestigious endowed chairs when he returns to academic life.

Consulting. This is very common in fields where the discipline has something to sell, as do most professional schools. Some professors are highly regarded by their peers and are often asked for advice. Academics, particularly those in fields where there is little to sell, tend to disparage such activities, but consulting offers to academics not only income but also opportunities to practice in their disciplines. It is a way to keep up with the field. Some disciplines, such as business, receive particular scorn for their consulting activities, particularly when it is widely believed that consultants in these fields earn fabulous outside incomes. A few do, but most do not. Like all other things in academic life, the relatively few fabulously successful practitioners are widely noted, but others are not.

Administration. Most university administrators are also academics, and administration offers a possible alternative career. The money payoff is usually higher than for teaching only, but a full-time administrator rarely has much time for research, writing, public service, or consulting. He also loses touch with his own discipline rather rapidly if he stays away from it for more than a few years.

Administrators and managers have many special problems, as this book suggests. They catch hell from all sides, and the goal deviations and other pressures of modern academic life may make the price too high for many who seriously consider such a career. Universities and colleges can always find someone to do the job, though not necessarily the person they would like. Administration means more money, a chance to change things, and a feeling of being where the action is. Only after some time does disillusionment set in and does the feeling arise that there are other ways to win the game. One result is that many administrators are those who cannot win well in other ways, which can cause internal status problems. If the real winners are seen as respected or true scholars, then those who get into administration may not be the most respected men around. Efforts to lead from a position of internal weakness can be frustrating.

Optimizing Strategy

Given all of this, it is clear what many young professors should do. First, they should do research in their areas of professional competence. Second, they might write textbooks or other instructional materials that can be published and distributed extensively. And if they have any time or energy left, they can do anything else which appeals to them, such as teach, administer, or do public service.

Given this strategy, it is clear why so many outsiders and students are disturbed by the modern university. The best ways for professors to optimize are contrary to what others want and expect from faculty. Here is the real problem in terms of goal divergence. If the faculty member optimizes for himself, he will create a situation that does not meet the needs of the university as seen by others.

For over a century, American universities have been run for their faculties. Now most professors, keenly aware of what is significant in their own discipline, realize that the way to create a great university and to achieve individual acclaim is to operate as suggested above. But financial patrons want very different things from their universities, things that were, until a decade or so ago, forthcoming anyhow. The basic issue we now face is that the professional prestige pattern described above meshes very badly with our desires for students, society, and the rest of the environment. As the university and college system has grown in size, it has gotten out of touch with the needs of the rest of the world.

This aloofness would not matter much if the system were still small, but it is not. And, in the end, any organization has to adequately meet the needs of those who pay the bills. Because this professional prestige system is so firmly entrenched in most academic disciplines, it will require massive attitudinal changes among faculty to bring about major changes on a broad scale, which is why academic institutions are so hard to manage these days.

Actually, this deviation may not be as great as it seems at first. Most effective researching professors are quite good teachers. They know more about what is going on in their fields, and they are at the forefront of knowledge in their areas. An imaginative person who can get good ideas down on paper rarely is dull when speaking to a small group. But the image remains of faculty busy with research and writing while neglecting their students.

The paradox for administrators is that university quality is judged by the caliber of the faculty, and this caliber is judged by research and writing. It is possible to have an almost perfect university with relatively little teaching going on. This seems to be one of the major complaints of young students in such highly regarded universities as Berkeley, Chicago, and Harvard. Outside it looks great; inside it can be seen as a real mess. Resolving this conflict is a major task for top managers and administrators.

Outsiders and Insiders

The ideal academic, from the professional point of view, is frequently the outsider, the man who is known and respected in his profession. The insider, the man who cannot achieve greatness in his own discipline, moves toward local activities. He teaches, does local public service, and performs middle-management administrative functions in the university.

These two types are the opposite ends of a spectrum, and most professors fall somewhere between. But both kinds will be found on every large university campus. They present real dilemmas for administrators, because the insiders make the place function, while the outsiders give the school whatever reputation it may have. Hence some balance is needed.

Schools with too many insiders tend to be seen as dreary cow colleges, full of well-intentioned but not terribly exciting people. This is unfair, because many good teachers and administrators are insiders and they like to work this way. But if a brilliant young student is pondering where to go for his graduate program, and if he asks his best professor for advice, a place full of insiders is not likely to be first choice. After all, no one has ever heard of the professors there, and while they may all be good, it seems better to suggest a place full of brilliant, published scholars with major reputations. Rating scales of quality in departments will take due note of the apparent lack of professional competence, and rankings will be lower as a result. The academic image will be one of modest competence but not of much interest to the real intellectual world outside.

Schools full of outsiders have high prestige and are full of intellectual excitement and activities. Often they are also the ones under attack from students and outside supporters—particularly if they are state supported. If everyone in the department is busy doing writing and research, internal administration may well be chaotic, because no one is interested in such trivia. Some courses are not scheduled; others are planned for twenty students and get ninety-five. Students may see the professor two or three times per semester instead of the scheduled fifteen. The professor is badly needed in Washington for key consultations, and the students can wait. Examination papers may be returned ten weeks late, or not at all. After all, there was that special conference to attend.

All of this can be frustrating to administrators. If heat is applied to outsiders to get them to behave like insiders, they may move on. In a few years, persons outside the school are saying things like, "Oh, yes, since Smith became president of State the place has deteriorated badly. Boswell in English and Steinmetz in physics have both left, you know. Tragic how one man can wreck a good school." Most administrators are academics too. It takes a tough man to carry out this strategy.

Here again we see major goal divergence. The scholars want one thing; students, state legislatures, and others want something quite different. Actually, what they want is the exciting outsiders behaving like insiders, at least in terms of meeting classes, teaching students, and behaving more or less conventionally toward others in the system. Once in a great while you can have it both ways, when a very unconventional outsider arrives and stays. The Nobel prize winner happily teaches freshman chemistry; the servant of kings and presidents just happens to like to sit around and chat with his students; or the great botanist with an international reputation serves with good humor, administrative skill, and considerable insight as chairman of his department. But such people are truly rare.

Economic conditions of the 1970s may alleviate this problem

somewhat, because the outsiders do not have as many good places to go. Budgets are being cut or seriously constrained almost everywhere. The risk of alienating really good scholars is considerably smaller now than it has been for decades. Yet the truly great man can go anywhere, which is one reason why administrators are often reluctant to shift goals away from the academic view. To do so can be very costly, particularly in terms of internal support and prestige. Even the lesser lights on the faculty are keenly aware of the great men, and if the great men are unhappy, the insiders and budding outsiders may also be unhappy. Only when the budget heat is really on do top administrators take the risk of offending their great men. Remember that such men are good grantsmen too, so their departure can mean lost dollars. However, the days of the juicy grant with lots of overhead also are nearly over, so once again the pressures lead to goal system change.

Use of Time

Given the above, any good university will generally try to structure the professors' work tasks to meet the conditions, as perceived by professors, for good professing. This means providing as much secretarial support as can be financed, the best computers, ample laboratory facilities, and small teaching loads. These sorts of perquisites attract outsiders, who are typically the ones wanted. But insiders get these things too. They may even get more than their share, because they are often the administrators who allocate space, secretaries, and computer time.

This pattern leads to the second major problem with professors. About 10 percent of the faculty may do about 90 percent of the desirable external activities. Yet virtually the whole faculty has the time to try. Professors typically have much free time. Moreover, most professional tasks are open ended. One can spend five minutes, five hours, or five weeks grading a student term paper, and no one can say for sure which is optimal. One professor may write a learned article over a busy weekend; another may spend a year on the same number of pages. Both may feel (correctly) that they are working hard.

Thus the faculty can make time for whatever they see as

important. They can do well, which requires sound managerial planning tied in with suitable control, evaluation, and reward systems. Far too often in modern universities, administrators pay high personal prices for failure to consider the problem of how faculty members can make the most effective use of their working time.

Image

Most professors in large universities have advanced degrees arduously obtained from other relatively good universities. Most of them have had long years of apprenticeship in their scholarly disciplines. This leads to a professorial self-image, created in the tradition of nineteenth-century English and German universities. We all have nice self-images, and the one most academics have relates directly to their goal systems and work attitudes.

This self-image appears to be about as follows, in its extreme form. It involves very high status in the community. The scholar or man of learning is one to be looked up to, a wise man who deserves and gets significant public support. The image is one of a small elite of scholars. Many try; few are chosen to lead the scholarly life. It involves the feeling that the world out there has deep affection and appreciation for this sort of person. The image includes seeing oneself as carrying on the intellectual traditions of the society, which often involve nothing very practical or pragmatic. But it does mean that the values and ethics of the society are deeply imbedded in and carried on by professors. Students are seen as a small elite who will rise to positions of prominence, both economically and socially, in the system. Hence there is a critical responsibility to handle them properly and train them well.

All of this was probably true in Victorian England, when less than 1 percent of college-age students were in universities. Some of it may still. There are no bolts to tighten on the assembly line and no tight schedules to meet for customers. A few professors just goof off and become semiretired gentlemen of leisure; some politic endlessly within the university for various reforms; others worry about real or imagined ills; and still others raise general hell. All types are familiar to any seasoned administrator. And many of them will focus some of their attention on the administration. Whatever an administrator does will be evaluated, discussed, criticized, and written about endlessly. Most administrative actions are public, and so this activity is inevitable. Administrators and managers coming to universities and colleges from more structured work assignments are often baffled or hurt by such activities, but they are a normal part of multiversity life.

The managerial solution to this problem is difficult. The usual way to handle it is to give particularly noisy professors jobs as administrators or as chairman of committees charged with plastering up troublesome interfaces. Another possibility is to adjust duties. Give those professors who are doing research enough time to do it, but give those who are interested in other things many more duties to fill in the empty hours. This could lead to variable teaching loads, for example. Some professors might handle up to fifteen hours of teaching; others might get along nicely with three. It is difficult to decide who should do what; remember that insiders tend to be chairmen, and asking them to take on extra work may not be seen too favorably. Moreover, the quiet professor who seems to be loafing may be writing (over a ten-year period) the monograph that will shake his discipline. But more fine tuning could be done than is. The astute manager will utilize a contingency approach in deciding how to deal with various professors. This requires an adequate understanding of their personal goals, interests, and capabilities.

The basic trick is to have everyone working hard at tasks that be true in a few Ivy League type, private universities. But this image is wildly at variance with what is really going on in most state-supported institutions and private schools. This self-image explains in part why there is so much goal divergence between the academic institution and the outside world. What is expected and wanted from any faculty is not exactly what is seen as critical by the faculty itself.

There are exceptions. Professional school faculties may see themselves in quite different ways. (And in many cases various professional schools are really not accepted internally. After all, they are not accepted in most English universities even today.) And individual professors, particularly the successful outsiders, are often much more sensitive to the market than the above self-image would suggest. If one is to obtain a fat grant from a willing donor, whatever is being produced has to be sold. But as a general rule, faculties see themselves as something they could be only in some wistful, nostalgic corner of some never-never academe. Administrators have to accept this self-image and try to move on. Any proposal or action that tends to force reality on the faculty will be intuitively resisted, and a lot of debate and argument will ensue before reality is accepted. The self-image makes the university that much harder to manage.

Outside Reactions

Events of the past several years have shocked the professorial world and self-image. Why, those people out there do not really like us! Budget cuts, pressures to teach more, and biting criticisms of faculty activities seem unreal. But they are very real, and when, for the fourth straight year, pay raises fail to reach even the level of inflation, faculty are not only bewildered and hurt but also angry. Which strategy should be followed to regain lost prestige? How can the present fuzzy goal system, which optimizes for professors, be kept without jeopardizing the money and the students necessary to support the institution.

Most professors perceive themselves as rather poor. After all, salaries which range from $9,000 to $35,000 per year are not large in American economic terms. But the faculty salary median for better schools (those in the top half) is over $15,000, and numerous fringe benefits received probably push this to $17,000 or more. This is not much when compared to the income of a medical doctor, a successful lawyer, or a business executive, so professors feel poor. Even the superstars in the really prestigious universities rarely get over $30,000 or $35,000 per year.

American family median income is around $10,500. The working man, worrying about his taxes and wondering where the next car payment will come from or contemplating his child's dental bill, considers professors very affluent indeed, and by golly, they should suffer, too! Nevertheless, it is common for professorial interest groups to compare academic salaries to those of highly skilled, highly paid professionals and executives and conclude that academics receive far too little. Faculty members typically agree. The universities and colleges have been run for the professors for a long time, so it is reasonable to expect that the professors' view of poverty is the one accepted. In all ranks, fields, and categories, there are some professors who deserve what they get, and who may indeed be underpaid. But there are many others who would find it very difficult to obtain even 80 percent of what they now earn if they went elsewhere. As the squeeze continues, more state budget analysts see this, and the heat is on.

The professional reaction is to fight hard for retention of tenure, since with tenure, the economic rent continues. The countering reaction, increasingly common, is not to raise salaries and to let inflation take the toll. At even 5 percent inflation, a professor's real income can be reduced by 50 percent in under eight years.

So we get to collective bargaining (Howe, 1971; McConnell, 1971; Perkins, 1973, Chap. 10). Professors, increasingly annoyed at both pay and prestige losses, ponder bargaining in trade union fashion for money, working conditions, and job security. A number of schools have already gone this route, and both the American Federation of Teachers (AFT) and the AAUP have formed bargaining units or offered to do the job.

The real key to collective professorial bargaining is productivity control, although most discussions to date have dealt with pay. It would do the profession little good to get 30 percent pay increases, only to have the staff cut 30 percent because the total payroll cannot be increased. Crucial, then, is whether the financial backers will go along with significantly larger budgets, not whether the top administrators will cave in over the bargaining table. One likely outcome is that the top administrators will give in, only to find that they have to fire that 30 percent because the state legislature or private donors or parents will not provide the extra cash.

We will probably see much more collective bargaining in the rest of the 1970s, as the economic condition of universities continues to deteriorate, which seems likely given present moods in most state legislatures and also among many private sources. Because better or higher paying jobs cannot be obtained by most faculty members, reductions in pay will not usually mean people will move on. They will be stuck and often bitter. Effective academic management should develop contingency plans for dealing with collective bargaining and its likely impacts. This course is much wiser than waiting for unionization to occur before strategies or policies for dealing with it are formulated.

One serious result of collective bargaining will be the destruction of the professorial self-image. Gentlemen of means and leisure do not go out on picket lines. If professors do, they will change, perhaps for the better, perhaps not. Few so far have evidently thought through the implications of this change. Unionization might lead to increased faculty power over pay and material benefits, but it may also lead to a significant loss of power over academic and other matters.

Retaining Power

Earlier we suggested that one of the major power losers in the new academic game would be the faculty. If this is true, what can they do to regain power or keep the losses to a minimum? Figure 2 in Chapter Six indicates in detail what could be done. One obvious way to regain power is to control budgets. But unless those budgets can be made larger, this power cannot be used to expand professorial pay, perquisites, or protection. Only selected fields and individuals would win, and the internal result might be more dissension, as faculty groups wrestled with questions of who gets what. It is unlikely that professors can get budget power because administrators are reluctant to give up their major power base and trustees are even more reluctant to. At some institutions, such as Princeton, faculty representatives have been getting significantly more influence in the budgeting process. But this is very far from faculty budgeting control. When a group of faculty members does get a lot of influence or power in preparing the budget, as in the situation discussed in Chapter Two, the administration is placed in serious jeopardy. Another route to power would be to take what business managers might call the total market approach. What does the university offer that others want? If this is known, then professors can expand the supply of these services while contracting expenditures on things not wanted. The market demand is for training that will equip students for good jobs and for relevant universal education that will enable graduates to get ahead economically. Business schools and other professional schools are familiar with these demands and they are willing to move in this direction, but liberal arts colleges usually are not. So far the total market approach has won little acceptance with most professors at nonprofessional and nonvocational schools.

Still another route to power is in taking control of the information system. The more an individual knows about what is going on, the more powerful he is likely to be. But this course of action takes lots of time and lots of work. One must be knowledgeable in such fields as computer technology, management, and systems analysis, which are not even interesting to many professors. A few will become knowledgeable and will probably end up as administrators or managers as a result, but most will not.

Many professors are likely to opt for collective bargaining—particularly after pay has been frozen, or nearly frozen, for a few more years. They will bargain hard and effectively with administrators, and they may get interesting pay gains. But the total financial pie will not grow significantly, so something has to give. The thing that gives will be jobs. As pay goes up, the same percentage of faculty will be released. We will see more of what we are already seeing in many fields, namely an inside elite, well paid and tenured, with a large number of riff-raff, equally qualified but unable to find work at going rates, outside the gates. Only if professors as a group —or their administrators—can persuade financial backers to put up more cash for the same results will this picture change, and it is unlikely that they can in most cases.

Conclusion

A basic administrative problem is suggested by this analysis. Perceived academic payoffs are frequently quite different from those wanted by external university or college supporters. And it is difficult to get these divergent perceptions of payoff to mesh. The very things that tend to make a university great—at least to professors—are often the things that make it difficult to manage the university along the lines wanted by outsiders. The administrator—especially an ineffective one—who pushes his faculty too far may discover that he has acquired a reputation as a wrecker.

Although the successful, prestigious, well-paid professor is often subjected to massive scorn and derision by students and outsiders, professors have had good reasons, up to now, for trying to maximize in the areas they have. If one tried to plot a maximizing strategy, the image of the professorial outsider and research-oriented professor described earlier might be the most effective one for professors to pursue.

This basic problem relates directly to university and college goal divergence problems. Somehow the managers and administrators have to get the job done, even though their most important inputs are frequently activities completely at odds with all notions of efficiency, institutional goal achievement, and sound university management. The major thesis of this book is that states and other financial backers will eventually put enough heat on faculty and administrators to force dramatic change during the remaining years of the 1970s and beyond if adequate changes are not brought about through internal initiative. If we are right, the game will change quickly and dramatically. And it is not likely to be an easy change for either professors or administrators.

Chapter XII

Students

It is possible to write an entire book about university management without paying any attention to students, and many have done so. The more prestigious the school, the less regard often given to students, because most activities and power centers in such a school often have almost nothing to do with students. Since 1945 some of the most prestigious academic posts (from the academic viewpoint) have been in think tanks like Bell Labs or RAND, where there are no students. Peripatetic academics who visit many schools are aware that frequently the lower the school in the academic pecking order, the more important the students. Lower-level schools do not have much research output, so they worry more about students.

Parents, employers, and others outside the academic world tend to believe that students who attend a university full of prestigious scholars that the student never sees are better educated than students who go to a school where such luminaries are absent, even though at the latter school the student would get more faculty attention. The prestigious schools get more than their share of first-rate young minds, although these are the schools where fine minds are frequently most neglected. This is one reason why student upsets, anger, and disorders also occur at places like Stanford, Berkeley, Columbia, and Harvard.

Student riots make headlines, and administrators whose private papers are published in the underground press may have to resign, so it is useful to consider the problems students have, particularly in the so-called good colleges and universities. If the administrator can head off nasty incidents, he will have a longer and happier professional life. Moreover, the better the administrator makes his school academically, the more likely it may be that he may have student troubles.

Deterioration of Educational Quality

The financial trends noted in previous chapters suggest that educational quality will deteriorate during the 1970s. Large state multiversities (and various private institutions in serious financial trouble) are most likely to suffer, although others will not have an easy time. This follows from the financial vulnerability of the state multiversity. Its cost per student is high; this attracts state legislators looking for easy targets. Its students are often most prone to radical behavior; this also attracts attention.

This deterioration will take some predictable forms. Classes will be bigger. Since roughly 80 percent of a large university's costs are labor, the second thing to be cut will be faculty per student. The first thing to be cut will be paper clips, secretaries, and minor capital purchases, but even reducing these costs to zero will not make much difference, so this second cut will come quickly in many cases. As a result, more students will be handled by fewer professors. Students will get less personal attention. This is partly the result of larger classes and small faculties, but it also stems from other manpower cuts. Professors will have fewer assistants and secretaries, so they will have more to do and less time in which to do it.

All sorts of mechanical and computerized teaching will be encouraged. Much instruction can be done better by teaching machines than by professors; this is particularly true of drill materials at lower levels (for example, the first year of languages and of math). Relationships between students and professors will be even more impersonal than they are now. A related development in schools noted more for research than teaching will be that professors will feel abused and withdraw more. This behavioral pattern is common around budget cutting time. "I'll do exactly what you tell me, if you push me around," is the attitude many have when their pet research project is cancelled or classes reach ridiculous sizes. Small classes will be taught by teaching assistants. Some schools may find that even this cannot be done. If the demand for doctorates declines or stagnates, many doctoral programs will shrink, decreasing the pool of graduate students used as teaching assistants. If this happens, the number of small classes will also shrink.

Drop-out rates may accelerate. Even if these rates stay the same, they are ominous. Presently only about half of starting students finish their degree programs at many schools. If private firms had this reject rate, they would have been bankrupt years ago. At prestigious private schools with carefully selected freshmen, 90 percent or more of the students finish; a big multiversity is lucky if significantly more than half finish. In the past, students persisted to graduation because that assured them of a job. But this is no longer true—the jobs are not always there, and many young people are dropping out. If budgets are based on body counts, this drop-out rate could spell big, big trouble for the universities.

This problem relates to the professorial image. Professors want to teach the elite, but they are getting more vocationally oriented students. The students get frustrated and drop out, so the professor has less to do with teaching, which is fine—until the budget cuts come.

If a school can predict even the likelihood of these kinds of deterioration, its management would be wise to consider these trends in its planning and to develop some contingency plans for avoiding, minimizing, and dealing with the effects of diminishing budgets and enrollments. We have more to say about this in Chapter Thirteen.

The percentage of eighteen-year olds attending four-year colleges has declined somewhat in the years since 1970. Academics regard this as a temporary aberration and believe that many students are just taking a year off. If this is not a temporary problem, then everything said earlier in this book will happen a lot sooner than expected. Adult education will become even more crucial for institutional survival. State support of schools is based on enrollments. If enrollments decline, budgets will follow very fast. And tuition is essential to the viability of private schools. The fifteen to twenty-four age group in the United States grew by 12 million in the 1960s, but is expected to grow by only five million in the 1970s and to decline by six million in the 1980s.

Students constantly complain about the treatment they are getting, but so far they have only talked. If the best job option is a routine, menial job in a factory and graduates find that they can earn no more after four expensive years of college than they could have after high school, why should they bother to go to college? The young people may be voting with their feet, and that means real trouble ahead for universities and colleges.

The professional schools are not as hard hit as are institutions of general liberal education. To become a professional, you have to be certified, so students come. But to become a used car salesman, you do not have to go to college. There was a time not too long ago when one went to a university to discover culture, but now much pop culture is something you do in spite of, not because of your university training. If a person works to gain income to have fun, he can earn enough without going to college to finance his interests.

Students want something that few schools offer. What they would like is the intimate, personal, small seminars, given by wise and compassionate instructors who want only to impart wisdom to a handful of students. We catch occasional glimpses of the dream in the truly magnificent professor who does this, and to hell with the rest of the academic world. He also has to be extraordinarily wise to the ways of chairmen and administrators, because anyone of this sort found around a major campus is likely to end up teaching some freshman basic class of two thousand students. But they can only be found by the dozens in the whole United States, while we need them by the tens of thousands to give the students what they really want. Such education necessarily becomes elitist, given the tremendous shortage of human talent. As long as we have a mass or universal higher education system, such dreams will forever elude us. If they were ever real in the United States in this century, it was probably for a year or two in 1935 or 1936 at Harvard or Chicago, in some obscure field with few students then or now.

Many students and faculty do not believe that real resources are limited and must be rationed. It is curious how so many otherwise intelligent people think one can buy anything with money. All the money in the world would not buy the thousands of compassionate professors to do the job the way the students want it done. They just do not exist. Students will never give up on the dream, so we must face up to how to handle the problem better without having the resources to achieve it.

Student-University Relations

Most professors and administrators went through a more elitist higher education system than now exists. Fewer and often better students were in college thirty, twenty, and even ten years ago. Those whose own academic careers began in the 1930s and the 1940s lived in a totally different world, where only about 5 to 15 percent of eighteen-year olds went on to college. Today over 30 percent of the eighteen to twenty-four age group is enrolled. In many states, 40 percent or more of the high school graduates enter college. Universities are now mass education systems and are becoming universal ones. There are also more young people around to educate. Absolute numbers have gone up steadily—but they are likely to fall off before very long.

The result is that relatively few of us are emotionally prepared for our present system. It has different kinds of students and quite different educational purposes superimposed on all of the older goals. Students sense this clearly, but educators rarely do. Multiversities suffer more than other state schools, because they tend to see themselves as prestige universities. A new junior college, formed to handle the new students, will not be in so much trouble, nor will a typical new nonresidential four-year state college.

Mass or universal education implies some developments that schools will eventually have to accept, like it or not. Here are some that are worth considering when preparing contingency plans for a given university or college. *In loco parentis* is dying rapidly, and it will be dead before 1980. It worked reasonably well in an elitist system, but it tends to fall apart in a mass system. There are too many types of students for any administration to handle them all like a bunch of immature children. Students will be treated just like anyone else. If they get in serious trouble, the local police will handle them. This development will have positive benefits for universities. They can avoid police costs, and safety officers on campus can earn their pay by giving out traffic tickets and directing strangers. And student affairs offices will be free for more useful work than discipline for criminal offenses.

Expulsion may well become easier. Organizations try to survive, and survival is hindered when protesting students keep annoying the system. If schools decide that the business of the school is education, they may decide to exclude those who have other ideas. If a worker goofs up and cannot do the job within the given constraints, he may be fired. One university goal is to prepare people for jobs which usually involves some kind of job discipline. A related development may be closer policing of admissions for potential activists. Just as a government agency will not hire certain types, or as firms rarely hire known Communists, universities may not admit persons who meet formal entry requirements but could cause serious trouble.

It is possible that higher education financing will be done through educational vouchers or chits. Present proposals suggest that each young person be given chits of given value for a year's education. He or she could use these at any school that would accept him and could select the school he or she considered most relevant to his or her needs. This is a pretty recent and quite revolutionary idea. It would mean that the schools most attractive to students would get them. No matter how good a college or university, it would be only as good as students think it is, regardless of what professors or administrators believe about it. Universities would have to become much more market oriented than they now are. Already some pilot work has begun with chits in California high schools. A further pressure toward use of federal chits may come from present court cases involving out-of-state tuition. Students have taken universities to court for charging out-of-state fees when they have some justification (for example, marriage to a resident, or voting in a state) for claiming resident status. If state universities, particularly good ones, cannot charge more for out-of-state students, one solution would be to give all students federal chits. This system would enable a student to pick a school anyplace in the country, and the schools deemed undesirable by students would have to improve, or else.

Good schools, defined here as those that provide students with the best opportunities for achieving their goals, might be swamped, and poorer schools will be frantically scrambling for students. If this trend continues, there will be even more pressure to get institutional goals in line with student goals.

If schools move closer to job markets in training, it is likely that student dissatisfaction and protest will decline. Most students want to learn something useful for the future. Professional school students, aware that whatever they are learning has a pretty sure payoff, rarely strike (although they complain a lot!). Protests usually begin in the unfocused arts—the areas most likely to be cut back. Students will get locked into career channels earlier, and they will not complain so much. Career-oriented students can wait. When they are certified doctors or lawyers or managers or accountants, they can burrow from within, as many young professionals are doing. Rebelling too soon merely cuts item off from their chosen profession. A few years ago at the height of student protest, it seemed that revolution and chaos were imminent on many campuses. The very rapid decline in protest surprised many. The wilder types left school because this form of revolution went nowhere. Many followers, faced with grim job markets, shaped up and tried to learn something useful. Others who might have drifted aimlessly through school choose not to attend. The remaining students are fairly serious, and are interested in the traditional class jumping and vocational training that American universities and colleges have always provided.

The image that emerges is of the university as a factory whose major output is relevant educational services. Students get processed through the system as efficiently as possible; professors do their thing in the classrooms; administrators try to make the whole system run as smoothly as possible, balancing as best they can the claims and pressures of all interested parties. It looks pretty grim to the present mainstream academics and arts students. Because it does, there are certain to be many counterpressures. Most will fail, because those wanting a different system typically do not have either the political muscle or the financial resources to make schools over in some other image.

Because some persons feel very strongly about this—enough so that they are willing to give up future income, prestige, and social status—we will probably see considerable development of free universities, various forms of communal educations, and similar developments outside of the formal university structure. How significant such developments will be depends on the dedication and enthusiasm of the persons willing to sacrifice to make such schools work. One thing they will not have is lots of resources, except voluntary or underpaid ones. If they turn out to be fairly large in the aggregate, and more significant than conventional universities, we may see a new development of considerable significance within higher education. However, this does not seem to be very likely in the foreseeable future.

If new ideas do have impact, it will be because society will move away from its present certification psychosis. There is evidence to suggest that many are questioning our present premises. But to date, not much has been done to change them. We are even making efforts to get more previously uncertified persons (for example, Blacks) into the system. If employers and society will accept a man who is educated in any way, we might get someplace. Such a development seems rather unlikely in the next ten years.

Informal new systems, operating outside formal certification groups and state sanctioned systems, are not likely to attract the mainstream students or faculty. (Administrators are totally out of this game, since most of these informal schools have relatively little administration.) They will attract some dissatisfied and bright people and they could eventually affect formal university and college developments. Administrators might well observe carefully the development of these informal systems. The more structured and conventional mainstream universities become, the more strident the objections to them will become, and the more likely it is that intriguing developments will occur outside the mainstream university system.

Those committed to radical change as manifested in free universities have been very disappointed to date. Such universities and colleges have flourished briefly, then have declined to nothing as eager supporters lost interest. Unless longer-term committments of resources can be found than have been to date, such utopian developments are likely to be far into the future.

Professors as the Real Enemy

In a more structured, vocationally-oriented university, it is likely that students will finally recognize that their real enemies are professors. Most student demonstrations have been directed at administrators, but it is the individual professor who fails to interact with his students, who gives failing grades, and who acts as the quality control sieve barring entry into his discipline. As these things become more important, students may react against individual professors or departments rather than against administrators who could not make professors conform to student desires even if they tried.

Administrators may soon find themselves trying to arbitrate disputes between angry students and stubborn faculty, without great success. We have moved a long way from the 1930s, but many faculty were educated then and have not changed very much. If there is a significant generation gap, it will show up here. This point was overlooked in the 1960s because some administrative reforms (for example, changing policies on *in loco parentis*) helped ease the situation. Also, there were (and are) many faculty whose version of the good life consists of student-faculty control of the university, with the faculty, of course, playing the dominant role. Many of these faculty members encouraged protests. It remains to be seen if they will encourage protests against other faculty, who happen to be unfair in grading or whose courses are dull.

At a growing number of campuses where there are faculty unions or serious consideration of faculty unionization, student leaders and activists have been expressing increasing interest in participating in collective bargaining, or in opposing it for the faculty without student participation. The students see the faculty and not the administration as their major opponent, and administrators in the future may well try to form coalitions with students to oppose or resist the faculty on various issues (McConnell, 1971; Perkins, 1973, Chap. 10; Shark, 1972 and 1973; *Chronicle of Higher Education,* April 16 and 30, 1973).

Declining Value of Higher Education

There was a time when a scribe earned money because he was literate. Mass primary education killed this monopoly. Later the college man, the one in a hundred, had good status and earning power because he was a graduate. Still later, in the present generation, the man with a doctorate is the high status person, and it should be no surprise that young strivers should want this status symbol.

But as more people get more higher education, the dollar value of education diminishes. This is one of our present difficulties. Most older people still feel that any college education is as good as any other. But the quality of a school, and the kinds of things it teaches, are becoming very significant. Employers are looking for applicants with specific, useful training—for accountants and engineers and schoolteachers, for lawyers, doctors, optometrists, and mathematicians. The broad gauge man of letters who can do anything is gradually disappearing. This is frustrating to students and faculty alike because it implies that those parts of the university that are job or career oriented will get ahead, while those more concerned with noneconomic and nonapplied pursuits will be shortchanged.

Students are perceptive, and studies of enrollment changes in American universities suggest that growing numbers of students are trying to get into fields that promise payoff. If you need a good job at the end of your education, it is wise to study something the world thinks relevant.

But we have never lived in a world where 40 percent or more of all adults have some higher education (only California now has a total as high as this, which may explain some of its peculiarities). We will be well into this world by 1980, and by 1990 it will be the real world for most of the United States. As we move millions of students through the system, it is likely that some totally unexpected developments will occur. No matter what an individual's aspirations or expectations may be, they will be unrealized, because the model on which they are built (be it from the world of last year or of Socrates) is already obsolete. Students coming into the university find that their intuitive models, put together by adults of all ages and types, are wrong. It is traumatic for them, but it is also traumatic for all university and college personnel.

If everybody gets to college, the fellow who gets ahead may be the one who just keeps on studying. This is particularly true in rapidly developing fields such as management or business. A student is partially obsolete the moment he walks out the university door. The comers and climbers may demand much more continuing adult education than they have in the past, and one growth area—which presently has very little status or money—is in extension work, part-time programs, and adult education.

Again one of our models collapses. This time it is the notion of a block of educational time, which turns out the complete citizen, ready to work productively for forty years or more. Now, the poor ex-student discovers, after a year or two, that he is falling behind. So back to school he goes, probably at night in a continuation center, and probably for job and profession-oriented study (strike one more blow against the liberal arts)—because only in this way can he avoid being swamped by bright younger people who know much more than he does.

The rapid development of continuing education fits our new model neatly. Education for use, job linked, easily financed (because most of it is rather cheap, along with being politically popular), fits the new educational image. But this model also reduces the significance of traditional, formal education. Students will have to adjust to a longer-term process of education than they now do, and as many adults already have.

Power

Students typically have very little real power in the university or college—something they always complain about. In recent years, many students have gained access to committees, but when they arrive at the meetings, disillusionment follows. Old professors mumble incantations about problems and people the students know nothing about. After a few meetings, they do not even bother to come. One of the harder tasks for a chairman of any university committee these days is to get his student members even to show up. Not having studied our power map (Tables 3 and 4 in Chapter Three), the students do not realize that university or college power is terribly diffuse and ill-defined. They tend to react by feeling that somehow they have been cheated—power has got to be around someplace! But it isn't. Student participation in matters affecting them is likely to increase at many schools, but this does not mean that they will get or share in much more real power. If transient students did share significantly in decision-making authority or official power, this could have highly undesirable consequences for the institution (Brewster, 1971, Chapter 4).

Students could gain power exactly the way faculty could, by gaining control of budgets and information. It is unlikely that they will ever gain any real budget control, although a student is occasionally found on a faculty budget committee—that can recommend but not control. Given the complexity of modern budgets, young students are in a poor position to evaluate them efficiently, because they do not yet have enough practical knowledge or experience. The old pros on the committee can easily argue them down.

This leaves information, and again youth and lack of knowledge precludes very effective work. By the time any student really learns enough about the complex operations of the university, he graduates. Serious study of even minor points of university operation can take years. Students may feel that the power plant is polluting the campus, but by the time they find out the facts, let alone do anything about it, the school year is finished.

There is one simple information system that students could develop that could lead to real power. They could keep careful records on every ex-student—of the job he or she obtained, whether or not the university department or school was helpful in getting students to their desired goals, and whether or not the education received was relevant to the student. All of this material could be compiled and published, much as teaching ratings now are. The results could lead to major internal institutional shifts. Consider a freshman picking up this manual the first year it was published. He is interested in studying history, so he turns to the section of this department. He finds a notation to the effect that the history department not only does not know what happened to its undergraduate students, and it does not care. Scattered information from graduates shows that a few went to good graduate schools, a few found high school teaching jobs, but the majority are either unemployed or working as shoe clerks.

Our student looks at the optometry school. He finds that every graduate is employed, that the school knows where they are and what they are being paid, and that most students felt that the school was very helpful in getting them useful and creative positions. Similarly the chemistry department knows about most of its graduates, as does the math department. Other schools and departments have mixed records. Some just don't give a damn about their students.

Guess where our freshman will end up. Such information could cause massive shifts in majors and resources, as students followed the fields that at least tried to help them out on graduation. After a few years of rapidly falling enrollments, even the most recalcitrant department would be eagerly trying to train and place its students. Too bad this will never happen because politically oriented students rarely are interested in such dismal proceedings. But of all the things students could do, this one information system could be most effective in giving them useful power.

One wonders how many students passing through a university or college really want to extend power and influence in decision-making and policy formulation beyond a few areas that directly affect them. In the search for Harvard's current president a few years ago, the selection committee sought advice and inputs from 16,000 students, but only 196 responded. Were the students just not interested, or were they cynical enough to believe that their inputs would make little difference to the outcome?

About the only chance students have to gain significant internal power is to seize control of some information system. They may also exert indirect power by not coming to or withdrawing from a particular school. Other avenues look dim indeed, most notably the traditional one of marching on the president's office. Confrontations may be fun, but they do not lead to power—at least not for more than a fleeting moment. One reason is that the particular kind of power they want is often not there. It is scattered all over the power maps we have shown, and until students realize this, they will remain impotent.

Trying to figure out what students will do is much more difficult than most other university forecasting. Students reflect the whole society and the way it handles its young, and proper forecasting involves predicting how society will change. One can see a whole set of potential developments, depending on what happens beyond the university boundaries. In spite of much uncertainty, effective academic managers will develop contingency plans based on different assumptions and sets of conditions that have a fairly significant chance of becoming reality. Being prepared is much sounder management than fighting fires. It seems clear that whatever happens will be rather surprising to those who fail to do meaningful contingency planning.

Chapter XIII

Policy Implications and Institutional Change

It is clear that universities and colleges are under strong pressure to change, and that such pressure is unlikely to go away in the future. Academic institutions, whether they like it or not, are becoming increasingly open systems as they function in increasingly turbulent, changing, and competitive environments. Pressures from the external environment and from students will force academic institutions to become more structured—though not necessarily less democratic—and more concerned with clearer and ordered goals. Priorities will have to be clarified and changed at many schools if the schools are to be viable and adequately successful. Clearcut decisions will have to be made about what is to be done in universities and colleges. This is really what much of the student turmoil of several years ago was about, and it is what budget-cutting and stringent financial constraints in the 1970s are about.

Various publics or constituencies are disenchanted with academic institutions, and they want change. Rising costs are also a major factor necessitating institutional change. The job of top management, and especially of the chief executives of universities and colleges, is to get effective change related to the institution's viability and success as fast as possible. This chapter considers some policy implications and operational guidelines for change.

If and when goal systems change, some members within the academic system will gain or lose power. If they do not change, power will increasingly shift externally to outsiders at many institutions. We can expect that those who lose will fight bitterly against such changes; others who will gain will feel that the new directions are sound and sober reflections of reality. Some parties will go down fighting; others may try to figure out how to shift directions and join the new movements. One purpose in this chapter is to suggest how such groups can win—or at least not lose nearly as much—if they choose to change.

Current Developments

We have been observing recent past trends and projecting them into the future with a cloudy crystal ball. Here are some of the developments that may have major impacts on universities and colleges and their immediate environments.

The financial crunch will undoubtedly continue. There is no evidence to suggest that this crunch will not get a lot worse for many schools before it gets better. University costs continue to escalate at 7 to 10 percent per year; potential budget resources suggest that 4 or 5 percent per year more money is all that most schools can realistically expect to get. There should be fairly continuous budgetary stringency throughout the higher educational system in the United States in the foreseeable future. Of course there will be a few exceptions. A handful of laggard states may try to catch up, and their systems may get

20 percent additional cash per year for the decade. But most bigger states have already made their major expansion push. A handful of favored private, prestige schools may also escape, but even the better endowed private schools are now getting into quite serious trouble.

State governments, reflecting what is clearly a widespread nervousness about the goals of institutions of higher education, will push for their goal system in preference to the academic one, with varying degrees of success. Bills already in the legislatures of California and Ohio would require that professors must teach twelve hours per week, and that professors must be on campus forty hours per week. Although these measures were killed quietly in committee, others may not be. Michigan has already passed a similar bill, although it was recently struck down by the state supreme court.

Administrators will eagerly seek optional sources of financing. The most likely source is the federal government, and the most desirable arrangement would be government funds with no strings attached. Federal support may increase, but such funds will not be unrestricted. Federal strings, to pressure schools to meet federally sponsored goals, may be more desirable than pressure to meet state goals, but not much better. Moreover, the states will not back off from university funding, so any federal funding will be supplemental, not total. The states will have a major say about university goals.

Research money will still be available, but most of it will be: (1) tied to specific projects, such as energy, air pollution, specific developments in physics, and some social problems; (2) mainly for projects with specific payoffs, which means that much soft, esoteric research, pure research, or research not having significant contemporary relevance may be very difficult to finance because results in these areas have not been impressive and sponsors are losing patience; (3) given to schools with proven records, when specific results are wanted (the general, "pass the money around to see what happens" approach is losing ground, and if soft federal financing continues, the amounts will be relatively small). Schools seeking funds had better be good in applied areas, and prepared to prove their expertise with short-term research results of the proper quality. Those who cannot meet such conditions will not survive very well, if at all, in the 1970s grantsman's race.

The university system growth rate, in terms of total students of traditional college age will slow down in the mid-1970s, with major reductions in growth likely by 1980. This development is largely demographic, and it has already begun. Some of the drop might be partially offset by higher percentages of young people going to college, but the days of explosive growth in numbers are over. A smaller percentage (39) of eighteen-year olds started college in 1973 than in 1970 (43 percent). This development will undoubtedly have much bearing on financial support in the second half of this decade.

Inflation rates of two major things universities and colleges buy—high-skill manpower and buildings—show no signs of slackening. Costs rise by 10 percent per year, while the economy gains by 4 or 5 percent per year. Universities unfortunately need exactly the kinds of things that inflate faster than the average. One major reason for building cost inflation is that current buildings include sophisticated heating systems, extra telecommunications equipment, computer facilities, and air-conditioning, and they also require large parking areas. If universities could make do with ultrasimple, barracks-like buildings, costs would fall, but few persons would advocate this course. Price inflation could come to a halt rather fast if the present surplus of academics, combined with the lessened need for more buildings, lead to lower expenditures. Around 75 to 85 percent of operating budgets are typically for personnel, and over 50 percent are for professional personnel. Already many states and schools have responded to budget crunches by not raising wages. Academic employees object, but given their poor alternatives, there is not too much they can do about it. The declining rate of increase in student enrollments may make new building construction rare, creating a saving on the capital budget.

Given this cost pressure on schools and the resulting need for much more private and state support, states and others will become much more inquisitive about how funds are used. This should mean more concern about goal systems and more pressure to get them in line with deeply held external convictions and values. This point also interrelates with the apparent deep-seated suspicion of academics and young people quite common in many states. Such suspicion leads quickly to efforts to cut budgets and pass laws to get things in line. We can expect that both these things will happen in many states. Private schools may also be in for some deep trouble as their backers express similar doubts and fears. It is clear that in many institutions the whole academic game will change sharply as these pressures mount. Much of the above bothers most academics, because it implies that unpleasant changes are in store. We would just as soon fumble on in our own pleasant and accustomed ways, ignoring that cold and hostile world outside. But we are not likely to be able too.

To achieve the needed goal system changes, the university or college will have to work out a better fit with the goal systems hoped for by the state and federal governments, major private donors, students, parents, and various other outside groups. Few universities will ever have goal systems that mesh completely with the desires of their major financial backers, but they will be forced to move in that direction. Such changes will involve both the efficiency or cost dimension of academic institutions and the revenue, demand, or market test dimension. If a given institution does relatively well with regard to the latter, the former would usually not present critical problems.

Efficiency and Cost Pressures

There will be much stress on efficiency in all dimensions. There is already a very extensive literature about efficiency measures, and the upshot is that it is extremely difficult to measure the efficiency of something as complicated as a university or college. We will have to try much harder in the future.

In many dimensions, academic institutions are terribly inefficient. Most waste space and other plant; most misutilize expensive personnel badly; and most perform housekeeping and maintenance functions poorly. If no one knows what output is supposed to be, there never is any reason to worry about the size of any individual's output. Hence, whatever he does is as important, significant, and relevant as anything done by anyone else. But infinite goals mean infinite costs and resources.

Here are some inefficiencies that are very common in most universities and colleges today, along with some modest proposals to increase efficiency. Minor changes in policies could cause large efficiency gains.

Professional Efficiency. If we accept the state goal of mass or universal college education as important, then one way to hold costs down is to have more students per professor. The typical modern state multiversity—as well as most other schools—tends to have a faculty-student ratio of from ten to twenty-five to one. Thus each professor should handle about fifty to one hundred students per semester or quarter, assuming each student takes about five separate classes. Most university professors do nothing of the sort. One major escape hatch has been extensive use of teaching assistants, selected from among the (hopefully) brighter and more competent graduate students. Students tend to resent this type of teaching, as do legislatures. Most of it occurs in the freshman or sophomore years, but one can find major university departments in good schools where the majority of *all* undergraduate instruction is taught by apprentices who receive low wages.

What are the professors doing? Working long and hard with a handful of graduate students; spending lots of time on research; and, if externally successful, spending much time off campus consulting, trying to get another grant, or performing some public service. Many good and successful faculty men optimize by following this pattern. Relatively few know or care who a great freshman teacher is, but Nobel prize winners make national headlines (to say nothing of pulling down an eighty-thousand dollar prize, tax free, and being swamped with offers of tenured, endowed, chairs—and salaries of over forty-thousand dollars—from every major university in the world). Let others mess with the freshman!

Many university administrations even now do not know what real loads individual professors are carrying—the information system is totally undeveloped. It was never important before. But the financial attractions of making professors work more with students will become increasingly appealing. The crude economics of the situation are suggestive. If the university manages to obtain two thousand dollars per student per year (in state support, tuition, and all other sources), if each professor handles about 60 percent of the contact hours for these students; and if the student-faculty ratio is around twenty to one—then the whole professional payroll can be met by moving up to a norm of fifty to sixty student contact hours per semester.

This reasoning suggests that all professors do is teach, when in fact in the modern university this is but a small part of what they do. But note the change in goals here. If the state demands that they teach, this sort of crude measuring stick using contact hours (with the inevitable exceptions, plus and minus, built into the system) will be increasingly utilized. Faculty with propensities to do other things may object, but they may be forced to teach more. This is not only an efficiency point, but also a major goal system change for most universities.

Research Efficiency. This will take the form of working on projects with payouts. One does research that can be sold. If the scholar can convince someone to pay his costs for research, then it gets done. If he cannot, he goes back to the classroom. This would also be a major goal system change. Many professors are interested in goals we have labeled as *truth,* and many of these cannot be priced on any market. But this kind of research will be curtailed, or at least cut back sharply, because—with the various efficiency measures suggested here—there will be no place to hide such expenditures, and there will be no one willing to pay for them.

Plant Efficiency. The easy way to get more space, laboratory facilities, library use, and so on is to work more hours per day. Universities vary on this point, but most have low utilization rates. When buildings fill up five or six hours per day, the usual administrative advice is to buy more buildings. But an optional (and much cheaper) solution is to use the buildings eight, ten, or twenty-four hours per day. Professors are gentlemen, and students are busy, so few are willing to work at 8:00 A.M. on Saturday, from 3:00 P.M. to 5:00 P.M. on Fridays, or at other unusual hours. But classes scheduled at such times—particularly classes using scarce facilities such as laboratories—could save $10 or $15 million—the cost of a new building. Few persons in universities even know what utilization rates are, and fewer do anything about improving them. Administrators may have data about utilization, but it is often incorrect. Students and professors do informal rescheduling without letting anyone know about it.

This whole question might be solved quite easily, as we

suggested in Chapter Four, by paying premiums to professors who are willing to teach at inconvenient or unconventional hours and offering small reductions in fees to students who sign up for such odd-hour classes. Why do we operate from nine to five? Because we do. Quite a few students and professors might be pleased to have classes at 11:00 P.M., or even on Sundays. At least it's worth a try.

This suggestion repels virtually all faculty and administrators, to say nothing of students. It seems somehow so mechanical, so technocratic, so dehumanizing, so nasty! Yet it is quite likely that many universities will have improved their utilization of space by the 1980s.

Job Market Efficiency. Rarely have Americans worried much about what students study. If one person is a poet, while the second plods through the business school, it has not mattered much. But it may matter a great deal in the future. Some fields (for example, management or business) are getting so complicated that one has to study the field systematically before he can hope to be hired. Other fields are turning out graduates who are employable at the same wage rate they could have received if they had gone to work directly out of high school. If the state and federal governments are going to put their scarce funds into education, they are quite likely to insist on relevant education, as they see it.

Relevant means having some payoff desired by the financial backer. We already see this in federal grants to selected areas (for example, public health, medicine, transportation, energy, pollution, dentistry). Some fields are more relevant than others from the market point of view. States want more electronic technicians, more engineers of certain kinds, more geologists, and more business and management students. This pressure for relevance will result in much more interest in the job market. We are in the mass or universal education business in a major way, and the old notion of education for a small elite of idle gentlemen with independent incomes is definitely out. Most young people are probably in college largely to prepare for a relevant career, and the universities must restructure their programs and majors to adjust to this fact.

Few universities can give a complete breakdown of jobs now held by last year's graduates, let alone any earlier graduates. This was none of the university's business, so no one really paid much attention to the problem and the information system is underdeveloped. Most professional schools are more likely to know, because their prestige, importance, and well-being depend on acceptance of their graduates as well-qualified professionals.

It is not too difficult to build the information system needed to reveal who is getting the biggest payoff from his college education. The federal government is sponsoring long-term studies of manpower demand. And so we come to the concept of controlled majors. Entering students will be told about the job market in fields of interest to them. Only where there appears to be the likelihood of a good job at the end of training will students be admitted to a major field. Where pay is good and job satisfaction is likely to be at least adequate, the department will expand in students and faculty. Those departments that are not interested in the problem (and hence do not know what is happening to their graduates) and those in areas of labor surplus will tend to diminish in size and stature. Persons working in high-demand areas like this notion, because for them it implies considerable gains in prestige. Often these are areas that are not totally respectable intellectually, such as management, business, dentistry, public health, and engineering. Objections to controlled majors come from those in areas where the first job has never been seen as terribly crucial. The idea cuts deeply against the philosophical grain of such disciplines.

Information Retrieval Efficiency. As we mentioned earlier, there is not much point in collecting information unless there is a need for it. Now such information does matter, so it will be collected. Information processing and retrieval are getting cheaper, thanks to computers. About every five years, the cost of getting information processed drops by 90 percent. Shortly, it will be too expensive not to compute, and universities and colleges will join other complex organizations in obtaining all the information they need to operate reasonably efficiently.

Another aspect of university information retrieval relates to libraries and related research materials. This is another area subject to the financial crunch. It costs more than ten dollars just to get a book catalogued, and costs continue to rise. It seems unlikely that we will see many new multimillion volume libraries. More likely are systems of facsimile reproduction, new means of bibliographical search, interlibrary loans, and other means of retrieving information more efficiently. The overall result may be lower unit cost for any given university.

All of these efficiency changes will be resisted by most universities. But they will come, either by reform from within or as the results of external pressure. One problem for faculty, particularly excellent faculty of the old school, is that many good schools will be having financial problems simultaneously in the foreseeable future. Threats of resignation, traditionally made in an effort to prevent change, will no longer be meaningful because, in fact, there will be no place to go. As this is written (in 1974), we have already seen a noticeable softening of most academic markets, and quite a few unhappy people are not moving. There are not many lush opportunities a few states away, and the prestigious private schools are not expanding.

This factor will strengthen managers' or administrators' hands in the crunch. It is easy to forecast initial reactions—such as mass protests, unions, indignant letters, and resignation threats—to the above changes. But unless markets for academics change through unforeseen causes, goal systems can and will be shifted.

Generating Income and Demand: The Market Test

Academic personnel frequently are reluctant to acknowledge that they are in the marketing game, because for them this implies vulgar salesmanship, hucksterism, and other horrors better left to private profit-making businesses. But anyone who has looked at any college catalogue or brochure is quite aware that selling is the name of the higher education game, now more than ever. Many schools have recently added business, marketing, and public relations specialists to their staffs, and some have been using such experts as consultants. If you cannot attract students, you are in deep trouble regardless of who your financial backers are. As traditional elitist schools also have more trouble attracting students (even poorer ones), they, too, will place more overt stress on marketing and salesmanship.

In general, however, what is needed at numerous institutions, far more than salesmanship or marketing or advertising, is serious marketing research, innovation, and general educational and program changes. If an institution is trying to market an unwanted, unattractive or defective product, salesmanship alone is not likely to do much good over time, especially in a relatively sophisticated buyers' market. Perhaps Ralph Nader and his Raiders should investigate the higher educational sector next!

Universities and colleges were able to escape the market test for a long time because the product they offered was historically considered to be so good, and was so restricted, that only those with enough cash and brains could buy it. But by around 1965, the game clearly began to change, and many who got the precious degree found that it did not necessarily bring them riches and status. Hence the disillusion of financial sponsors; the disturbed students; the unhappy faculties; and the strong pressures for goal system changes. Sometime around 1965, many people discovered that in the end, the university, like any other institution, could only thrive and prosper if whatever it offered was at least in large part what its clienteles wanted. Universities and colleges long have advertised a product that would have led to legal charges of fraud if they had been private companies. Now the supporters and clienteles have found the academic institutions out, and many colleges and universities are examining their inflated claims, false advertising, and disillusioned students. In similar circumstances, many private companies would go bankrupt. Hopefully the universities and colleges will, instead, change.

A university or college need not focus all of its resources, talents, and energies on responding to external demand and pressure, or in meeting the market test for its services. However, it must do enough in this regard if the institution is to continue to have enough resources, soft money, and discretionary funds to do the things that many of the faculty and various administrators feel should be done and want to do. Facilitating the growth of those parts of the institution that are stronger in terms of external demand and opportunities will enable subsidization of the weaker parts.

The following are some of the ways that many universities and colleges could gain added revenues, respond more effectively to external demands and opportunities, and meet the market test. Some related concrete examples are presented in the next section.

Career Preparation and Jobs. The simplest way to do this is to expand or create professional, semiprofessional, and vocational programs, courses, majors, and degrees that provide the relevancy, quality, methodology, and content which are still important in attracting students and enabling them to get good jobs. It is a mistake to consider only pay scales for graduates—many students are more interested in relevant, interesting, and significant careers than the highest possible pay.

Career preparation and training can be facilitated through work-study programs, internships, and field projects not just in professional schools or majors in vocational programs but in many other areas as well. There can be vocational training in liberal arts programs. For example, if courses in editing, printing technology, information analysis, communications, and public relations were offered in the English department, English majors would be more competitive on the job market. Most English departments would resist this, but it may well come, particularly after quite a few of the English faculty are dismissed for lack of student demand. Similarly, courses in stenographic and office management training could be added in various liberal arts programs. And lower level and more practical materials could be added to the curricula of many science and more theoretical and esoteric engineering programs. An interdisciplinary, cross-departmental approach can be used to make career preparation more effective. Majors in liberal arts or science fields could be provided with considerably greater leeway to take courses, minors, or even dual majors in the professional, semiprofessional and vocational programs. This would increase enrollments in the arts and sciences. And a university with strong professional schools that are permitted to flourish is likely to attract good undergraduates in other fields who plan to enter one of these professional schools for graduate work.

On the other hand, if students from career-oriented programs are required, encouraged or permitted to take a substantial number of courses—or to pursue minors or dual majors—in liberal arts or science departments, the enrollments in these departments will benefit through a derived demand effect. And many of the better professional and vocational schools do encourage such broad education and training for their students. However, here too, the noncareer oriented courses will attract more students only if they are seen by the students as relevant, interesting, and worthwhile.

In sum, career training versus nonvocational education does not—and in our view, should not—have to be an either or proposition. An adequate balance between the two tends to be desirable for both the student and the institution. But the values, attitudes and beliefs of many faculty members at many schools will have to be changed before this balance is achieved. In turn, this will mean significant modifications, changes, and innovations in courses, curricula, and programs, as well as considerable redeployment of faculty resources. Those who are not willing to change stand a good chance of being among the losers.

Part-Time Education. This can be for undergraduates or graduates, for degree credit or not; during the day or in the evening; during the summer or during the regular academic year; and for live-in or commuter students. It can be career oriented, nonvocational, or leisure-time in nature. It can be for employed people, housewives, senior citizens, or the underprivileged who want to get up to college entrance level.

A growing number of schools are now offering programs that use the same core of faculty for both full-time and part-time students. Students are also permitted to switch from part-time to full-time and vice versa. If a given full-time student does not want to pass up a good job opportunity that comes his way, he can switch to the part-time program to finish his degree work. If a part-time student can get leave from his work, he can switch to the full-time program. Many employers have shown a willingness to cooperate with both their employees and the schools they attend in scheduling work.

There are virtually endless part-time education market opportunities for universities and colleges, if they are really interested. The idea of part-time education is not new, but not many schools have done very much about it to date. As our society grows more affluent, as people have more leisure time and also live longer, and as more people acquire a more lasting thirst for knowledge, education, and career improvement and change, the potential market for part-time education increases. Some major part-time programs, like the University of California Extension, have been in operation for more

than fifty years, and many of the institutions that have such programs are among those that are relatively well off today. Even some
of the prestigious private schools have shown increased interest in
part-time programs as traditional enrollments have dropped.

The California example is interesting in efficiency terms. The
state provides the facilities (buildings, lights, and so on), which are
cheap because they are there and are not used at night. The classes
are held if enough students sign up to cover the professors' costs plus
a small overhead. This leads to courses in everything from basket-
weaving and marital problems to postdoctoral physics, depending on
what the people want. And many of the courses turn a very nice
profit for the university.

Most of this extension work is nondegree, but some schools
have begun to offer degrees and more will. If the market demands
something, and if there is money to be made (either directly or
through body count state funding), someone will try it. Shades of
Madison Avenue huckstering.

Open University and Lifelong Learning. This can be a varia-
tion of part-time programs, and it can also include correspondence
courses with or without degree credit. These programs can be operated at relatively low cost and with considerable efficiency. Some do
permit mature students who never graduated from high school but
who have certain qualifications or pass certain examinations to enter
undergraduate programs, and some permit students without undergraduate degrees to enter graduate programs. Good schools that
have been experimenting with mature student admissions have found
that such students typically perform better on the average and also
often get significantly more out of their higher education than do
the regular students.

The open university—also referred to as the extended university—is more common in Britain than in the United States at
present. However, there are vast opportunities for American higher
education in this sphere. In an open university prior formal academic preparation and formal examinations may be waived as
requirements for admission, graduation, or both in lieu of other
qualifications. An open university also provides correspondence
courses and other off-campus learning. Such programs and courses

vary in length and may or may not involve the pursuit of degrees, diplomas, and certificates.

In lifelong learning individuals continue to be educated, in the ways they want, throughout their lives. Programs include business administration and management; retreading for engineers, technicians, and scientists; retraining and upgrading for educators; and medical, nursing, and health care seminars. Much of lifelong learning is job related because many people want knowledge that will help them get ahead in their profession or trades; universities and colleges have much to offer in this area. Vocationalization of traditional curricula may disturb some, but if the students do not come in sufficient numbers to traditional offerings, then one answer is to find other market opportunities and capitalize on them. (In the end, the market test determines the viability of much of higher education.) Lifelong learning also involves nonvocational programs and courses related to hobbies, leisure time, senior citizen interests, intellectual and cultural pursuits, and personal and social problems. And many programs include both vocational and nonvocational dimensions.

Taking the Classroom Off-Campus. This can be a variant of the two previous approaches, or it may involve regular or part-time students. The classroom can be taken to plants, offices, military bases, hospitals, airports, other schools, prisons, or wherever any group wants some education and is willing to pay for it. It can also involve programs in outlying areas, abroad, on ships, and in or at many other locations.

Relevance. Elimination of many of the anachronistic admission, prerequisite, course, and graduation requirements would attract many students. Qualified students could be granted deferred admission enabling them to enroll in the institution within a period of several years, or to leave and return within an extended period of time. And a great deal can be done at numerous schools to change and upgrade the content and quality of many programs and courses. Work-study programs, student internships in more fields, field projects, and more study in other locations would attract many students. The same is true of more appropriate student activities, special seminars, smaller classes, and tutorials for undergraduates, especially for freshmen and sophomores in the bigger and more impersonal universities.

Cooperative Programs. Many kinds of cooperative or joint educational and research programs involving two or more institutions could lead to more relevant education and more options for students, and also would have synergetic effects resulting in greater operating efficiency. The cluster college concept, like that of the Claremont University complex, can also lead to significant benefits.

Public and Community Service. Many of the adult education programs are actually an important kind of public or community service. Apart from directly generating more income for the school, they can also build greater support for it in other important ways. By becoming more of a cultural and information center in the community and opening its libraries and other facilities to outsiders, a university can build external support. The same is true of focusing more research and courses on critical community or societal problems, and having more faculty members and other personnel engage in outside activities where they can make a meaningful contribution.

Examples

Within the richness and diversity of California higher education can be found many examples of the kinds of steps academic institutions are taking to alter their goals and increase their enrollments. We have chosen a few of the most interesting and effective new programs—there are many more, within the state and throughout the nation.

UCLA. UCLA is one good example of a university that is working to generate income and demand through educational change and innovation. This university has recently implemented six part-time undergraduate and graduate degree programs through its extended university program. One of them, the part-time MBA program, is now in its second year, and has more than one hundred students. The demand for this program has been strong, and enrollment is expected to grow significantly in the future. Part-time master's degree programs have also gotten underway in public health, architecture, and education. There is also a human services part-time program leading to a BA degree. The newest part-time program is a liberal studies degree program focusing on the humanities, social sciences, and sciences. The major aim of these programs is to provide educational degree opportunities for adults, who for various reasons could not complete college. This includes housewives and others, not just people working full time. UCLA employees are also permitted to enroll if certain conditions are met.

UCLA's extension programs offer many courses off-campus in locations convenient to those interested in enrolling in them. And the University of California's extension operation has experienced an upsurge in interest in independent study courses at home or at work. Among the students are shut-ins, servicemen, seamen, housewives, people who live in rural and isolated areas, and people working in towns and cities. This kind of education is relatively low cost and can be very efficient.

UCLA has done a number of significant things to increase the satisfaction of and improve educational opportunities for lower division undergraduates in particular. Undergraduate education has recently been given more genuine emphasis as a relatively high priority goal at this institution, which is so big that many undergraduates have found it to be too impersonal. Now undergraduate applications are rising substantially. Special freshman seminars have recently been introduced, with classes limited to ten or fifteen students. They have been placed under the director—Stanley Wolpert, a senior history professor—of a new Office of Academic Change and Curriculum Development.

During the 1973–1974 academic year, over fifty experimental seminars were taught by senior faculty, and more are being designed. The aim is to offer seventy to one hundred such seminars each year in the future. They have thus far proven to be very popular and have long waiting lists. The current seminars have been made possible by UCLA's share of a $1 million grant, authorized by the California state legislature on the governor's recommendation, to improve undergraduate teaching in the UC system. However, most of the faculty involved in these seminars have voluntarily accepted teaching overloads that reduce the time they spend on research and other activities. As early as 1971—before the state grant—some departments were offering freshman seminars. Students typically find these seminars to be more intellectually demanding and intimate than other courses. Most of the seminars focus on current and relevant topics and are built around student and faculty interests rather than rigid fields or disciplines. Students prepare research reports and defend them in the seminar. Professor Wolpert has conducted a seminar on Gandhi and Executive Vice-Chancellor David Saxon has given one on the "physicists universe."

Several years ago a special UCLA task force set as a goal the creation of an improved sense of community involvement that would give students a greater sense of belonging in a big urban university. The vice-chancellor for student and campus affairs accepted this goal as a personal challenge. There are now about 350 special student activity groups run by students. These include academic discipline, living, and special interest and activity groups. One group of twenty-six students is working in a community project involving the reentry of released mental patients into society. Most of the students are seniors in psychology and sociology. They have been recruiting community volunteers to provide for continuing assistance.

Recent studies have shown considerable interest among UCLA alumni, community, and other supporters for a current institutional fund-raising campaign, even though general economic climate is not good. The regents have approved a $20 million fund-raising campaign for UCLA. It is very likely that the target will be met, if not exceeded, because of the many significant contributions UCLA has made and is making to the southern California community which, in turn, sees the great potential UCLA has for becoming an even better and more valuable academic institution in the future.

The funds—all from private sources—will be used to enrich various programs, for endowed teaching (not research!) chairs, student fellowships, and research endowments. It will provide the university's budget with greater flexibility and more discretionary funds to pursue more goals effectively. It will provide the extra margin needed for even greater academic distinction. The capital funds in the $20 million plan will be used in large part to serve community and external interests. The plan includes a new alumni and development Center, renovation of Royce Hall auditorium—which is used for many events that are open to the public—and conversion of the women's gym into a studio for UCLA's graduate dance program, which gives public recitals.

California State College at San Bernardino. California State College at San Bernardino went into shock in the winter of 1972 when applications dropped 55 percent (*Los Angeles Times,* March 10, 1974, Part II, p. 1). After a flurry of task force meetings, reports, and recommendations, the administration and faculty agreed to scrap many of the old liberal arts and educational notions. Top management, including the vice-president for academic affairs, played the central role in this process, although there was also a good deal of genuine faculty participation. Career education has since been given top priority—a sharp change for this institution, which started out a decade ago with a strong liberal arts emphasis. Many members of the founding faculty had hoped that the college would be known as the Darthmouth of the West. But a white-collar, high-quality liberal arts college was not what the working-class families of predominantly blue-collar San Bernardino wanted.

The college has been meeting the demands and needs of its community by sharply expanding and introducing a variety of vocationally or career-oriented degree programs. These include both business and public administration, child development, criminal justice, environmental studies, and nursing. Masters degrees as well as undergraduate degrees are offered in the administration program. The college is also planning additional applied degree programs, and is considering certificate programs involving clusters of related courses for students not ready for the full four-year program. Undergraduate enrollment in administration has grown by 20 percent in the past year, and another 120 students—including many middle and lower management employees of local industry and government agencies—enrolled in the master's program, which is taught largely at night.

Some fifty-eight students enrolled in the criminal justice program in the fall of 1973, even though final approval for the program was not received from external officials until a few weeks before classes started. About thirty more students signed up for the winter quarter, and about one hundred were expected by the spring term. In the nursing program, which has not yet been approved, eighty-six students are already enrolled. Most of them are registered nurses without a bachelor's degree who want to upgrade their skills or move into managerial jobs, or both. The chairwoman of the nursing department feels that demand for nursing in the area is so strong that the program could have one thousand nursing students within a few years. However, the official college plan calls for only 210 nursing majors by 1980.

While statewide enrollments in the California nonjunior college system have been leveling off, San Bernardino's enrollment has been increasing by 13 percent annually in the past few years, since it began its strong career emphasis. In 1973 enrollment rose four hundred, to 2,608 students. However, enrollments are down significantly in most liberal arts departments—for example, 51 percent in history and 21 percent in anthropology. Although the chairman of the English department, among others, has warned of the real danger of educational imbalance with an excessive career training emphasis, he feels that the enrollment decline has had a good effect on his department. The department has had to rethink its curriculum in terms of what students want to take, not just what the faculty thinks they ought to take. As a result, the enrollment of this department has dropped only 10 percent, much less than for most of the other liberal arts areas. The administration hopes that other liberal arts departments will follow the example of the English department.

An effort is being made to include sufficient liberal arts courses in the vocational programs. For example, there is a philosophy course in the criminal justice program. The chairman of the administration department stresses the importance of a broad background in management or administration, and he himself has a wide knowledge of art and music. Majors in administration must take seventeen of thirty-six courses outside of this department. This is a broader general education requirement than that maintained by almost any other department in the college.

San Bernardino has also dropped its general educational requirements from ninety to seventy units, most of which can be taken in a junior college before transferring. The college-wide foreign language requirement has also been dropped, as was a writing proficiency test and the comprehensive exams most departments required students to take before graduation. The college has stepped up its publicity and recruiting in nearby high schools and community colleges, and has worked hard to eliminate problems that had made it difficult to transfer junior college academic credits to San Bernardino.

Scripps College. Scripps College, a women's school, still clings tenaciously to its liberal arts curriculum (*Los Angeles Times,* March 10, 1974, Part II, p. 1). It has 560 students and 51 faculty. Applications for freshman classes have been less than the college would like, but it has not reached the panic point yet. In spite of growing pressures, Scripps has not yet had to reconsider in significant ways its antipathy toward vocationally oriented education. "Art bakes no bread" is one of its mottos. Its primary motto since its founding in 1926 has been to "develop in its students the ability to think clearly and independently and the ability to live confidently, courageously, and hopefully." Scripps' students are mostly from middle- and upper middle-class families; the annual cost is about $4200, and hard work is stressed. The head of the college still feels that it is a certain kind of college for a certain kind of woman.

Scripps will likely survive and also continue to be adequately successful in its niche. However, it has recently felt it necessary to make some concessions to the concern about jobs and other educational problems, and it will probably have to make more in the future. A part-time career counselor has been added to the staff, and these activities are to be expanded. Most students feel they will need additional graduate or professional training later, however. The alumni office has been intensifying its efforts to find out what happens to its graduates, a task it has been casual about in the past. Rigorous graduate requirements have recently been eased by changes in the science curriculum, language courses, and basic humanities sequence. There is now less emphasis on straight lectures and more on combined seminars and lectures. There is also greater stress on interdisciplinary approaches and on the contemporary relevance of the curriculum.

Pepperdine University. Pepperdine University has a loose affiliation with the Church of Christ, and most of its students come from relatively religious—and conservative—families, although not necessarily from this particular denomination. About twenty-five or 30 percent of the faculty are of this denomination, although it is a nonsectarian institution. Its founder, George Pepperdine, was of this denomination, and all board members must be, but this church does not support the institution financially. The land for what is now the main campus of this university, in Malibu, California, was donated by a wealthy Malibu family of a different

Protestant denomination several years ago. The $30 million Malibu campus was opened in September 1972.

Most of the full-time students and faculty are not from the Malibu area, but they are attracted to it in part because of the lovely setting of this interesting community. The values or character of the campus do not mesh that well with those of the community, although people from the community are increasingly enrolling in part-time and special courses and programs, and making use of the facilities and events open to the public.

The original campus of Pepperdine was in south central Los Angeles, which is now in large part a Black urban community. This campus has recently become an urban affairs college. Pepperdine also has a law school in Anaheim, and is affiliated with the Center for International Business in downtown Los Angeles. In total, Pepperdine has 3700 regular students—1200 of whom are at the Malibu campus—and 120 full-time faculty members, including 70 in Malibu. It also has 7000 students and many part-time faculty in its continuing education programs. The university offers its students a year-in-Europe program in Heidelberg.

One priority goal of Pepperdine's part-time education is to send the classrooms off-campus to various other organizations, especially for vocational or career training. Most of the part-time MBA program is conducted in this way, for example. Athletics as well as various kinds of student activities are important institutional goals. And the college is helping students find both part-time jobs while in school and full time jobs after they graduate. A sizable proportion of the students are from minority groups and poor families, and many of them receive scholarships, loans, or other kinds of financial aid. There is a $250,000 scholarship fund from private sources.

This university seems to be both viable and reasonably successful in its chosen role, in large part because it has a very able and dynamic chief executive, William Banowski, who has worked his way up the system since 1959. Banowski played the central role in raising most of the funds for the expensive Malibu campus. He did this in three years, from 1969 to 1972, during a period of economic recession. He has also played the key role in getting the scholarship funds. Banowski, who is only thirty-eight, has been seriously mentioned as a possible Republican candidate for state governor. He is co-host of an NBC television show—Inquiry, a director of several major corporations (including Coca-Cola) and nonprofit organizations (including the Los Angeles educational TV station). In general, there seems to be a good fit between this university and its goal system and the type of chief executive it has.

Others. The University of Southern California, in addition to giving in-house professional and career-oriented programs at various organizations in the area, also has been giving graduate programs in aerospace management at United States military bases around the world. USC is also profiting from the regional discussion centers it has established. Golden Gate College conducts MBA programs at military bases, and an experimental program at the Bechtel Corporation. The college plans to offer this program anywhere Bechtel has enough interested and qualified personnel who wish to enroll. William Rainey Harper Junior College in Illinois (Lahti, 1973) uses a management by objectives approach in many areas. Some of its specific development objectives have included a one hundred percent increase in continuing education by a certain date, thirty new business seminars, twenty-five new courses on hobby and leisure time activities, and twenty divisional and graduate courses stimulated and coordinated through this college for other universities and colleges. Chapman College gives classes aboard ship through its World Campus Afloat program. The ships also visit cultural centers all over the world. Each semester hundreds of students from several hundred other institutions have enrolled in this program. California State Polytechnic College in San Luis Obispo, Brigham Young, and the Oregon Technical Institute have recently cut down on their advanced mathematics requirements for the bachelor's degree in engineering technology. This has led to many transfers from other schools and significant increases in their enrollments. The cluster college concept applied at Claremont, and more recently in some other places, has resulted in considerable cost savings, greater student options, synergy, and improved operating efficiency in such areas as purchasing, faculty centers, food services, and cross-enrollments.

Unrealistic Options

Many persons, including most academics, probably will not like many of the forecasts, options, and analyses presented in this book. They seem so dreary, so entwined in money and crass values, so unlike the real world of higher education! However, very few if any real educational utopias exist. But many still feel that somewhere out there is a dream of something very precious and fine, not contaminated by money, budgets, accountability, efficiency, operational goal systems, management, the commercial value of degree, or other nonsense. These dreams typically take the following forms.

The free university: The students study what they want; the faculty teaches what they want, and out of the experience come some truly vital educational experiences. Instead of messing with credits, degrees, and required courses, the students and faculty share knowledge.

The un-university: In this vision, there would be no formal system. Instead, the students and faculty will share common experiences of brotherhood untrammeled by academic requirements or organization.

The student-run university: Here the students would control the system. The model is reasonable, since various medieval universities ran this way. If the faculty did not please the students, their salaries were cut.

The faculty-run university: The faculty could control the university, setting whatever goals and standards the faculty might want.

Good dreams, good utopias? Perhaps. But they are not likely to succeed. To gain power and run a modern academic institution of any significant size, you need first to obtain economic resources. If you do not have budgetary control, plus sources of funds, you need instead large numbers of very dedicated and very knowledgeable and skilled students and teachers. Admittedly some of these persons exist, but not enough to change the whole United States higher educational system into a utopian system, or even to change one complex institution.

Second, you need control of inputs. If you cannot control the quality of faculty and students, you probably cannot control the quality of outputs, and this means that you get erratic results. If you get erratic results, outsiders may be unwilling to finance you. You have to be able to sell your output. The output may be services, scholarship, or graduates, but if you do not demonstrate to the world that what you are doing is useful, you will not last long.

All optional universities and colleges suffer from the same defects. They seek to avoid duties for which outsiders pay universities, most notably the job of sorting out persons for social roles. We may not like this duty, but it is the way academic institutions get money. Students and faculty in particular may object to this social sorting process, but realistically it is what universities do.

All of the above is disturbing to many true scholars. They rightly claim that the business of universities is truth and scholarship, not the vulgar affairs of the body politic. But in the real world of higher education today, universities must prove to financial backers that the product is worth the money spent on it. When we realize and accept this, we may be able to manage universities more efficiently. Central to all of this is the operationalization of the goal systems of universities and colleges.

Management and Operationalization of Goal Systems

Only a small number of major universities are in a position to pursue more than a limited number of goals and related priorities in a reasonably effective and efficient manner. These are institutions that are large enough, diversified and prestigious enough, have relatively strong capabilities in many varied areas, and have had adequate resources in the past to do this reasonably well. They include such private institutions as Harvard, Stanford, and Chicago, and a few public universities such as UCLA, Berkeley, and the University of Michigan.

UCLA has long been relatively strong in graduate and professional education in quite a few fields and in research, extension education, public and community service, and even athletics. It has been at the forefront of social egalitarianism efforts and has been relatively innovative, efficiently run, and well managed. Presently, it is placing high priority on effective undergraduate teaching and student involvement, as well as on its extended university concept involving new part-time degree programs. The goal system and priorities have not remained static, and the ability to change has been and is one of the basic strengths of UCLA. It has been able to redeploy its faculty capabilities and resources to a sufficient degree when external conditions have warranted it. Quality and effectiveness—in a relative sense at least—and a good sense of priorities are obvious characteristics of management.

Even though UCLA is a relatively strong performer with regard to many of the thirty-one goals discussed in Chapter Three, USC, a private university also in Los Angeles, continues to be a viable and successful academic institution. It has not tried to emulate UCLA across the board, nor has it tried to attract the same kinds of students. USC has built good niches for itself, capitalizing on those areas where UCLA has not been strong and limiting efforts in areas where it cannot compete effectively.

Most universities and colleges cannot effectively or efficiently pursue the range of goals and priorities that a major public or private institution can. However, the need for niches, limited priorities, and adequately operational goal systems is not really recognized by numerous universities and colleges in all parts of the country.

An academic institution should first have a pretty good and realistic idea of what it is and what it is doing before it decides where it should be heading. Each must make a meaningful assessment of its capabilities and limitations, its strengths and actual and potential competitive advantages, its limitations and weaknesses, its available overall resources, and the resources and additional students it can realistically expect to get if it changes in certain ways and moves into new spheres. Each institution must do long-term, medium-range, and short-term planning, as well as adequate contingency planning involving the redeployment of capabilities and resources, among many other things. Such planning should focus both on external environmental conditions and internal operations, and should integrate the two dimensions in a meaningful way. Management, and especially top management and the chief executive, must take the lead and play the central roles in all of this, and must serve as the key catalyst and as the most important information and communication center. If management does not do this, who will?

Clark Kerr mentions that Robert Hutchins, during his tenure as president of the University of Chicago from 1929 to 1945 and as chancellor from 1945 to 1951, was the last university chief executive to shape a goal system and bring about a great deal of change and innovation. Hutchins, in a recent conversation with Richman, expressed the belief that many university and college presidents could do far more today than they have been doing. Relevant goals and priorities, along with strong and effective leadership and managerial capability, are needed. And there are many ways in which an academic institution can be relevant in a pluralistic and diverse society, depending on who it wants to serve and what it wants to accomplish.

Incidentally, Hutchins, when asked, selected Kingman Brewster of Yale as his example of a currently effective and successful university president. Hutchins' primary criterion for his choice related to Brewster's influence on and contributions to Yale's goal system and priorities.

The president is likely to be able to get at least adequate external support from resource providers, internal support from the faculty, and enough students, if his proposed goal system is adequately operational and placed in the context of plans for accomplishing it. Even if the goal system and related plans indicate a short-run cut in the budget and in the faculty of a few percent, while all other available proposals and likely prospects suggest considerably larger and durable cuts, then it is likely that adequate faculty support can be generated. Of course, the president need not, and usually should not, dictate his desired goal system, priorities, and plans in an authoritarian manner. He should consult widely, and provide for participation and related democratic processes in order to help in formulation and in gaining workable support. But this cannot go on forever, and at some point top management must either go ahead with the formalization and implementation stages or scrap the plans and goal system.

All of the managerial functions are critical. Not only effective planning is called for, but also sound information systems and effective control both during the planning and implementation stages. Effective leadership, direction, communication, and motivation are also needed. Sound organizational design is required, because various parts of the institution will have to be reorganized and new structures and relationships will have to be developed. Staffing is important, because some personnel changes, additions, and perhaps resignations will be involved. This means managerial attention will have to be devoted to appraisal, recruiting, selection, training, advancement, and demotion involving various academic and nonacademic personnel and positions. Some of the basic questions that should be very seriously considered in operationalizing and restructuring the institution's goal system and priorities include the following:

Who should we try to educate, in what fields, for what purposes, and in what ways, given our capabilities, limitations, resources, and the market opportunities we are in a position to capitalize on with reasonable success? What additional resources will be required to capitalize more effectively on our capabilities and potential competitive advantages, and can we realistically expect to be able to get them? If so, from where, when, and how?

How much emphasis should we place on research? What kinds of research—if any—should we give highest priority to, given our capabilities and external needs, as well as our actual and potential resources for research?

What kinds of public and community service should we pursue and emphasize? What are we likely to be able to do that we are not now doing, and what can we do more effectively? What are the significant gaps in our community and beyond that we can realistically do something about? How much will this cost approximately, and what benefits are likely to be forthcoming to the institution?

How important are other goals—for example, athletics, social egalitarianism, cultural or religious assimilation—to the success of our institution? Can we really pursue them effectively, and at the same time that we pursue our other goals?

The institution's goal system should be in dynamic, not static, equilibrum. Priorities will have to be shifted over time in response to changing conditions. Through effective planning this can usually be done in an evolutionary way, rather than through revolutionary, abrupt upheavals—though the latter may also be beneficial under some conditions.

San Bernardino College shifted emphasis to career training and jobs for its graduates, and this priority became the key maximizing goal for the institution. Within a year or two this goal system proved beneficial, as enrollments increased quite sharply. However, in the next few years, the college may well find that other goals should be given higher priority than career training in order to prevent serious imbalances and also to keep up with changing conditions. For example, San Bernardino may decide to place top priority on part-time programs, including or even exclusively non-vocational ones, or it may once again concentrate on building a liberal arts program. Career training will still be important, but enough will have been done in this sphere to treat it as a constraint goal—indicating the minimum amount desired—rather than a high-priority goal.

One of the newer approaches that management can use in formulating a given university's or college's goal system is the Delphi technique, which was first developed at the RAND Corporation (Dalkey and Helmer, 1963; Gordon and Helmer, 1964; Richman and Farmer, 1965, and 1970, pp. 329–339). This technique has been used in a few studies involving the goals of universities and colleges (Uhl, 1971a and 1971b). However, they have focused on the identification rather than the formulation of goals, and the respondents in these studies were not necessarily chosen for their objectivity or expertise.

The Delphi technique is a method for obtaining a consensus from experts about a matter not subject to precise quantification. It can deal with either the present or the future. This technique can be used to weigh relative values of a set of interrelated variables, or to indicate which variables are critically important for future events. It can also be used to identify the major contingencies on which future developments will depend, and this involves dynamic applications. The Delphi technique is not intended, however, to provide very precise or totally accurate information about a problem, but rather key insights about the nature of crucial information related to the problem.

A panel of experts is selected who are best suited to analyze the problem and determine what the relevant information is in a relatively objective way. They usually do not meet together, in order to avoid personality dominance. The experts present their weightings, opinions, information, and predictions, and the related assumptions about the problem under study in the first round. They quantify their responses in some way whenever possible. If there is a pretty high degree of argrement among the experts, a second round is not usually needed. If not, important information is fed back from all of the experts to all of them in subsequent rounds, until an adequate degree of convergence of opinion is reached, or until it is felt that it does not pay to continue. The respondents are asked to elaborate on their reasoning, to pinpoint the factors they consider to be the most relevant. They are also asked about the kinds of additional data they feel would enable them to make a better assessment or prediction. An effort is then made to obtain these data.

The management of a university or college can use the Delphi technique, along with one or more panels of experts, to determine what the institution's goal system really is. It can also be used in deciding what goal system should be implemented, taking into account accessments of the institution's strengths, capabilities, limitations, weaknesses, actual and potential resource position, relevant environmental trends, and the market and other educational opportunities open to the institution. In this case, the Delphi technique becomes a forecasting, planning, and marketing research tool.

The experts selected should be as open-minded and objective as possible about what would be in the best interests of the institution. Hence, you would not normally choose a department chairman or dean whose faculty is in very deep trouble, a trustee with very strong biases and rather narrow vision, a student activist who has strong vested interests, or an administrator or faculty member whose job is in serious jeopardy because of his performance. Outside educators or academic managers often make suitable experts, as do various kinds of citizens from the community. Some of the institutions' trustees, faculty, administrators, and students may be good candidates. The same is likely to be true of some alumni, prospective students, government officials, and major actual or potential private donors.

The institution's management must usually take the lead in using the Delphi technique, and in selecting the experts, if the effort is to prove worthwhile and effective. And top management involvement and support is also usually required. If it is handled properly, the benefits derived from using the Delphi technique can often outweigh considerably all of the costs entailed. Even if management chooses not to use it along with multiple rounds of feedback, some form of expert opinion is still very likely to be worthwhile, if not absolutely essential. Management should not operate in a vacuum. The Delphi technique, or some other kind of expert assessment, can also be used in connection with the goal systems of individual schools, faculties, or even departments.

If and when the university or college—or one of its major parts—designs and implements an adequately operational goal system, the problems of performance evaluation, goal verification, and accountability become easier to cope with. However, these problems will never be easy to handle. Considerable time, effort, and perhaps expense is likely to be required if goal verification is to be done properly. But the benefits, in efficient resource utilization, effective goal attainment, and often also increased financial support, are likely to outweigh the costs over time by a wide margin. Here are some of the kinds of assessment that can be useful.

Student Evaluations. Most schools could be doing much more with regard to student evaluations of teaching, instructors, courses, and programs. UCLA's graduate school of management, as one example, has put a great deal of serious effort into student evaluations. It has a student committee that coordinates the program, gathers information, and feeds the results and recommendations regarding teaching into the school's staffing committee, which considers faculty tenure, promotions, and merit increases. The class and instructor evaluation results for each course are run off and made available to anyone interested in them. The evaluation instruments have been refined, revised, and improved over time. Teaching effectiveness is given much weight in deciding on the advancement of faculty members. Since this evaluation program began in earnest, there have been many verifiable indications that the quality and effectiveness of this faculty's teaching has improved significantly, and many courses have been altered in major ways.

Alumni Feedback and Assessment. The alumni, or at least a useful sample of them, can be surveyed at different points in time about which parts of the educational process are proving to be of greatest and least value to them. Meetings can also be arranged periodically to discuss these questions in depth, rather than relying solely on mail questionnaires. Alumni may be in a position to provide valuable information, advice, proposals, and ideas. Keeping records on the career progress, pay, job satisfaction, and other important activities of alumni can also prove useful for goal verification. Favorable results can frequently do much in attracting students and in getting financial support from benefactors who need verification that the school is doing a relatively effective job in its education and training.

Student Placement. Indicators can be devised showing how effective the institution is in placing students in desirable jobs after they graduate and in part-time jobs so they can finance their way through school. Relatively good results here can help attract more students and obtain greater financial support.

Minority and Underprivileged Students. Assessment in this area becomes especially important if social egalitarianism is a priority goal. Measures can be designed indicating how effectively such students are brought up to par when this is necessary, how they progress through the educational process, and what happens to them after graduation.

Research. Here the market test can often be the best measure if outside funds are obtained and used for research. If subsequent external funding is obtained for related research projects, the research results have probably been useful and/or relevant. However, if internal funds are used for research, meaningful criteria are needed to determine how much to allocate to which projects. Such criteria are usually not easy to design, but they should take into account the capabilities of the researchers, the likelihood of a significant contribution, and the importance of the project in relation to the institution's goal system. Criteria are also needed to guide the institution and its major parts in determining what kinds of institutional research grants to pursue.

Public and Community Service. Although it is often very difficult to assess in a precise cost-benefit way the impact of various kinds of public or community service on the institution's viability and success, much more of this can be done. The institution is usually in a much better position to effectively offer some services than others, and some are much more important to or strongly desired by the outside world than others. The institution should give priority to those it is in the best position to offer, and should structure its reward and evaluation systems to encourage those services that are the most important or needed externally. Relevant external information is needed for this purpose. Attendance and use of facilities are good market test measures that can be employed in connection with various kinds of athletic, cultural, or other events and activities offered by the school. The same is true for the use of the libraries and other facilities by outsiders, and for the response to and interest in various publications, TV, and radio programs operated by the institution.

Operating Efficiency. Most universities and colleges can utilize more and better efficiency indicators than they do. This can be done in ways that really do not significantly sacrifice educational quality. We have already discussed many kinds of efficiency problems and measures in this chapter, and in earlier chapters.

Management Appraisal. Management should appraise the organization's goal system and determine how effectively and efficiently the goals are being attained. While there are likely to be many uncontrollable and partially controllable factors involved, an appraisal can usually be made taking into account the more critical uncontrollable factors. Managerial appraisal should also focus on how effectively and efficiently all of the basic managerial functions—first outlined in Chapter One—are performed, because all of them relate to the goal system. The central administration or top managers cannot do everything, and so many tasks will have to be delegated to other administrators and units down the line. One useful guideline regarding how much authority to decentralize or how much autonomy to give various units can be found in the profit center concept in business, and it also relates to management by objectives. Greater authority and autonomy should generally be given to those schools, faculties, departments, or other parts of the system that have operational goal systems and competent managers and are relatively self-sufficient in terms of their expenditures in relation to the revenues they generate. If they are earning a sizable surplus for the institution, all the better, especially if this is expected to continue in the future. Such units are typically the ones that will be confronted with less critical problems. It may well pay to let them operate quite autonomously. However, some kinds of budgetary, policy, and other controls and constraints will still be needed to avoid serious negative side effects, suboptimization, and coordination problems that could be detrimental to the institution's overall goal system and priorities. Even when a given unit has not been and still is not self-sufficient or profitable, it may pay to use the management by objectives approach and grant it quite a bit of autonomy, under some conditions. For example, if the management of the unit comes up with a valid set of priorities based on a sound and well-documented overall plan, and also has sound implementation plans that are likely to be accomplished, then top management may be wise to give the go ahead and exert only a limited number of strategic controls—unless and until some serious unforeseen problems seem to be emerging.

Power Change Implications

One fundamental reason why goal system changes are going to be so controversial at many academic institutions is that many traditional power bases will be diminished in importance and others will increase in importance. We now use the taxonomies, framework, and methodologies developed in Chapter Three to illustrate this more more vividly. We also trace through the power and interface changes that seem to be currently emerging at the same state university that we used for our example in Chapter Three. Once this is done, it is not very difficult to forecast the reactions of different parties to such changes, and to predict some of the strategies that might be used to win or minimize losses. Although we focus only on one university here, this has many significant implications for other universities and colleges.

In the taxonomies presented in Chapter Three, old weights are the first numbers in parentheses after each item, and the new or current weights are the second numbers in parentheses. If items are becoming more important, their weights rise; if they are less significant, the weights drop.

Schools have become slightly less important in the power game, while interdisciplinary groupings have become a bit more significant, as has the central administration functional subsystem. Placement is becoming considerably more important.

The social subsystem has declined in terms of power and influence in decision-making. As for the political authority subsystems, student government has become a bit more important, while the faculty council, AAUP, and central administration have become a bit less so. Deans are losing quite a bit of power, although some of the professional school deans continue to exert significantly more power than the others. Department chairmen generally are also now less powerful and influential. The biggest gainers in this group are the trustees, who are taking a more active and direct part in the governance of this university. Some of this greater centralization of authority at the board level may well have been avoided, if the trustees felt that the central administration was or is able to be more effective.

Data processing, public relations and information, and the registrar have become more important among the information subsystems. The university press and other university publications are now less significant in the power game.

Budgets have now become even more of a critical input. Therefore, he who controls or significantly influences budget size and allocations will be a significantly more important person. Students have also become much more important, and this gives them greater potential for exerting power and influence in the future—but they may not do much about this potential. Even more important potentially are the students who decide not to attend this university, thus creating a serious student shortfall. Fixed plant, equipment and supplies, and land have become less important inputs with regard to power and influence. However, the first two could gain in power in the future, if and as they become increasingly scarce in terms of related outputs.

Most of the external environment items have become significantly more important in the power-influence game. Alumni have not, and perhaps this university should be doing considerably more in building alumni support and exchanging information and ideas with them.

As for outputs or goals, jobs for graduates are becoming a much more important goal, and this ties in with the growing importance of placement activities and some of the environmental constraints. Undergraduate students have gained in importance, while graduate students have declined somewhat, as has research. Public and community service has increased significantly, while protection and benefits for professionals in the system have been losing considerable ground. Several of the other goals are also losing some of their former importance.

Thus, those subsystems relating in important ways to money or jobs go up, and most of the others stay the same or decline. This means that university personnel who have a direct interest in jobs or money will tend to gain power, while those who control more traditional functions will typically lose power. Externally, those who can better mesh the university goal system with the external environment will gain, while those who cannot will lose. The schools that show the world that they can produce the services needed and desired are likely to be the big winners in the remaining 1970s and beyond.

Table 9 uses the new weights to arrive at suggestive current external interface scores for each subsystem. Table 10 uses them to arrive at subsystem interface scores, and to compute a total power score for each subsystem item. Some items—typically those that have become more important, such as placement—now have critical interfaces with more parts of the overall system than in the past. A few others, which have become less important, now have fewer interfaces. This is shown by comparing Tables 3 and 4 in Chapter Three with Tables 9 and 10 here.

Table 11 shows the current suggestive total power scores for each subsystem, as well as the plus or minus rank order changes compared to Table 7 in Chapter Six. The biggest relative power and influence gainers in terms of rank order changes at this particular university are currently placement, the registrar, and data processing, followed by the trustees and university TV and radio. The losers are social subsystems, deans, department chairmen, the faculty council, other student organizations, student government, AAUP, and the central administration political authority system.

The trustees currently seem to clearly be the most powerful group, replacing the central administration at the top of the list. However, if the trustees and the central administration are unified with regard to a certain issue or decision, they are probably in a better (more powerful) position to act than they were a few years ago. This would tend to be the case, because authority and power have become more centralized, and it is harder to form coalitions

Table 9.

EXTERNAL INTERFACE RELATIONSHIPS

SUBSYSTEMS	INPUTS									ENVIRONMENTAL CONSTRAINTS									OUTPUTS OR GOALS										TOTAL EXTERNAL INTERFACE SCORE
	Budgets	Professional Manpower	Other Manpower	Fixed Plant	Equipment and Supplies	Land	Students	Alumni	Private Donors	State Government	Federal Government	Local Government	Other Pressure Groups	Manpower Users	Other Colleges and Universities	Secondary Schools	Professional Groups	Parents	Truth	Graduate Students	Undergraduates Students	Athletics	Benefits and Protections for Professionals	Benefits and Protections for Other Employees	Public and Community Service	Research	Cultural Assimilation	Jobs for Students	
(weight)	40	15	5	3	2	2	15	5	6	11	5	1	4	12	8	7	7	4	2	6	8	3	5	2	8	5	2	8	
Functional S-1																													
1.1 Schools	X	X	X	X	X		X	X	X	X	X	X	X	X	X	X	X	X	X	X	X		X	X	X	X	X	X	196
1.2 Interdisciplinary Studies	X	X	X	X	X		X	X	X	X	X	X	X	X	X	X	X	X	X	X	X		X	X	X	X	X	X	124
1.3 Central Administration	X	X	X	X	X	X	X	X	X	X	X	X	X	X	X	X	X	X		X	X	X	X	X	X	X		X	197
1.4 Placement	X	X	X				X			X	X	X	X	X	X	X	X	X		X	X		X	X	X		X	X	115
Social S-2	X	X	X			X	X	X		X	X	X	X	X	X	X	X	X	X	X	X	X	X	X	X	X	X		71
Political-Authority S-3																													
3.1 Student Government		X								X			X							X	X	X	X		X		X		60
3.2 AAUP	X	X	X				X	X		X	X		X							X	X		X		X		X		81
3.3 Unions		X	X							X			X								X	X							46
3.4 Central Administrative Group	X	X	X	X	X	X	X	X	X	X	X	X	X	X	X	X	X	X	X	X	X	X	X	X	X	X	X	X	195
3.5 Deans	X	X	X	X	X		X	X	X	X	X	X	X	X	X	X	X		X	X	X	X	X	X	X	X	X		163
3.6 Department Chairmen							X						X							X	X						X		68
3.7 Other Student Organizations							X											X		X	X	X					X		50
3.8 Faculty Council	X	X	X				X			X				X	X	X	X		X	X	X	X	X	X	X	X	X		79
3.9 Trustees	X	X	X	X	X	X	X	X	X	X	X	X	X	X	X	X	X	X	X	X	X	X	X	X	X	X	X	X	201
Informational S-4																													
4.1 Data Processing	X	X	X	X	X		X	X	X	X	X	X	X	X	X	X	X	X	X	X	X	X	X	X	X	X	X	X	158
4.2 Public Relations and Information	X	X	X	X	X		X	X	X	X	X	X	X	X	X	X	X	X	X	X	X	X	X	X	X	X	X	X	139
4.3 University Press			X		X		X		X				X	X	X				X	X	X	X	X		X	X			53
4.4 Other University Publications	X	X			X		X		X				X	X	X				X	X	X		X		X	X		X	113
4.5 University TV and Radio					X		X				X				X					X	X				X	X		X	66
4.6 Library System	X	X	X	X	X		X			X				X	X				X	X	X		X		X	X	X		81
4.7 Registrar	X		X		X		X	X	X					X		X	X	X	X	X	X		X		X	X	X	X	73

Table 10.
SUBSYSTEM INTERFACE RELATIONSHIPS

EXTERNAL INTERFACE SCORES (Fig. 2 ÷ 10)	S.1.1	S.1.2	S.1.3	S.1.4	S.2	S.3.1	S.3.2	S.3.3	S.3.4	S.3.5	S.3.6	S.3.7	S.3.8	S.3.9	S.4.1	S.4.2	S.4.3	S.4.4	S.4.5	S.4.6	S.4.7	A — Total Subsystem Interface Score	B — Subsystem Weight (From Figure 1)	C — Total Power Score (A×B)
	20	12	20	12	7	6	8	5	20	16	7	5	8	20	16	14	5	11	7	8	7			
Functional S-1																								
1.1 Schools		X	X	X	X		X		X	X	X	X	X	X	X			X		X	X	197	14	2758
1.2 Interdisciplinary Studies	X	X	X	X	X		X		X	X	X	X	X	X	X			X		X	X	148	10	1480
1.3 Central Administration	X	X		X	X	X			X	X		X	X	X			X	X		X	X	209	13	2717
1.4 Placement	X	X	X				X		X	X	X	X	X	X	X			X	X			156	8	1248
Social S-2	X	X	X	X		X	X	X	X	X	X	X	X	X	X	X	X	X		X	X	191	2	382
Political-Authority S-3																								
3.1 Student Government	X	X	X	X	X				X	X	X	X	X	X	X	X						169	5	845
3.2 AAUP	X	X	X		X		X		X	X	X		X	X								144	6	864
3.3 Unions			X		X	X																77	4	308
3.4 Central Administrative Group	X	X	X	X	X	X	X	X		X	X	X	X	X	X	X	X	X			X	214	14	2996
3.5 Deans	X	X	X	X	X	X	X		X		X	X	X	X	X	X	X	X			X	192	9	1728
3.6 Department Chairmen	X	X	X		X	X	X		X	X		X	X		X	X		X			X	174	5	870
3.7 Other Student Organizations	X		X		X	X	X	X	X		X							X				133	5	665
3.8 Faculty Council	X	X	X	X	X	X	X		X	X	X		X		X	X	X	X			X	152	6	912
3.9 Trustees	X	X	X	X	X	X	X	X	X	X	X	X	X	X	X	X		X			X	202	18	3636
Informational S-4																								
4.1 Data Processing	X	X	X	X	X		X	X	X	X		X	X	X	X		X	X		X	X	152	13	1976
4.2 Public Relations and Information	X	X	X	X		X	X	X	X		X	X		X			X	X	X	X		184	10	1840
4.3 University Press		X	X		X	X																71	2	142
4.4 Other University Publications	X	X	X	X					X	X	X	X		X	X		X				X	135	7	945
4.5 University TV and Radio	X	X			X				X									X				98	7	686
4.6 Library System	X	X	X	X					X	X			X	X	X	X					X	153	11	1683
4.7 Registrar	X	X	X	X					X	X				X	X	X	X			X	X	112	6	772

Table 11.

CURRENT SUBSYSTEM POWER RANK ORDER

	Current (from Table 10) (scores in brackets)	Change from Earlier Rank Order (*Table 7 of Chapter 6*)
Rank		
1.	Trustees (3636)	+1
2.	Central Administration: Political Authority Subsystem (2996)	−1
3.	Schools (2758)	0
4.	Central Administration: Functional Subsystem (2717)	0
5.	Data Processing (1976)	+2
6.	Public Relations and Information (1840)	0
7.	Deans (1728)	−2
8.	Library System (1683)	0
9.	Interdisciplinary Studies (1480)	0
10.	Placement (1248)	+7
11.	Other University Publications (945)	+1
12.	Faculty Council (912)	−2
13.	Department Chairmen (870)	−2
14.	AAUP (864)	−1
15.	Student Government (845)	−1
16.	Registrar (772)	+3
17.	University TV and Radio (686)	+1
18.	Other Student Organizations (665)	−2
19.	Social Subsystems (382)	−4
20.	Nonacademic Unions (308)	0
21.	University Press (142)	0

with enough power to effectively oppose a unified effort by the trustees and the central administration.

All of this suggests that those in academic institutions who wish to retain power, or get more, had better get involved in projects and activities that will be important in the future. If budgets, career training, jobs for students, and part-time programs become more important, the biggest losers are likely to be those who do not deal with these problems.

Ominous for professors at numerous schools is the sharp loss in power confronting or soon to confront them both internally and externally. If faculty members want to win big, the obvious strategy is to become involved in budgetary activities (including control of expenditures, not just advice) and manpower planning activities, including jobs for students. Student government could gain power by doing the same. This could be relatively easy on the job side, because students could, without much objection, become very active in placement activities. The more they do, the more important they will become.

It is unlikely that those who now control budgets (trustees, central administration, deans, schools) will give up much power—they have not in the past one hundred years. Student groups and faculty press constantly for advisory roles in budget-making, and they often get them, but they rarely control budgets. But the new university game more directly involves students in two ways, and both student and professor groups could easily gain more power by trying to find jobs for students and former students. They could also relate more closely to external organizations that could help with jobs, such as professional organizations, alumni, and government agencies. It is unlikely that this will happen, given student involvement with internal activities and traditional faculty distaste for vulgar job-seeking activities.

If we unpacked the taxonomies more carefully, we would find that those schools and deans (and their faculties) that are more market-related in terms of student jobs will tend to gain power—or lose less power—relative to more traditional schools. The professional schools have been most interested in where students go and these (except perhaps education) are the only likely power gainers so far in the 1970s. Education is a special case on the demand side—

changing demographic trends have seriously dampened the market, and interest in what students do cannot help if there are no jobs for them.

Students and faculty who can attract more new students also will gain power. Students typically come if they are reasonably sure that they can obtain a decent job and good career prospects after they obtain diplomas, and the schools that take care of their graduates now tend to get bigger shares of the entering classes, both graduate and undergraduate. It is a mistake to consider pay scales alone, because many students are not as interested in the highest possible pay as they are in significant careers. But careful training that leads to no job at all will rather quickly lead also to declining enrollments in the new university game.

The strategy for top university or college management is clear, if these general trends continue. On the marketing side, the school has to attract students by offering them things they want, and very often these things include jobs in relevant careers. This represents a major shift in goals, but it will have to be done for the majority of schools. A few prestigious Ivy League and other schools can escape, but not the typical university or college. If the goal shift is this way, then the management is faced with major resource shifts. The chief executive will have to face the inevitable fact that his institution cannot be all things to all people if financial resources are not infinite. This will lead to phasing out or cutting down weak areas, particularly those where no payout can be expected.

All these changes cannot be made overnight. Given the likely resistance from many parties, it may take many months to get adequate agreement on general future thrusts, let alone on important ones. But some major changes and improvements and many beneficial minor ones can usually be implemented while these planning, negotiating, debating, and compromising processes go on. Such changes, as well as comprehensive planning for the future, have to take place either with or without faculty approval. Because a general decline in faculty power is occurring at many institutions, faculty members will usually agree to management proposals as long as management is suggesting a sound goal system, has realistic plans, and knows what it is doing and trying to accomplish.

Convincing present faculty that change is needed will

typically be difficult. Present faculty are largely tenured, and most of them will still be around ten years from now. Top managers will have to look at existing strengths, then build on these a new kind of institution that will lead these people into new and perhaps exciting paths, many of which should be adequately market-oriented.

This type of management also leads very directly to the need for very good information about what is going on. If management has adequate and accurate information about activities right before or after they happen, it can evaluate and decide whether or not to contract or expand, where, and in what ways. Management that lacks this information operates in a vacuum of ignorance, which is where most universities and colleges are now. Most universities are going to have to construct rational information systems to evaluate activities.

Few persons or institutions take the loss of relative power and prestige lightly. One can forsee the AAUP drifting into trade union activities; future top administrators may have quite complex labor-management problems unless they move cautiously. Lots of deans and chairmen will resign indignantly, because they often reflect faculty viewpoints; really competent replacements may be hard to find. And capable trustees may be even more difficult to find, because some of the things they now do will be more difficult and will require more time and conscientious attention. The impact on universities and colleges could be profound if lesser caliber men are all that can be persuaded to serve. The next ten years are going to be quite exciting and tense, if anyone manages to last long enough in positions of power to see them through.

Conclusion

We began this book with the proposition that universities and colleges have to be managed like other complex organizations, and we observed that relatively little had been written about such management in a very systematized way. Our study has been written primarily—but by no means exclusively—for academic managers or administrators, and so it has a focus that may bother various other readers. Unlike most authors who write on higher education, we have not been chiefly concerned here with questions of academic freedom, truth, student or professorial rights, or various other issues so widely discussed in American higher education today. Our focus has been on how a university or college manager or administrator, especially a top-level manager, could do at least a reasonably good job, survive, and hopefully even make some major contributions to his institution and society.

This book has utilized a comprehensive open systems approach in its study of academic institutions and their management. This has been coupled with a contingency approach orientation. The focus has been on the goals or outputs of the system, the inputs into the organization, the internal subsystems and relationships involved in the input-output transformation process, and the external environmental constraints that confront the institution. We have attempted to build useful taxonomies of the overall system and its major parts, and to develop some useful related methodologies for analysis and decision-making. Our concern has been with predictive and prescriptive dimensions of management and organizational behavior, as well as descriptive and explanatory aspects.

Of primary importance has been the vexing problem of institutional goal systems and priorities. Most universities and colleges have highly ambiguous goal systems, and we have dealt with ways in which effective management and leadership might go about operationalizing these goal systems. Serious conflict situations frequently arise from goal divergence between different groups or constituencies, both internal and external to the organization. If priorities are obscure and goal systems are not adequately operational, it is usually not possible to get the most suitable inputs or to use them very efficiently or effectively to achieve the goals. Much of the environmental constraint action confronting academic institutions stems from the attempts of interested outsiders to change institutional goal systems and priorities. A key task of management is to structure the goal system in ways that maximize advantages and minimize disadvantages to the institution. This has required systematic consideration and analysis of the goals problem.

Because our approach has attempted to be both realistic and dynamic, much attention has been given to power and influence, as well as to conflict among various individuals, constituencies, and units that have a major interest in the institution and its management. Power has been taxonomized in managerial and political terms, not merely in a legalistic or formalistic manner. We have constructed a road map of power or, if you like, a guide to winning—or at least keeping one's losses to a minimum.

Power, goals, and management are intimately related in reality. If goal systems and priorities are changed, power usually shifts. Conversely, power changes are typically needed to bring about significant changes in goal systems. We have demonstrated this in many ways. If goal systems are adequately operationalized, this can do much to clarify power, authority, and other role relationships. Similarly, if power, authority, and role relationships are clarified, this can do much to bring about clearer and more effective goal systems and priorities. Our analyses, guidelines, recommendations, and conclusions have stemmed from the following facts, predictions, trends, and prospects.

Universities and colleges typically have fuzzy goal systems and outside financial supporters and students frequently have quite different orders of priority than those within the institution, especially the faculty and the administration. The financial crunch will continue and probably force even more academic institutions into major budget crises before the end of the 1970s, unless they effectively implement major changes very soon. The crunch will force academic managers and administrators to cut costs or increase revenues considerably, on both. How costs are cut will be largely a function of the goal system, as will success in increasing revenues. If costs are cut as the faculty would like, the financial supporters will rebel in numerous cases. But if the administrators cut costs the way supporters would like, there will be many disgruntled faculty members, or even faculty rebellions at institutions that lack effective management and leadership. Similarly, if faculty goal preferences dominate, rather than those of the fund-providers and students, revenues are not likely to increase significantly at many or even most schools, and they may in fact decline. However, unlike most earlier budget crises, even most of the better schools could be in trouble at once, so discruntled faculty probably will not be able to move easily to other schools. For this reason in particular, faculty power and influence will be limited, but many faculty members will respond in other ways in an attempt to protect their interests.

If costs are to be cut, a meaningful action plan would be most useful. The same is true if revenues are to be increased. We have examined various university and college subsystems, suggesting subsystem interactions and how analyses might be made of what would happen if various items are cut and how revenues might be increased. However, in most cases where major changes in goal systems are not soon implemented effectively, cost-cutting of considerable magnitude is likely to be needed because adequate revenue increases will probably not be possible. Most persons seeking power within academic institutions are doomed to disappointment, unless they can control or exert considerable influence over budgets, information, student recruitment, career preparation and jobs for students, and perhaps new kinds of part-time and adult educational programs. Since most individuals are unlikely to do so, many of them will lose or fail to attain power and influence in decision-making. Academic managers and administrators who lack power—and especially those who are not very effective managers and leaders—are in an uncomfortable situation. They are the interface buffers between the world outside, the trustees, and their faculties, students, and other personnel. Given the goal divergence between the various groups, most of the time someone will be angry at numerous universities and colleges, unless management is able to cope effectively, creatively, and often courageously with the goals and power problems. Those who are running major modern universities or colleges are stuck with this buffer job; and, given goal divergence and cost cutting problems, it is not going to be easy. A lot of university and college presidents will be functioning as hatchet men during the second half of the 1970s and beyond, and not very many will be popular within their institutions. Outsiders may find such people attractive, but most insiders will not.

Goal divergence has not been a major or very pervasive problem until quite recently because we were in an unprecedented period of university and college expansion, which is now coming to an end. Most people, when confronted with the awkward choices now required, will argue that the problem really is not very serious. They will point out that federal funds may be available; they will push the new campaign to get more cash from state and private donors; and so on. All of these things may well succeed in some cases for a year or two, but a 15 percent compounded cost curve means that costs double in money terms every five years. A large university with an operating budget of $100 million in 1974 would have a budget of around $3.2 billion in 1999 when we retire.

If the fundamental problem of goal system operationalization, verification, and restructuring is not handled carefully and effectively during the rest of the 1970s and in the 1980s, much of the vitality, originality, and delight of the modern American higher educational institution may well be destroyed. As academics and administrators, we are living in a fool's paradise if we do not recognize what is coming; but we can do a lot to make sure that a sufficient number of the changes made are in the direction we see as desirable. There will be some universities and colleges in the future run by academic managers who see this argument. Their own faculties may well hang them in effigy, at least for a while. Their own strong internal supporters may be relatively few for some time. And they may have to take steps that will be seen by various insiders as traitorous, unethical, and dangerous. But the proper question is, what are the options? An academically undistinguished and intellectually unattractive administrator appointed by an unsympathetic outside group—that has a much narrower view of higher education —who destroys in five years what has taken generations to create?

The kinds of educational utopias noted earlier do not provide realistic options, except perhaps for a handful of very small schools with abundant resources. Another option is to do nothing and hope the problem will go away. This is typically the inevitable reaction to the first tight budget. After all, the legislature did not quite understand the problem. We can do better next time, if we only work harder. Or, in our two-party state, we will win next time. Or more private funds will be forthcoming soon if we seek them more vigorously. Or the drop in student enrollments is only a temporary phenomenon. This kind of wishful thinking has often been adequate in the past. But given Baumol's numbers logic, and all of the other hard data now available, wishful thinking will not work in most cases for much longer. When the inevitable crunch comes or becomes even worse, many universities and colleges are going to be in really deep trouble.

Another kind of wishful thinking is the reaction that "if all those people out there really understood what we are doing, they would change their minds and let us go on with our own goal system." This has worked in the past—there are many examples of major states that have poured big money into higher education in the past two decades because their lawmakers believed that it paid off. New York is a recent example. However, the game is getting too expensive for this to work much longer.

But it will be tried. Scholars will make speeches, administrators will follow the chicken and gravy circuits around the state making their pleas, and students may picket the state house. In a few cases short-term success will be gained, and that will encourage others in less fortunate states to try the same gambit. In the end, though, facts will have to be faced—and acted upon.

A third possibility is to get the federal government to pick up a large part of the new extra costs without any strings attached. There are many efforts along these lines now in progress, and pressure will increase as desperation mounts. Federal funds may help, perhaps for as long as a decade. But given all the other demands made on our central government, the possibilities of open-ended grants to major state universities—or private schools—increasing at about 10 percent per year, seem rather remote at present.

The most realistic, viable, durable, and potentially effective option is informed, effective management and leadership of universities and colleges. This requires appraisal and alteration of institutional goal systems, wise uses of power and influence, creative conflict resolution, and improved operating efficiency.

Many scholars and academically oriented individuals among our readers are probably quite depressed. What we have presented will seem dreary to those interested in traditional academic goal systems. But numerous academic institutions will be facing goal divergences and scarce resources for the remainder of the 1970s and beyond. The goal systems at numerous institutions are going to be changed. The emphasis should be on how such changes can be made to minimize disadvantages and maximize advantages to the institution. Systematic consideration of the goals problem seems to be the most important thing that an academic manager or administrator should be doing now.

Hopefully, this volume will help those responsible for

managing universities and colleges to be better prepared and more effective. If such managers and administrators can survive the 1970s in better shape than one would expect given recent performance and conditions, it is quite possible that academic institutions of the 1980s may be much better places to be.

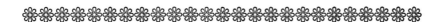

Bibliographical Essay

This essay presents some contemporary sources dealing with management and organization theories. These are books that do not focus on academic institutions but may be of considerable value to those interested in the management of universities and colleges. The essay is organized along the different basic orientations or approaches to managerial and organizational problems.

The management process approach focuses on the common functions of management, such as planning, control, organizational design, staffing, leadership, direction, motivation, and communication. This is also referred to as the operational management approach. The following important books fall into this overall category:

DALE, E. *Management: Theory and Practice.* New York: McGraw-Hill, 1969.

KOONTZ, H., and O'DONNELL, C. *Principles of Management.* New York: McGraw-Hill, 1972.

MINER, J. *The Management Process.* New York: Macmillan, 1973.

NEWMAN, W., SUMMER, C., and WARREN, K. *The Process of Management.* Englewood Cliffs, N.J.: Prentice-Hall, 1972.

BOWER, M. *The Will to Manage.* New York: McGraw-Hill, 1966. (This book not only deals with various managerial functions, but also emphasizes the will to manage, as suggested by the title.)

Richman and Farmers' forthcoming book, *Management and Organizations,* to be published by Random House in March 1975, also focuses on the functions of management. In addition, it utilizes open systems and contingency approaches to a greater extent than the above books.

The following recommended books focus intensively on one or at most a few of the basic managerial functions, rather than on the management process as a whole:

STEINER, G. *Top Management Planning.* New York: Macmillan, 1969.

ANTHONY, R. *Planning and Control Systems.* Boston: Division of Research, Harvard Graduate School of Business Administration, 1965.

NOVICK, D. *Current Practice in Program Budgeting (PPBS).* New York: Crane, Russak, 1973.

FREMONT, L., and MILLER, G. *Planning, Programming, and Comprehensive Budgeting.* Chicago: Markham, 1972.

BONINI, C. P., *Management Controls.* New York: McGraw-Hill, 1964.

DALTON, G., LAWRENCE, P., and LARSCH, J. *Organizational Structure and Design.* Homewood, Ill.: Richard D. Irwin, 1970.

KOONTZ, H. *Appraising Managers as Managers.* New York: McGraw-Hill, 1971.

FIEDLER, F. *A Theory of Leadership Effectiveness.* New York: McGraw-Hill, 1967.

DAVIS, K. *Human Relations at Work.* New York: McGraw-Hill, 1967.

VROOM, V. *Work and Motivation.* New York: Wiley, 1964.

Two of the best books on management by objectives are:

RAIA, A. *Management by Objectives.* Glenview, Ill.: Scott, Foresman, 1974.

WIKSTROM, W. *Managing by and with Objectives*. New York: National
Industrial Conference Board, 1968.

The most highly recommended books that focus on contingency approaches to management and organization include:

KAST, F., and ROSENZWEIG, J. *Contingency Views of Organization and
Management*. Palo Alto, Calif.: Science Research Associates,
1973.
HELLRIEGEL, D., and SLOCUM, J. *Management: A Contingency Approach*. New York: Harper and Row, 1974.
MORSE, J. *Organizations and Their Members: A Contingency Approach*.
New York: Harper and Row, 1974.
LAWRENCE, P., and LORSCH, J. *Organization and Environment*. Homewood, Ill.: Richard D. Irwin, 1969.

There are still not many books with a real open systems
orientation. Among the best available are:

MAUER, J., ed. *Readings in Organizational Theory: Open Systems Approaches*. New York: Random House, 1971.
KATZ, D., and KAHN, R. *The Social Psychology of Organizations*. New
York: Wiley, 1966.
CHAMBERLAIN, N. *Enterprise and Environment*. New York: McGraw-
Hill, 1968.
FARMER, R., and RICHMAN, B. *Comparative Management and Economic
Progress*. Bloomington, Indiana: Cedarwood, 1970.

Within the last decade or so there has been a rapid increase
in interest and work on various other comprehensive or general
systems approaches to the study of management and organizations.
The distinguishing feature of the following sources is that they view
organizations and their managements in a more systematic way than
various other approaches, examining comprehensively the interrelationships among different subsystems that comprise the overall organization:

Academy of Management Journal 15 (December 1972) 4. The theme of
this issue is general systems theory and its relevance to management
and organization theory.

KAST, F., and ROSENZWEIG, J. *Organization and Management: A Systems Approach*. New York: McGraw-Hill, 1970.

JOHNSON, R., KAST, F., and ROSENZWEIG, J. *The Theory and Management of Systems*. New York: McGraw-Hill, 1973.

SHODERBEK, P., ed. *Management Systems*. New York: Wiley, 1967.

CARZO, R., and YONOUZAS, J. *Formal Organizations: A Systems Approach*. Homewood, Ill.: Richard D. Irwin, 1967.

In recent years the overall field of management information systems has also been mushrooming, and this will no doubt continue in the future. The rapid growth, complexity, and diversity of organizations, further advances in computer technology, growing interdependence in society, the need for larger and larger amounts of information from both the external and internal organizational environments, greater emphasis on long-range planning, and more rapid environmental change and turbulence—these are among the chief reasons for the growing emphasis on management information systems of all types. The following books in this category are recommended:

BRIGHTMAN, R. *Information Systems for Modern Management*. New York: Macmillan, 1971.

LI, D. *Design and Management of Information Systems*. Palo Alto, Calif.: Science Research Associates, 1972.

MORTON, M. *Management Decision Systems: Computer-Based Support for Decision-Making*. Boston: Division of Research, Harvard Graduate School of Business Administration, 1970.

RAPPAPORT, A. *Information for Decision-Making*. Englewood Cliffs, N.J.: Prentice-Hall, 1970.

BLUMENTHAL, S. *Management Information Systems*. Englewood Cliffs, N.J.: Prentice-Hall, 1969.

The newly emerging field of human resource accounting can be considered as a subfield of management information systems. This subfield involves the development of methodologies, theories, and techniques for measuring the value of the productive capacities of an organization's human resources. Through experimental applications in various organizations, significant progress is being made in detecting and measuring changes involving the human organization, related quality of working life factors, and conventional productivity and efficiency trends. Among the most important works in this area are:

FLAMHOLTZ, E. *Human Resource Accounting.* Encino, Calif.: Dickenson, 1974.

LANDEKICH, S., and CAPLAN, E. *Human Resource Accounting: Past, Present, and Future.* New York: National Accounting Association, 1974.

LIKERT, R. *The Human Organization: Its Management and Value.* New York: McGraw-Hill, 1967.

Human Resource Management, a quarterly journal published by the Graduate School of Business Administration, Division of Management Education, University of Michigan, Ann Arbor.

Along with steadily increasing technological complexity and growing concern for the higher and more complicated needs of human beings and the quality of working life, there is growing interest in achieving a more effective integration between human factors and technology in organizations. This has led to a sociotechnical systems approach. The following are recommended sources:

DAVIS, L., and TAYLOR, J. *Design of Jobs.* Baltimore: Penquin, 1972.

EMERY, F., and THORSRUD, E. *Form and Content in Industrial Democracy.* London: Tavistock, 1969.

TRIST, E., HIGGEN, H., MURRAY, H., and POLLACK, A. *Organizational Choice.* London: Tavistock, 1963.

WOODWARD, J. *Industrial Organization: Theory and Practice.* London: Oxford University Press, 1965.

TAYLOR, J., ed. *The Quality of Working Life: An Annotated Bibliography 1957–1972.* Los Angeles: Center for Organizational Studies, Graduate School of Management, University of California, 1973.

There are a number of modern behavioral science approaches dealing with organization theories and, to a lesser extent, with operational management theories. Many behavioral scientists who contribute to organization theory do not see themselves as management theorists, although quite a few do make—either directly or indirectly—some valuable contributions to the study and practice of management. Such behavioralists typically do not focus on the management process or managerial functions with the aim of developing prescriptive management theories or guidelines, and they view management as just one of the components or subsystems of organizations and organization theory. Most behavioral scientists working on the development of organization theory emphasize description, observation, explanation, and verification. They often use an inductive approach, as compared to the more normative, deductive, intuitive, and distilled experience stress of the management process approach.

Management theory and organization theory are clearly interrelated and have a good deal to contribute to each other. In fact, many scholars now draw considerably on both, regardless of what their primary concerns may be.

Modern behavioral approaches to the study of organizations and management tend to focus on motivation and behavior in organizations, groups, and individuals. They draw mainly on psychology, sociopsychology, sociology, and to a lesser extent anthropology. Three basic levels of analysis are involved, and many behavioral scientists now consider more than one. The first is the level of the individual, with his personality, motives, drives, attitudes, values, learning and adaptation abilities, and skills. The second is the level of the group, with its norms, values, sentiments, interaction patterns, problem-solving and decision-making processes, adaptation and change mechanisms, conflicts, and formal and informal behavior. Finally, there is the level of the total organization, often viewed as a complex human system. The following books dealing with behavioral approaches and organization theories are among the most valuable with regard to management theory and practice:

ARGYRIS, C. *Integrating the Individual and the Organization.* New York: Wiley, 1964.

ETZIONI, A. *Modern Organizations.* Englewood Cliffs, N.J.: Prentice-Hall, 1964.

GIBSON, J., IVANCEVICH, J., and DONNELLY, J. *Organizations: Structure, Processes, Behavior.* Dallas: Business International Publications, 1973.

LIKERT, R. *New Patterns of Management.* New York: McGraw-Hill, 1961.

MARCH, J. *Handbook of Organizations.* Chicago: Rand McNally, 1965.

MARCH, J., and SIMON, H. *Organizations.* New York: Wiley, 1958.

MC GREGOR, D. *The Human Side of Enterprise.* New York: McGraw-Hill, 1960.

PERROW, C. *Organizational Analysis: A Sociological View.* Belmont, Calif.: Wadsworth, 1970.

SCHEIN, E. *Organizational Psychology.* Englewood Cliffs, N.J.: Prentice-Hall, 1965.

SCHMIDT, W. *Organizational Frontiers and Human Values.* Belmont, Calif.: Wadsworth, 1970.

SCOTT, W. *Organization Theory: A Behavioral Analysis for Management.* Homewood, Ill.: Richard P. Irwin, 1967.

THOMPSON, J. *Organizations in Action.* New York: McGraw-Hill, 1967.

Since World War II, a growing number of modern quantitative approaches have emerged that can be very valuable to management practice. These include operations research; critical path method (CPM), also referred to as program evaluation review techniques (PERT); simulation models; linear programming; industrial dynamics; and game theory. These and various other mathematical models, techniques, methodologies, and tools are viewed as part of the overall management science approach or school. These approaches typically focus on rational decision-making by using quantitative methods and scientific analysis. They deal with organizations primarily as economic or technical systems, or both, rather than as human systems or subsystems. The following readings in management science are recommended:

ACKOFF, R., and SASIENI, M. *Fundamentals of Operations Research.* New York: Wiley, 1968.

BECKETT, J. *Management Dynamics, the New Synthesis.* New York: McGraw-Hill, 1971.

FORRESTER, J. *Industrial Dynamics.* Cambridge, Mass.: MIT Press, 1961.

HEIN, L. *The Quantitative Approach to Decision-Making.* Englewood Cliffs, N.J.: Prentice-Hall, 1967.

MILLER, D., and STARR, M. *Executive Decisions and Operations Research.* Englewood, Cliffs, N.J.: Prentice-Hall, 1970.

MORRIS, W. *Management Science.* Englewood Cliffs, N.J.: Prentice-Hall, 1968.

RAIFFA, H. *Decision Analysis*. Reading, Mass.: Addison-Wesley, 1966.

SCHELLENBERGER, R. *Managerial Analysis*. Homewood, Ill.: Richard D. Irwin, 1969.

SCHLAIFER, R. *Analysis of Decisions under Uncertainty*. New York: McGraw-Hill, 1967.

SHAFFER, L., and RITTER, J. *Critical Path Method*. New York: McGraw-Hill, 1965.

SMYTHE, W., and JOHNSON, L. *Introduction to Linear Programming, with Applications*. Englewood Cliffs, N.J.: Prentice-Hall, 1966.

STARR, M. *Management: A Modern Approach*. New York: Harcourt Brace Jovanovich, 1971.

WAGNER, H. *Principles of Operations Research with Applications to Managerial Decisions*. Englewood Cliffs, N.J.: Prentice-Hall, 1969.

Within the last several years a still limited but growing number of books have appeared which emphasize both management and organization theory. Some also stress modern quantitative approaches. These books are eclectic, although most do not go very far in integrating or synthesizing the different approaches. For example, the managerial functions, behavioral theories, and quantitative methods are typically treated chiefly, if not entirely, in separate sections. The following books are recommended:

DONNELLY, J., GIBSON, J., and IVANCEVICH, J. *Fundamentals of Management: Functions, Behavior, Models*. Dallas: Business Publications, 1971.

FILLEY, A., and HOUSE, R. *Management Process and Organizational Behavior*. Glenview, Ill.: Scott, Foresman, 1969.

FLIPPO, E. *Management: A Behavioral Approach*. 2nd ed. Boston: Allyn and Bacon, 1970.

HAMPTON, D., SUMMER, C., and WEBBER, R. *Organizational Behavior and the Practice of Management*. Glenview, Ill.: Scott, Foresman, 1968.

RICHARDS, M., and GREENLAW, P. *Management: Decisions and Behavior*. Homewood, Ill.: Richard D. Irwin, 1972.

MC GUIRE, J., ed. *Contemporary Management: Issues and Viewpoints*. Englewood Cliffs, N.J.: Prentice-Hall, 1974.

The following sources are recommended for those readers

interested in empirical studies of what managers of various types of organizations actually do—their roles and behavior in reality. The Cohen and March study dealing with university presidents is contained in the main bibliography of this book and is not listed here.

DALE, E. *The Great Organizers.* New York: McGraw-Hill, 1960.

DALTON, M. *Men Who Manage.* New York: Wiley, 1959.

MC GREGOR, D. In C. McGregor and W. Bennis (Eds.), *The Professional Manager.* New York: McGraw-Hill, 1967.

MINTZBERG, H. *The Nature of Managerial Work.* New York: Harper and Row, 1973.

SAYLES, L. *Managerial Behavior.* New York: McGraw-Hill, 1964.

STEWART, R. *Managers and Their Jobs.* London: Macmillan, 1967.

Because of the rapidly changing, complex, and turbulent environments in which organizations and their managers must function, and the increasing internal complexity of organizations, organizational change and organizational development (OD) have recently become major new approaches to management and organization theory. The differences between organizational change and organizational development studies are becoming more blurred. Many people consider them to be essentially the same, because both focus on organizational change, innovation, adaptation, and learning. Change is viewed as a natural process rather than as a special phenomenon. Specialists in this area—and most of them are behavioral scientists, although some are also very interested in the management process— feel that the process of change can be incorporated and welded into the many other process of managerial and organizational life.

Organizational development is commonly viewed as a planned, organization-wide effort, managed from the top, to increase organizational effectiveness and health through planned intervention—using behavioral science knowledge—in the organization's processes. Most of the literature to date is descriptive and based largely on actual cases and individual experiences. Organizational learning and innovation, intervention theory, the use of change agents and both internal and external consultants, client systems, temporary systems, matrix organization, managerial grids, organizational analysis and diagnosis, sensitivity training, individual and group therapy, planned change of a systematic nature, and implementation programs—all form part of organizational change and organizational development studies. The recommended books in this overall category include:

ARGYRIS, C. *Management and Organizational Development.* New York: McGraw-Hill, 1971.

ARGYRIS, C. *Intervention Theory and Method.* Reading, Mass.: Addison-Wesley, 1970.

ARGYRIS, C. *Organization and Innovation.* Homewood, Ill.: Richard D. Irwin, 1965.

BECKHARD, R. *Organizational Development: Strategies and Models.* Reading, Mass.: Addison-Wesley, 1969.

BENNIS, W. *Changing Organizations.* New York: McGraw-Hill, 1966.

BENNIS, W., BENNE, K., and CHIN, R., eds. *The Planning of Change.* New York: Holt, Rinehart and Winston, 1969.

BENNIS, W., and SLATER, P. *The Temporary Society.* New York: Harper and Row, 1968.

BLAKE, R., and MOUTON, J. *Building a Dynamic Corporation Through Grid Organization Development.* Reading, Mass.: Addison-Wesley, 1969.

DALTON, G., LAWRENCE, P., and GREINER, L. *Organizational Change and Development.* Homewood, Ill.: Richard D. Irwin, 1970.

MARGULIES, N., and RAIA, A. *Organizational Development: Values, Process, Technology.* New York: McGraw-Hill, 1972.

Peter Drucker's new and very comprehensive book *Management: Tasks, Responsibilities, Practices,* published by Harper and Row in 1974, does not really fit neatly into any of the above categories but is highly recommended. Drucker is regarded by many management scholars and practitioners as the doyen of contemporary management writers and thinkers. He is also a very successful and widely sought after management consultant and an educator. His new book pulls together many threads that have run through his dozen or so earlier books, such as the concept that planning is part of the manager's everyday job and the notion of discontinuity in economic and political life. But more than any of its predecessors, this book portrays heroes. Although the focus is primarily on business enterprises, there are some chapters on nonbusiness organizations, and much of the book is also relevant to the management of academic institutions. The book is true to its subtitle, since its treatment of the tasks, responsibilities, and practices of management is comprehensive and relevant.

References

ALTBACH, P. "The Champagne University in the Beer State: Note on Wisconsin's Crisis." In D. Riesman and V. Stadtman (Eds.), *Academic Transformation: Seventeen Institutions Under Pressure*. New York: McGraw-Hill, 1973.

American Council on Education. *College and University Business Administration*. Washington, D.C.: 1968.

BALDRIDGE, J. V. *Power and Conflict in the University*. New York: Wiley, 1971a.

BALDRIDGE, J. V. *Academic Governance*. Berkeley, Calif.: McCutchan, 1971b.

BARZUN, J. *The American University*. New York: Harper and Row, 1968.

BAUMOL, W. "Macroeconomics of Unbalanced Growth." *American Economic Review*, 1967, 57 (3).

BELL, C., BROWNLEE, H., and MOOD, A. "Allocation of a University's

Resources to Instruction." In A. Mood, C. Bell, L. Bogard, H. Brownlee, and J. McCloskey (Eds.), *Papers on Efficiency in the Management of Higher Education.* Berkeley, Calif.: Carnegie Commission on Higher Education, 1972a.

BELL, C., BROWNLEE, H., and MOOD, A. "Can Mathematical Modes Contribute to Efficiency in Higher Education?" In A. Mood, C. Bell, L. Bogard, H. Brownlee, and J. McCloskey (Eds.), *Papers on Efficiency in the Management of Higher Education.* Berkeley, Calif.: Carnegie Commission on Higher Education, 1972b.

BENNIS, W. *The Leaning Ivory Tower.* San Francisco: Jossey-Bass, 1973.

BERELSON, B., and STEINER, G. *Human Behavior.* New York: Harcourt Brace Jovanovich, 1964.

BOGARD, L. "Management in Institutions of Higher Education." In A. Mood, C. Bell, L. Bogard, H. Brownlee, and J. McCloskey (Eds.), *Papers on Efficiency in the Management of Higher Education.* Berkeley, Calif.: Carnegie Commission on Higher Education, 1972.

BREWSTER, K. "Politics of Academia." In H. Hodgkinson and L. R. Meeth (Eds.), *Power and Authority.* San Francisco: Jossey-Bass, 1971.

BROWN, J. *The Liberal University: An Institutional Analysis.* New York: McGraw-Hill, 1969.

CHEIT, E. *The Depression in Higher Education: A Study of the Financial Condition at 41 Colleges and Universities.* New York: McGraw-Hill, 1971.

CLARK, B. "The Wesleyan Story: The Importance of Moral Capital." In D. Riesman and V. Stadtman (Eds.), *Academic Transformation.* New York: McGraw-Hill, 1973.

COHEN, M. and MARCH, J. *Leadership and Ambiguity: The American College President.* New York: McGraw-Hill, 1974.

Committee for Economic Development. *The Management and Financing of Colleges.* New York: October 1973.

CORSON, J. *Governance of Colleges and Universities.* New York: McGraw-Hill, 1960.

DALKEY, N. and HELMER, O. "An Experimental Application of the Delphi Method to the Use of Experts." *Management Science,* 1963, *9* (3), 458–467.

DEMERATH, N., STEPHENS, R., and TAYLOR, R. *Power, Presidents, and Professors.* New York: Basic Books, 1967.

DUNN, J. "Old Westbury I and Old Westbury II." In D. Riesman and V. Stadtman (Eds.), *Academic Transformation.* New York: McGraw-Hill, 1973.

FARMER, R., and RICHMAN, B. *Comparative Management and Economic Progress.* Homewood, Ill.: Richard D. Irwin, 1965, and Bloomington, Ind.: Cedarwood, 1970.

FILLEY, A., and HOUSE, R. *Management Process and Organizational Behavior.* Glenview, Ill.: Scott Foresman, 1969.

FRENCH, J., and RAVEN, B. "The Bases of Social Power." In D. Cartwright and A. Zander (Eds.), *Group Dynamics.* (2nd ed.) Evanston, Ill. Row, Peterson, 1960.

GALBRAITH, J. *The New Industrial State.* Boston: Houghton Mifflin, 1967.

GIBSON, J., IVANCEVICH, J., and DONNELLY, J. *Organizations.* Dallas: Business Publications, 1973.

GODDARD, D., and KOONS, L. "A Profile of the University of Pennsylvania." In D. Riesman and V. Stadtman (Eds.), *Academic Transformation.* New York: McGraw-Hill, 1973.

GORDON, T., and HELMER, O. *Report on a Long-Range Forecasting Study.* Santa Monica, Calif.: RAND, 1964.

GOULD, J. *The Academic Deanship.* New York: Teachers College Press, 1964.

GOULD, S. "Trustees and the University Community." In J. Perkins (Ed.), *The University as an Organization.* New York: McGraw-Hill, 1973.

Governance of Higher Education: Six Priority Problems. New York: McGraw-Hill, 1973.

GRANT, S. "A Network of Antiochs." In D. Riesman and V. Stadtman (Eds.), *Academic Transformation.* New York: McGraw-Hill, 1973.

GRIFFITHS, D. *Administrative Theory.* New York: Appleton Century Crofts, 1959.

GRIFFITHS, D. (Ed.) *Developing Taxonomies of Organization Behavior in Educational Administration.* Chicago: Rand McNally, 1969.

GROSS, E., and GRAMBSCH, P. *University Goal and Academic Power.* Washington, D.C.: American Council on Education, 1968.

GROSS, E., and GRAMBSCH, P. *Changes in University Organization: 1964–1971.* New York: McGraw-Hill, 1974.

GROSS, E. "University Organizations: A Study of Goals." In J. V. Baldridge (Ed.) *Academic Governance.* Berkeley, Calif: McCutchan, 1971.

HARTNETT, R. *College and University Trustees.* Princeton: Educational Testing Service, 1969.

HARTNETT, R. *The New College Trustees: Some Predictions for the 1970s.* Princeton, N.J.: Educational Testing Service, 1970.

HARTNETT, R. "Trustee Power in America." In H. Hodgkinson and L. Meeth (Eds.), *Power and Authority.* San Francisco: Jossey-Bass, 1971.

HENDERSON, A. "San Francisco State College: A Tale of Mismanagement and Disruption." In D. Riesman and V. Stadtman (Eds.), *Academic Transformation.* New York: McGraw-Hill, 1973.

HODGKINSON, H., and MEETH, L. (Eds.) *Power and Authority.* San Francisco: Jossey-Bass, 1971.

HOWE, T. "Roles of Faculty." In H. Hodgkinson and L. Meeth (Eds.), *Power and Authority.* San Francisco: Jossey-Bass, 1971.

KAST, F., and ROSENZWEIG, J. *Contingency Views of Organization and Management.* Palo Alto, Calif.: Science Research Associates, 1973.

KERR, C. "Governance and Functions." *Daedalus,* 1970, *99* (1), 108–121.

KERR, C. Foreword to *The University as an Organization,* J. Perkins (Ed.). New York: McGraw-Hill, 1973.

LAHTI, R., *Innovative College Management.* San Francisco: Jossey-Bass, 1973.

LAING, J. "Power, Dependence, and Interpersonal Comparisons of Utility in N-Persons Supergames." In J. McGuire (Ed.), *Contemporary Management.* Englewood Cliffs, N.J.: Prentice-Hall, 1974.

LEE, E., and BOWEN, F. *The Multicampus University.* Berkeley, Calif.: Carnegie Commission on Higher Education, 1971.

LITCHFIELD, E. "Notes on a General Theory of Administration." *Administrative Science Quarterly,* 1956, *1* (1), 3–29.

LUMSFORD, T. (Ed.) *The Study of Academic Administration.* Boulder, Colo. Western Interstate Commission for Higher Education, 1963.

MANGELSDORF, P. "Swarthmore Knocks on Wood." In D. Riesman and V. Stadtman (Eds.), *Academic Transformation.* New York: McGraw-Hill, 1973.

MAUER, J. (Ed.). *Readings in Organization Theory: Open System Approaches.* New York: Random House, 1971.

MC CLOSKEY, J. "Innovations in Private Colleges and Universities in California." In A. Mood, C. Bell, L. Bogard, H. Brownlee, and

J. McCloskey (Eds.), *Papers on Efficiency in the Management of Higher Education.* Berkeley, Calif.: Carnegie Commission on Higher Education, 1972.

MC CONNELL, T. "Faculty Government." In H. Hodgkinson and L. R. Meeth (Eds.), *Power and Authority.* San Francisco: Jossey-Bass, 1971.

MC CONNELL, T. *The Redistribution of Power in Higher Education.* Berkeley, Calif.: University of California Center for Research and Development in Higher Education, 1971.

MC GRATH, E. "Who Should Have the Power?" In H. Hodgkinson and L. R. Meeth (Eds.), *Power and Authority.* San Francisco, Jossey-Bass, 1971.

MEETH, L. "Administration and Leadership." In H. Hodgkinson and L. R. Meeth (Eds.), *Power and Authority.* San Francisco: Jossey-Bass, 1971.

MILLETT, J. *The Academic Community.* New York: McGraw-Hill, 1962.

MILLETT, J. *Decision Making and Administration in Higher Education.* Kent, Ohio: Kent State University Press, 1968.

MOOD, A., BELL, C., BOGARD, L., BROWNLEE, H., and MC CLOSKEY, J. (Eds.) *Papers on Efficiency in the Management of Higher Education.* Berkeley, Calif.: Carnegie Commission on Higher Education, 1972.

Newsweek, Dec. 10, 1973, pp. 40–48.

OLIVE, B. "The Administration of Higher Education: A Bibliographical Survey." *Administrative Science Quarterly,* 1967, *11* (4), 671–677.

PARSONS, T. Introduction to *The Theory of Social and Economic Organization,* by M. Weber. New York: Free Press, 1947.

PERKINS, J. "The Campus: Forgotten Field of Study." *Public Administration Review,* 1960, *20* (1), 1–2.

PERKINS, J. (Ed.) *The University as an Organization.* New York: McGraw-Hill, 1973.

PETERSON, R. *College Goals and the Challenge of Effectiveness.* Princeton, N.J.: Educational Testing Service, 1972.

PETERSON, R. *Goals for California Higher Education: A Survey of 116 College Communities.* Berkeley, Calif.: Educational Testing Service, March 1973.

PETIT, T. "Alternative Approaches to Power, Influence, and Authority." In J. McGuire (Ed.), *Contemporary Management.* Englewood Cliffs, N.J.: Prentice-Hall, 1974.

PICHLER, J. "Power, Influence, and Authority." In J. McGuire (Ed.), *Contemporary Management*. Englewood Cliffs, N.J.: Prentice-Hall, 1974.

RAUH, M. *The Trusteeship of Colleges and Universities*. New York: McGraw-Hill, 1969.

RAUH, M. *"Internal Organization of the Board."* In J. Perkins (Ed.), *The University as an Organization*. New York: McGraw-Hill, 1973.

RIESMAN, D., and STADTMAN, V. *Academic Transformation*. New York: McGraw-Hill, 1973.

RICHMAN, B. "New Paths to Corporate Social Responsibility." *California Management Review*, 1973, *15* (3), 20–36.

RITCHE, M. *The College Presidency*. New York: Philosophical Library, 1970.

SHARK, A. "A Student's Thought on Collective Bargaining." *Journal of of Higher Education*, 1972, *43* (7), 552–558.

SHARK, A. "The Student's Right to Collective Bargaining." *Change*, 1973, *5* (3), 9–10.

SIGMUND, P. "Princeton in Crisis and Change. In D. Riesman and V. Stadtman (Eds.), *Academic Transformation*. New York: McGraw-Hill, 1973.

Statistical Abstract. Washington, D.C.: Annual volumes published by the U.S. Bureau of Census.

Time, Dec. 10, 1973, p. 14.

UHL, N. *Encouraging Convergence of Opinion Through the Use of the Delphi Technique in the Process of Identifying an Institution's Goals*. Princeton, N.J.: Educational Testing Service, 1971a.

UHL, N. *Identifying College Goals the Delphi Way*. Durham, N.C.: National Laboratory for Higher Education, Topical Papers and Reprints Number 2, 1971b.

WEBER, M. *The Theory of Social and Economic Organization*. New York: Free Press, 1947.

WEISSMAN, H. *Overcoming Mismanagement in the Human Service Professions*. San Francisco: Jossey-Bass, 1973.

Index

355